time

for

childhoods

A VOLUME IN THE SERIES

*Childhoods: Interdisciplinary
Perspectives on Children and Youth*

Edited by
Karen Sánchez-Eppler
Rachel Conrad
Laura L. Lovett
Alice Hearst

YOUNG POETS
AND QUESTIONS
OF AGENCY

time
for
childhoods

RACHEL CONRAD

University of Massachusetts Press
Amherst & Boston

ISBN 978-1-62534-449-6 (paper); 448-9 (hardcover)

Designed by Sally Nichols
Set in Monotype Granjon

Cover design by Rebecca Neimark Twenty-Six Letters
Cover photo by Thomas Rooney, © 2013. Courtesy of the photographer.

Library of Congress Cataloging-in-Publication Data

Names: Conrad, Rachel, author.
Title: Time for childhoods : young poets and questions of agency / Rachel Conrad.
Description: Amherst : University of Massachusetts Press, 2020. | Includes bibliographical references and index. |
Identifiers: LCCN 2019019861 | ISBN 9781625344489 (hardcover) | ISBN 9781625344496 (paperback) | ISBN 9781613766927 (ebook) | ISBN 9781613766934 (ebook)
Subjects: LCSH: Children's poetry, American—History and criticism. | Children—United States—Intellectual life. | Child authors—United States. | American poetry—20th century—History and criticism. | American poetry—21st century—History and criticism.
Classification: LCC PS310.C5 C66 2020 | DDC 811/.9099282—dc23
LC record available at https://lccn.loc.gov/2019019861

British Library Cataloguing-in-Publication Data
A catalog record for this book is available from the British Library

"The Busy Clock" (chapter 1) and lines from "Narcissa" (chapter 2) by Gwendolyn Brooks, and quotations from Gwendolyn Brooks and Nora Brooks Blakely (chapter 2) are reprinted by consent of Brooks Permissions. "[A black, black cloud]" by William Carlos Williams (chapter 1), from *The Autobiography of William Carlos Williams*, copyright © 1951 by William Carlos Williams, is reprinted by permission of New Directions Publishing Corporation. "Different Worlds" by Elizabeth Thompson and "Masters" by Jennifer Edwards (chapter 1) are reprinted by consent of the estate of Sandford Lyne. "Death" and "Things" by Moral Thirus (chapter 2) are reprinted by permission of Moral Thirus. "I Am in a Trap" by Janet A. Docka (chapter 2) is reprinted by permission of Janet A. Docka. Quotation from Ian Osborn (chapter 4) is reprinted by permission of Ian Osborn and Charity Osborn. "Don't Worry, Mom, Don't Panic" and quotation by Cailena Bickell (chapter 4) are reprinted by permission of Cailena Bickell and Katie Bickell. Quotations from Katie Bickell (chapter 4) are reprinted by permission of Katie Bickell. "It's Raining" and quotation by Aaron Fox (chapter 4) are reprinted by permission of Aaron Fox, Craig Fox, and Gülden Ülkümen. "Eulogy for a Balloon" by Rose Foster (chapter 4) is reprinted by permission of Rose Foster and Shawna Foster. Quotations from Shawna Foster (chapter 4) are reprinted by permission of Shawna Foster. "When People Leave This Earth" by Theo Candlish (chapter 4) is reprinted by permission of Theo Candlish, Kristina Jensen, and Paul Candlish. Quotations from Terri Bush (chapter 5) are reprinted by permission of Terri Bush. "[sitting on the dock]" by Christopher Meyer (chapter 5) is reprinted by permission of Christopher Meyer. Quotations from June Jordan (chapter 5 and conclusion) are reprinted by permission, © 2018 June M. Jordan Literary Estate, www.junejordan.com. Texts from the June Jordan Papers at the Schlesinger Library, Radcliffe Institute for Advanced Study are reprinted by permission © 2018 June M. Jordan Literary Estate, www.junejordan.com. "In the Times of My Heart" by June Jordan (conclusion) from *Directed by Desire: The Collected Poems of June Jordan,* © 2005, 2018 June M. Jordan Literary Estate, reprinted by permission, www.junejordan.com.

For Emma, Sammy, Tom

Contents

Preface

IN THE EARLY 2000S, the Eric Carle Museum of Picture Book Art was built on an old apple orchard across from the Hampshire College Children's Center (later called the Early Learning Center) which my then-young children attended. The museum's bookstore offers a fabulous selection of illustrated texts for readers of a range of ages. In the Poetry section, alongside mostly standard offerings by adult poets including Langston Hughes, Shel Silverstein, Robert Louis Stevenson, and Jane Yolen, I found *Salting the Ocean: 100 Poems by Young Poets*, edited by poet Naomi Shihab Nye. This book stunned me with its respectful reference to children who write poems as "young poets," its glorious full-color illustrations by Ashley Bryan of racially diverse groups of children sailing on boats of poetry, the rich and varied projects of its one hundred poems, and the fact that the book sat on the Poetry shelf. The shock I experienced was instructive: Why had I never seen such a book before, in my decades of reading and studying poetry? Why weren't poems by "young poets" ever talked about in literature classes, in literary magazines, in scholarly criticism? Why weren't poems written by young people more visible and more a part of literary culture?

As I am a childhood studies scholar trained in developmental and child clinical psychology, my "other life" as a poet and reader of poetry provided me with an additional site in which to think about how adults view and value children and children's perspectives or attempt to construct child viewpoints. Poetry written by adults about children and childhood (what I myself was writing) is most common, followed by poetry written by adults for young audiences (which took up most of the few shelves of poetry at the Eric Carle

Museum bookstore, and is a less available form than prose for children's literature).[1] The typical absence of poetry written *by* children on Poetry shelves can be attributed to developmental assumptions about children as partial and in process, which leads to seeing their poetry as homework practice rather than art, as outcomes of adult teaching rather than youth-directed creative work.[2] Developmental judgments about children as "less" (capable, logical, thoughtful) than adults—judgments that rest on age-based timelines—leave little room for seeing children's ideas and creations as valuable or insightful. These developmental assumptions connect directly to questions of power and the social-political roles available to adults and children, and they often play out on a daily basis in relation to time.

As a parent of young children, I saw that cultural messages about children and adults were out of time with my own experiences of trying (at least sometimes) to accommodate my children's priorities. When my oldest child was in the preschool I mentioned above, there was a fifteen-minute time span within which parents and guardians could pick up their children at the end of the day. I could tell from Emma's demeanor that it mattered to her whether I picked her up at 3:15 pm or closer to 3:30 pm. While at age three or four she may not have been watching an actual clock, she was watching the clock of the arrival of other children's guardians, the ticking off of other children's departures. Though she loved the preschool, my arriving closer to 3:15 pm seemed to be satisfying and reassuring to her, whereas my arriving closer to 3:30 pm caused other emotions for her that she didn't have words to articulate—perhaps disappointment, perhaps worry, perhaps just the gnawing of unfulfilled anticipation. Seeing this, I tried whenever possible to pick her up closer to 3:15 pm so my arrival could be an opportunity for our positive reconnection. This daily drama schooled me to see that time can be valued and experienced differently, that a window of time seemingly small and arbitrary from an adult perspective (what did it really matter whether I picked up Emma at 3:20 or 3:30 pm if I was still in a conversation with a student or colleague?) was large and freighted according to my young child's sense of time, so I cut those conversations short to enter in the time window that mattered most to my daughter.

Through such experiences I began to increasingly recognize how pervasive time is in dynamics between children and adults. I realized that contestations over time—over whose clocks are legitimate and need to be followed, and who has the ingenuity to construct clocks—are central to child and adult roles in contemporary European American societies.[3] In recent Anglo-American books for young children, clocks are devices to teach children when it is "time for" this or that, and plastic "teaching clocks" are part of the technology of training children to follow adult time.[4] My graduate education in developmental and child clinical psychology left me dissatisfied that the methods of those fields could help me understand what it feels like to be a child, and whether adults have access to knowledge of children's subjectivities and priorities. Seeing the kinds of clocks that children construct and use in their daily lives—like the clock of comings and goings that my daughter used at the end of each day of preschool—helped me realize that children's ways of using and trying to control time, whether in daily life or in poetry, reflect what matters to them.

Poetry written by children offers a window onto how young people craft time for themselves in terms of their own ideas and priorities. How young poets make and mark time in their poems serves as a way to refract the sense of agency they claim through and in their writing. "Agency" is a term that is much in use among academics in the social sciences and humanities yet is difficult to define. Agency is not quite power, not quite capacity, not quite control, but refers to a person's active engagement in planning, thinking, making, and participating in relation to the roles available to them. After all, chronological time and cultural biases toward young people *as young* are primary reasons that children's creative works are not better respected. Writing poetry is thus a means for young people to shape time according to their own concerns and imaginative vision. Building from William Carlos Williams's reference to a poem as a "small (or large) machine made of words" (*Selected Essays* 256), I learned to read poems as time machines built to poets' specifications. Yet for poetry written by children to be read seriously as literary texts, adult readers must set aside prevalent cultural judgments about children to grant them credit as artists and creators.

In titling this book *Time for Childhoods*, I prompt readers to give credit to the time of childhood in, of, and for itself—time *from* children's perspectives and time *for* children's purposes, goals, and interests—rather than for or as the past, present, and future of adulthood. The term "Childhoods" also involves reflecting on cultural conceptions of "the child" and "childhood" as a phase of the life course, as well as how children encounter, respond to, and help shape these conceptions. A plural notion of childhoods is crucial for my argument that a diversity of perspectives, experiences, and representations should be considered the norm for poetics of childhoods. In the book's subtitle—*Young Poets and Questions of Agency*—the phrase "Young Poets" accords credit to people under the age of eighteen as writers of poetic texts that can be considered literary, that is, worthy of appreciation and attention as literature. Finally, the phrase "Questions of Agency" indicates that I do not presume to fully answer questions about agency, but to formulate and explore questions that can help further our understanding of agency, temporality, poetry, and childhoods.[5] I focus on youth-written poetry that entered public spaces (such as contests and anthologies) through the sponsorship of adult poets, teachers, and editors in order to spotlight the agency that young people express despite adult mediation. That two of these adults—Gwendolyn Brooks and June Jordan—were among the most dedicated adult advocates for young poets in the twentieth-century United States enables me to discuss how they supported young poets' agency.[6] And since questions of youth agency are ultimately questions of justice, these projects also afford attention to how young poets represent age-based and racial injustice.

Do children have the right to be recognized as artists and poets? How do they claim that right?[7] These questions center on *rights*, specifically on children's right to be artists, to participate in the cultural life of their societies, and to have their participation recognized. They also involve *perspective*, since by omitting works produced by children from our notion of what constitutes art, we lose access to creative works that emerge through young people's experiences of being children and their perspectives *as* young. Lastly, these questions hinge on *time*. Children have their own temporal priorities that may differ from those of adults, including the adults they themselves grow up to become. Young people's creative work can convey their artistic perspectives drawing from their imaginations, experiences, and ideas about the time of their lives, which is otherwise elusive to adults. For young poets to be recognized by adults necessitates shifting from thinking of children as potential artists training for a future in which they can express themselves and contribute to cultural life, and instead acknowledging that young people can be artists or poets in the present, now, *while* they are young.[8]

Acknowledgments

THIS BOOK TOOK shape amid the presence, attention, and support of many people to whom I express my gratitude.

First, to the poets whose work I discuss, some of whom I was able to contact directly, and others whom I was unable to reach. Thank you for your poetry and your making of time. Thank you for sharing your artistry. Thanks also to parents of poets who corresponded with me for sharing their interest and ideas about children and poetry.

To the late Gwendolyn Brooks and the late June Jordan, for their inspiration, power, and grace in modeling how to listen to young poets. To Terri Bush, for generously sharing her experiences and materials about The Voice of the Children workshop and helping it come alive through her warmth and engagement. To Christoph Keller, executor of the June M. Jordan Literary Estate; and to the staff of Brooks Permissions, for their support of this project.

With appreciation for generations of students and colleagues at Hampshire College, my intellectual home while developing the ideas for this book. Thanks particularly to students in my Youth/Poets and Poetry and Childhood courses over many years of thinking together in those generative spaces; and with special thanks to Casey Andrews, gabby fluke-mogul, and Cai Sherley. Thanks to my colleagues across the college, in the School of Critical Social Inquiry, and in the Critical Studies of Childhood, Youth, and Learning program. Thanks also to the wonderful teachers at the Hampshire College Early Learning Center for years of inspiring collaborations and conversations about children, poetry, and children's rights and agency. For support for this project over the years, I owe thanks to the School of Critical Social Inquiry and the Hampshire College Dean of Faculty office.

With my thanks to the librarians and archivists at Hampshire College and the other Five College Libraries, at the Bancroft Library at the University of California at Berkeley, and at the Schlesinger Library on the History of Women at the Radcliffe Institute for Advanced Study at Harvard University. And with special thanks to Laura Quilter at the University of Massachusetts Library at Amherst.

To the editors of the journals *Childhood*, *Jeunesse*, and the *Lion and the Unicorn* for supporting earlier versions of some of the chapters, and for granting permission to reprint that material.

For intellectual inspiration, my gratitude to Helen Vendler, for spending a semester with me while a senior at Harvard reading the poems of Yeats, and for decades of her incisive prose about poetry; and to Richard Flynn, for his sustaining work on poetry, children, and childhood, and for his faith in this project. Thank you also to Dara Wier for an early vote of confidence.

Thank you to my friends and colleagues in the Five College Childhood Studies group—Alice Hearst, Karen Sánchez-Eppler, and Laura Lovett—who joined forces in creating the interdisciplinary series *Childhoods* that then seemed like the perfect home for this book. Much appreciation to Mary Dougherty and Matt Becker at the University of Massachusetts Press for their support of the series and of this book, and an extra thanks to Matt and to Rachael DeShano for their patience in working with me throughout the process; thanks also to Sally Nichols and Courtney Andree for shepherding the book to print and beyond, and to Rebecca Neimark for her inspired cover design.

I have so appreciated having dear friends with whom to share the projects of writing and scholarship. With fond remembrance of the late Nina Payne for her creativity and generosity in crafting space to support other writers. Heartfelt thanks to Kimberly Chang for writing in adjacent rooms, for helping me find the angle on the book early on, and for her keen reading late in the project. Tremendous thanks go to L. Brown Kennedy, for over two decades of teaching together on the border of childhoods and literature, and for so graciously and generously reading the entire manuscript and using her brilliant eye to help me clarify my discussion. And thank you to Alison Greene for telling me to let it go.

With much love and deep gratitude to my mother, Rona Chayah Conrad, for her unfailing belief in me. With loving thanks to my mother-in-law, Ruby Marie Rooney, who passed away as this book was in production, for her steadfast love and caring, her "Tuff" grip, and all of her wonderful stories. With warm remembrance of my grandfather Albert J. Harris for helping me find my vocation, and to the memory of my father Edward H. Conrad who did not reach this in time. Huge thanks to Rona and to Emma for their expert assistance at the end of the project. And very many thank yous to the Conrad, Rooney, Smith, Wiener, Riley, and Schneeberg families for shared spaces of care.

And finally, to my beautiful and loving family, Tom, Emma, and Sammy, who have helped me move forward with this book across the minutes, hours, days, and years. To Tom, for sharing the best joint project ever, and for your gorgeous cover photograph. To Emma and Sammy, for living and loving the time of our lives together, as persons, as humans, as presences.

Grateful acknowledgment is made to the editors for permission to reprint material from these previous publications:

Conrad, Rachel. "'My future doesn't know ME': Time and Subjectivity in Poetry by Young People." *Childhood: A Journal of Global Child Research,* vol. 19, no. 2, 2012, 204–18. Copyright © 2011 Rachel Conrad. DOI: 10.1177/0907568211422748.

Conrad, Rachel. "'My sole desire is to move someone through poetry, and allow for my voice to be heard': Young Poets and Children's Rights." Special issue on Children's Rights and Children's Literature, *The Lion and the Unicorn,* vol. 40, 2016, 196–214.

Conrad, Rachel. "'We are masters at childhood': Time and Agency in Poetry by, for, and about Children." *Jeunesse: Young People, Texts, Cultures,* vol. 5, no. 2, 2013, 124–50.

time

for

childhoods

CHAPTER 1

"The Busy Clock"

Poetry and the Times of Youth

Youth Agency *Now*

AT THE MARCH for Our Lives demonstration against gun violence in Washington, D.C., on March 24, 2018 (with a crowd estimated between two hundred thousand and eight hundred thousand youth and allies), one of the most stirring speeches was given by Emma González, a survivor of the February 14, 2018, school shooting at Marjory Stoneman Douglas High School in Parkland, Florida.[1] After invoking each of the seventeen slain students and school staff, Emma González held the audience in thrall, and in silence, for the remainder of "six minutes and twenty seconds," the time that it took for the shooting to occur. Emma González concluded her control over this time of silence with these words: "Since the time that I came out here, it has been six minutes and twenty seconds. The shooter has ceased shooting and will soon abandon his rifle, blend in with the students as they escape and walk free for an hour before arrest. Fight for your life before it's somebody else's job." The boldness of Emma González's agency in and over time—what I term "temporal agency"—involved asserting control over the attention of hundreds of thousands of people, not just through her voice and ideas but through her strategic temporal command of silence.

I begin with this example because young poets' crafting of temporal perspectives must be placed in the broader context of other young people who are asserting their voices, claiming their right to speak to societal concerns, and imposing their own timeframes. Other powerful contemporary examples in which young people are demanding to be heard include youth involved in the Black Lives Matter movement, and youth collectively challenging the U.S. government over climate policies. Thandiwe Abdullah, co-founder of the Black Lives Matter–Los Angeles Youth Vanguards chapter, argues for the importance of young people allying in and across social movements to include not only youth involved in single-incident school shootings but also young people "which are particularly black and brown students—who are over-criminalized, over-policed, and see guns every single day. They face that threat every single day." In her emphatic repetition of "every single day," Abdullah uses redundancy—through pointedly inserting the word "single" and repeating the phrase twice—to make the clock run slower, so her audience must contemplate the relentless dailiness of the threat that black and brown young people face. In doing so, Abdullah deploys an awareness of time and its connection to social-political power that is fueled by temporal agency.[2]

Another contemporary example of young people's action that reflects their temporal agency is the current legal case *Juliana v. United States* in which a group of twenty-one youth, currently eleven to twenty-two years old (aged eight to nineteen at the time of the filing of the initial complaint), is suing the U.S. federal government over their constitutional rights to life, liberty, and property that they argue include the right to a "stable climate system" (Juliana v. U.S. 99).[3] These youth have allied with an environmental legal organization, Our Children's Trust, which describes its mission as "elevat[ing] the voice of youth to secure the legal right to a stable climate and healthy atmosphere for the benefit of all present and future generations." The U.S. government has repeatedly sought to block the case from going to trial, including multiple appeals to the U.S. Supreme Court that twice resulted in blocking the trial shortly before it was to begin (Our Children's Trust).[4] Sophie Kivlehan, one of the plaintiffs in the case and the granddaughter of climate scientist James Hansen, writes in an editorial that even though the lawsuit (also known as *"Youth v. Gov,"* as the website devoted to the case refers to it) is likely to take years to pursue (as it already has), "I feel strongly that it is my and my fellow plaintiffs responsibility to spread awareness about this to other young people—we must all take ownership of our future." Here Kivlehan invokes a collective sense of identity as "young people" acting as youth in the present to "take ownership of our future," which is in stark contrast to the standard view of young people as valuable for the future they will eventually reach when they become adults.

Though the United States remains the only member state of the United Nations that has not ratified the 1989 Convention on the Rights of the Child, these young people's actions are mobilized by their own sense of their rights. In their daily lives, young people act according to their working conceptions of their rights and thereby influence their communities. In formulating plans, taking action, and insisting on being heard, young people shape what youth agency is and can be in their social-political worlds. This idea of "living" agency is akin to Karl Hanson and Olga Nieuwenhuys's valuable concept of "living rights" ("Living Rights" 6) that encompasses how young people "become aware of their rights as they struggle with their families and communities to give meaning to their daily existence" (4), ideas that I discuss further in chapter 4 in considering implications of children's rights discourse for thinking about young poets.

One method for claiming the right to speak and create *now* is by remaking time on one's own terms. Typical Western views of cultural production follow a socialization model in which young people are apprentices who become inculcated in cultural traditions expressed by older members of their societies and are considered capable of cultural production themselves only once they "grow up."[5] The temporal hegemony of a developmental lens judges children by forward-looking values in terms of how they are "progressing" toward an older and more "developed," that is, more complex and more advanced, adult of the future.[6] In the 1980s, sociologists and anthropologists of childhood proposed a "new social studies of childhood" to counter the dominance of developmental psychology throughout the twentieth century; this framework conceptualizes children not as passive recipients of cultural knowledge and practices but as active interpreters, makers, and participants, as Allison James, Chris Jenks, and Alan Prout (197) discuss.[7] Philosopher Gareth Matthews (*Philosophy of Childhood*) argues for the necessity of challenging the socialization model in order to assert that children can be artists deserving of an audience outside the family and classroom.

In *Time for Childhoods,* I take on the problem of the invisibility of poets under the age of eighteen, that is, those classified as "children" or "youth," who are not accorded recognition as authors of literary texts worthy of critical attention but are instead commonly viewed as the objects of adults' efforts as teachers or editors, or are confined to the past as authors of the "juvenilia" of canonical adult poets. The second problem I grapple with is the difficulty of theorizing youth agency, by which I mean understanding young people's intentions and modes of everyday action in the contexts of psychological and social factors, familial, cultural, and political practices, and institutional structures. Both problems are shaped by cultural conceptions of youth that neglect appreciating young people's lives in the present.

Neglect of poetry written by youth and limits in theorizing youth agency are explainable in part by cultural beliefs and practices that obscure the possibility of valuing children's present knowledge, capabilities, intentions, and accomplishments. These include the idea that children are by definition less knowledgeable than adults, which explains why children are commonly seen solely as students or recipients of adult knowledge rather than as teachers or co-creators of meaning. A related belief, drawing on the idea that art requires long cultivation and refinement that necessarily favors adult sensibilities and lifespans, holds that poetry written by young people is merely apprentice work rather than art worthy of attention. Hence, ideas and works that children create are of less value than works produced by adults, and are noted only for their precocity or their insufficiency. Precocity adopts developmental logic in considering interesting work by children as appearing "before its time." A judgment of insufficiency shores up adult control over cultural production, and maintains children as objects and consumers of culture rather than as potential creators of culture and knowledge. Also relevant is an adult-centric view of time that conceives of time from a normative perspective of adult bodies and experiences, and in terms of adult goals and interests. A final limiting factor derives from the intertwining of time and agency, wherein youth agency is envisioned only through the temporal constraints of the concepts and practices that maintain childhood as a social institution. Exploring young poets' ideas and imaginings of temporality enables a view of youth agency that is not limited by considering children only as the past of adults or for the future of adulthood but instead conceptualizes agency through the time of childhoods.

Anna Leader, a prize-winning high school–aged poet whose blurb helps introduce the anthology *Leave This Song Behind: Teen Poetry at Its Best* (compiled by adult editors from poetry by young people published in *Teen Ink* magazine), calls on adult readers to "listen" to young writers not as "the voices of the future" but for what they are saying "right now": "Teen writers, if they are acknowledged, are often cited as being the voices of the future. But this anthology is not important because it 'showcases the voices of tomorrow'—it is important because it contains the voices of today. Right now, teenagers have things to say about art, religion, sex, happiness, and so much more—and right now, if you care about these things, you'll listen" (Leader, n.p.).

A Childhood Studies Method toward Theorizing Youth Agency

This project is a work of childhood studies, a relatively new scholarly field that draws from multiple methods and frameworks in exploring the experiences and conditions of children's lives as well as conceptions and representations of childhood, including those produced by youth themselves. Grounded in intersections of varied knowledge practices, childhood studies can serve as a model for other domains of scholarship that would benefit from interdisciplinary, and even transdisciplinary (Darian-Smith and McCarty), approaches. Scholars have begun to advocate for retaining the success of childhood studies while broadening its focus to enter into scholarly discussions in wider fields.[8] One such context is scholarship in the social sciences on agency and temporality, where, for example, Steven Hitlin and Glen H. Elder, Jr., argue for integrating social psychological and sociological research; yet interdisciplinary integrations can go much further.

Time for Childhoods integrates literary analysis with methods of critical social studies of childhood in order to critique developmental perspectives that limit consideration of young people's cultural productions, and to subvert typical literary practices of excluding writing by children from critical attention. To integrate, as I do here, modes of inquiry drawn from the social sciences with those from the humanities is not typical practice even in childhood studies, where scholars usually work across either humanities *or* social science disciplines. Ideally, integrative approaches should take into account conceptions of childhood, lived experiences of children, and cultural representations of childhood (by children, where possible).[9] Robin Bernstein refers productively to the tension in childhood studies between scholarship that explores representations of childhood and scholarship that investigates the lived experiences of children, and argues that the field needs to account for "the simultaneity and mutual constitution of children and childhood" (22). With texts written by children, for whom the process of writing engages modes of agency that counter dominant conceptions of children as cultural consumers rather than producers, the "simultaneity and mutual constitution of children and childhood" is in the hands of a young writer.[10] In *Time for Childhoods*, I focus on young people's representations of temporality in poetic texts, which are interwoven with these writers' working notions and lived experiences of agency.

My method is a transdisciplinary fusion of literary, critical psychological, and sociological analysis in order to reclaim and read texts that have been excluded from critical analysis because of the age of the authors and cultural attitudes toward children and children's productions. I use literary analysis to discern young people's poetic visions of temporality, age, and youth, or in other words, how young poets construct figures of lived experience in and over time. I use critical developmental psychology to critique developmental underpinnings of assumptions about children's "potential" that locate children on a trajectory toward future adulthood, depict children as potential rather than actual persons, and judge children's capacities as limited compared with those of adults. And I use sociology of childhood to unpack and underscore how age operates implicitly and explicitly in literary practices, including ideas of literary oeuvres, generic formations, opportunities for publication, and the bestowing of critical attention, as well as to explore how the social positions of child and adult are constructed in poetic texts by children. Along the way, I think about the roles that adult poets, teachers, parents, editors, and critics can play in helping to bring the work of young poets to public audiences. My guiding questions use age as a category of analysis, which is consistent with work of recent scholars who think about age as a fundamental process, akin to gender, class, and race, that can apply to all humanistic and social-political inquiry.[11]

In *Time for Childhoods*, I have three methodological through lines. One involves reading poems written by young poets with the sustained close attention usually reserved for poems written by adult poets. This is not a standard method of literary critical practice. The handful of scholars who have written about young poets have done so in the context of adult-produced literature and culture (see Katharine Capshaw's discussion of Kali Grosvenor and Robin Bernstein's discussion of Daisy Turner), in projects that are focused on the pedagogical processes and contexts through which young people produce poetry (see the work of Korina Jocson and Maisha Fisher), or in relation to particular historical periods in which young poets found adult interest and publishing opportunities (see Laurie Langbauer on young British Romantic poets and David Sadler on young writers in the 1920s). My practice of giving close literary critical attention to poems written by young poets is part of an argument that poems by young poets should be read as literary texts.

The second through line of my method in *Time for Childhoods* involves reading youth-authored poetry that came to public attention through projects that were initiated and controlled by adults. Doing so helps reveal the agency of these young poets despite the extent of adult mediation, and necessitates a view of artistic agency as interdependent rather than strictly autonomous. I focus on a selection of adult-mediated projects from the mid-twentieth- to early twenty-first-century United States—poetry contests, writing workshops, informal and formal publications—in order to consider decisions that adult mentors, teachers, editors, and publishers make in presenting work by young poets, and to learn from contexts in which adults treat poems by young people with seriousness and respect.

The third methodological through line is reading poems by young poets for their crafting of time. I am interested in how young poets write *time for childhoods*: time through young people's ideas and artistry and for their own purposes. In order to read poems written by youth for their shaping and use of time, I develop critical terms that enable me to examine young poets' temporal poetics in relation to agency. I use the term *temporal agency* for the agency that youth practice in relation to time, *dynamic temporality* for a strategy of practicing temporal agency through innovative and flexible imaginings of time that might involve alternative timelines or trajectories, and *children's temporal standpoints* for the ways that youth envision and grapple with temporality through their identities as young people. These concepts enable me to examine young poets' making of poetic times for their artistic purposes, and to explore how agency in relation to time— temporal agency—is a crucial component of youth agency. Ultimately, my goals are to advocate for greater visibility of and respect for literary texts written by people under age eighteen, and to contribute to our understanding of youth agency and time for childhoods.

In *Time for Childhoods*, I make a case for the literary merit of poetry written by young people, for the importance of temporality as a lens through which to consider young people's poetry, and for the value of reading youth-written poetry for conceptualizing agency. I do not undertake a broader argument here about the value of children's art in general, which would require consideration of other forms of literature, visual art, music, and additional media. Nor am I arguing that all poems written by children should be lauded, published, and written about—just as literary critics do not consider all poems written by adult poets—but I argue that interesting and well-crafted poems by young poets should be brought to light, talked about, respected, savored, and added to our cultural life. With some exceptions, it is typically not possible to read poems written by young poets in the context of their oeuvre—as they often don't have an oeuvre—and instead we must be satisfied with taking each compelling poem written by a young poet on its own terms, as a single and singular work of art. After all, the idea that an artist must have a substantial body of work in order to be taken seriously relies on a developmental idea, which categorically excludes youth, that only work that is sufficiently developed over time is worthy of attention. I argue that serious consideration of poems written by young people necessitates reading their poems for their present artistry, rather than waiting for, or judging against, a body of work they might "develop" in the future.

Conceptualizing young people's artistic agency requires reconsidering some standard assumptions that typically underlie considerations of agency, since agency is often conceptualized in a manner that presupposes adult-focused realities and positions adults as the center of reference. This is particularly the case with regard to notions of autonomy and the assumption that agency necessarily involves the independent action of an agent. In this common formulation, anything that suggests adults' involvement, collaboration, or even co-direction in children's activity is considered evidence against young people's agency, and thus youth agency can be dismissed, belittled, or considered near-impossible within standard age-based power structures.[12] Instead of accepting autonomy as a challenge to youth agency, I build on recent considerations of interdependence in relation to youth participation and agency. Such views have emerged primarily in working to decenter European American conceptions of youth agency and develop models that are more inclusive of cultural discourses and contexts that prioritize interdependence rather than autonomy and acknowledge children's embeddedness in social and community relationships.[13] Making visible a more interdependent notion of youth agency is a challenge taken on by scholars in a range of fields, including historians of childhood, such as

Mary Jo Maynes, who uses personal narratives to discern how "individuals strategize and act, not alone, but rather always embedded in social relations, in institutions, and in history" (119).[14] Victoria Ford Smith's scholarship on child and adult artistic collaboration in the nineteenth and early twentieth centuries (in the United Kingdom) is an innovative approach that helps expand notions of young people's artistic production. Madeleine Leonard's notion of "intergeneragency" (9) is also relevant in addressing the structural and relational frameworks within which children practice agency, as is David Oswell's exploration of multiple "spaces of experience, experimentation and power" (271) as contexts for a "distributed" notion of children's agency (7).[15]

In *Time for Childhoods*, I examine the work of young poets in the context of adult-facilitated projects in order to engage directly with questions of adult mediation. I consider forms of adult mediation in supporting, prompting, editing, or publishing young poets' writings to be aspects of the facilitation of young poets' agency and not evidence *against* young poets' agency. I discuss at some length the ideas and actions of adults involved with young poets in order to highlight adult values and decisions that can support rather than undermine the agency of young writers. Throughout the book, I center close readings of youth-written poems from adult-facilitated projects in the late twentieth- and early twenty-first-century United States, primarily from archives of adult-sponsored contests and published anthologies edited by adult poets, teachers, and editors. I prioritize young poets' artistry, and consider young poets the authors of their poems, rather than see their efforts as compromised by, secondary to, or "under the aegis of" adult teachers, editors, or writers. In this light, adult facilitation is a tool that children can use in the service of their own purposes and projects. Adult mediation need not threaten youth agency but can help make visible the agency claimed by young artists in their thinking, planning, and making.

A common confusion in our discussions concerns the role that adults can take in relation to children's agency. Adults cannot "grant" or "give" children agency, but they can recognize, acknowledge, facilitate, preserve, ignore, obscure, erode, or obstruct the agency that children claim, practice, or express. Children must be the active subject of youth agency: youth agency encompasses ideas, desires, and strategies that children envision, rehearse, practice, or enact. In conceptualizing agency as an active practice,

I don't find it productive to refer to agency as a possession that children "have," and instead agree with Madeleine Leonard's formulation that also emphasizes agency as "a practice not a possession" (154).

Taking young people's artistic agency seriously involves privileging it even apart from the visibility it can achieve in adult-dominated contexts. Indeed, the outcome of the actions of young artists might be more private than public. It might live in the realm of ideas, drafts, goals, perceptions, and processes, and might not be fully realized, let alone noticed or valued by adults. David Rufo refers to young artists in elementary classrooms creating works "in secret, the creators under constant fear of being scolded by teachers, and in the process, devalued as artists" (23). Rufo discusses how, in order for young artists to pursue their own creative processes and purposes and make their own creative decisions, adult control and expectations, which can interfere with children's artistic intentions, must be renounced. In Rufo's own classroom practice, "Giving up arbitrary control over creativity in the classroom allowed children to have ownership of their own creativity" (22).

In instructional contexts, young people's artistic agency can be supported through a kind of balance of power between adult and child. Vicky Grube, as the "teacher" of an after-school drawing club, has observed elementary-age children's "self-initiated art making" (n.p.). Grube writes about her vision of the delicate balance of "both student and teacher as learners" and as constituting "a humane crossing" by drawing on Paulo Freire's and bell hooks's ideas of critical pedagogy: "The teacher has clarity of direction and skills to listen, to respect what the child knows, and to put forward new techniques, subject matter, and collaborative exchanges. . . . I see both student and teacher as learners . . . and in this grace a humane crossing launched" (n.p.). In *Teachers as Cultural Workers*, Paulo Freire writes of the mutuality of listening between "democratic" teachers and learners: "by listening to and so learning to talk with learners, democratic teachers teach the learners to listen to them as well" (115). Grube argues that in order for young artists to create a "new reality," the teacher must refrain from imposing "traditional" control: "If the teacher imposes obedience to an adult-tested aesthetic, the opportunity to learn much from the young artist is lost" (n.p.). In order to learn from young poets and acknowledge their agency, adults must recognize and even be guided by young poets' own artistic—and temporal—imperatives.

Exercising Agency in Relation to Time: Temporal Agency

In the psychological realm, time is not a separable dimension of subjectivity, but is part of the interplay of experiences that constitute human subjectivity generally, or what it feels like to be oneself. Agency makes use of this temporal foundation of subjectivity, which phenomenological philosopher Maurice Merleau-Ponty helps conceptualize not as a fixed sense that is rooted in time but as a continual process of coming into being in relation to one's experiences and other subjectivities: "Subjectivity is not in time, because it takes up or lives time, and merges with the cohesion of a life" (422). Subjectivity is what structures our experience of time, and is itself the temporal fabric of human lives.

A leading edge of scholarship on agency involves conceptualizing it in terms of human lives experienced in and across time. In the context of sociological understanding of the interplay between individual agency and structural elements of society, Mustafa Emirbayer and Ann Mische have argued that agency must be "reconceptualize[d] . . . as a temporally embedded process of social engagement" (963). For Emirbayer and Mische, the complexity of social action can only be understood "if it is analytically situated within the flow of time" (963), given that persons "at any given moment" choose to orient themselves "toward the past, the future, and the present" (964). Theorizing agency in relation to "temporally constructed engagement" (970) is also relevant when thinking specifically about youth agency.

Conceptualizing youth agency should take into account children's own implicit ideas of what kind of agency one thinks one has when one is a child. Children's art, ideas, lives, and communities are informed by their own theorizing about what it means to be a child, what children can do, and how much control children have (or imaginatively conceive) over time. The notion of "childness," or children's ideas about what it's like to be a child, has been described by psycholinguist Jenny Cook-Gumperz as the "understanding that children have of themselves as a social category" (208), which can incorporate intersections of size and age.[16] Young writers may invoke "childhood" or "adulthood" as a space of commentary in their literary representations and can complicate youth as a category of identity that intersects with other forms of social identity such as race and/or gender. The constraints on children's lives posed by age and time, by age-based ideologies and temporal practices, can also be opportunities for the emergence of agency, as James, Jenks, and Prout have suggested: "age, generation and time are . . . important constraints on the form taken by childhood in any culture. However, significantly, they may also be ones through which the agency of children arises" (59). Young poets' representations of time can reflect their critical engagement with what James and Prout term the "time of childhood" (the bracketing of the life span into age-based segments, such as "childhood" and "adulthood," and the ideologies and assumptions that accompany them) and "time in childhood" (how cultures of temporal practice impinge on children's ideas and experiences), as well as what they imagine beyond adult-controlled frames ("Representing Childhood" 231).[17] The concept of *temporal agency* encapsulates agency in and "over" time as a crucial component of youth agency, with "over" carrying the double meaning of "across" and "against" time.

"Temporal agency" is a form of agency that is available to young people in their ideas and daily lives. This agency is often out of view of adults because of a temporal hegemony that positions as cultural default the models of time based on adult bodies, experiences, and priorities. Young people's temporal agency involves their ideas, practices, and imaginings of time that demonstrate their working awareness of time, temporal order, and temporal valuation. Temporal agency does not depend on an elaborated abstract understanding of time or on perfect comprehension of clock and calendar, but involves a person's use of time and temporal practices to contemplate or accomplish one's own goals.[18] For children, exercising control over time—even imaginatively—opens a space for transforming temporally based social relations and fixed social roles, and for making more malleable the rigid clocks and calendars they find all around them.[19]

My interest in children's temporal agency and imaginative constructions of temporal possibilities goes beyond existing scholarship on time as an organizer of societal views of children,[20] and on differing priorities among youth and adults over the use of time.[21] Current research demonstrating that children can wrest control of time from adults is constrained by centering children's resistance to adults' temporal demands rather than putting children's own temporal goals at the forefront. For instance, sociologist William Corsaro's research in preschool settings in the United States and Italy showed how children used a range of strategies (including collaborative strategies among peers) to avoid or delay responding to teachers' demands to clean up, which Corsaro sees as a form of children's "common resistance" to adult rules in order to co-opt time for themselves (141). Considering such behavior as demonstration of young people's *temporal agency*—their agency in relation to time—reframes children's action from resistance to adults' control over time to a positive focus on children's own temporal priorities and goals.

When my children were young, leaving the house for school or for doctors' or dentists' appointments too often involved a predicament that I viewed as my daughter's and son's stalling or resisting as they put on their socks and shoes in slow motion, without any apparent regard for the urgency I felt. These daily differences in temporal strategies—their slowing down when I needed them to speed up—provoked me to think about the different temporal priorities, experiences, and values that were at stake for each of us. I could also see that these types of interactions are part of the fabric of child and adult roles; indeed, they help constitute those roles. In my household during those years, adults were people who cared about hurrying to keep a schedule and children were people who didn't. I asked my son Sammy when he was eleven years old about those slow-motion leave-takings as a young child, which were well-known to him because his father often explicitly referred to him as "moving in slow motion" at those times, and he readily responded at length.[22] Sammy explained that when his father or I said "It's time to go," he took that to mean "We're going to change the mood, the way we're acting, and the setting. I didn't think it meant we were going to very quickly do something else, because if it was done too fast, I would feel stuck on the thing that we'd been doing before." He felt this still explained why he moved slowly during certain transitions: "Like if it was to go to the dentist to get yucky stuff in my mouth, I'd want my mind to be still stuck on the thing I'd been doing before, so I'd go even slower" in order to process "what's going to happen."

Hearing my son's account, I was properly chastened, as this was a far richer, more insightful, and more logical formulation than I had ever ascribed to him at those frustrating thresholds, when I had considered my own urgency to be the only possible temporal logic. As this common example suggests, adults too often view children's actions in terms of their implications for adults' goals (hurry up or we'll be late) rather than as indicative of children's own goals and agency (I'm going slowly for a purpose, to prepare myself for this transition). My son's slowing down for a purpose is an expression of his agency in relation to time. To view his actions only as resistance to my temporal imperative is to fail to fully recognize his own temporal agency.

A striking historical example of a young person exercising temporal agency involves young poet Daisy Turner asserting her poetic agency in the midst of an all-school assembly in 1891 when she was about eight years old. This event, preserved because of her memory and repeated practice of her poem, was recounted by Turner at age 102 in 1985 in oral history interviews conducted by Jane C. Beck (Beck; Turner). For an assembly at which her white classmates were assigned dolls and poems representing specific European countries, Daisy, the only black girl in her class in a small Vermont school, was assigned by her white teacher to hold a doll representing "Africa" and recite a poem written by her teacher which began "My doll was born in Africa / My doll was born in the sun" (cited in Bernstein 196). However, Turner, who had been reluctant to perform her teacher's poem to begin with, made the spontaneous decision to compose and recite her own poem instead. Her account of this event emphasizes the expansiveness of her agency: "instead of saying the piece that the teacher had taught me to say, I was saying what I wanted to say on my own" (Turner).[23] Here, elder Daisy Turner conveys a threefold articulation of her agency—"I was saying" (voice), "what I wanted to say" (desire and intention), "on my own" (ownership and autonomy)—in a manner that accentuates the manifold agency she claimed as a child through her rejection of the teacher's poem, spontaneous composition of her own poem, and recitation of her self-authored poem. In doing so, she rejected the past-tense racist inheritance represented by her white teacher's poem ("My doll was born in Africa") to act with a present-tense boldness that is shared by the "dolly" and the speaker who she verbally crafts in her poem, the last stanza of which is as follows (Turner; Bernstein 195):

> So stand up dolly
> And look straight
> To the judges at the right.
> And I'll stand right by your side
> If I do look a fright.

Evident here is the present-tense immediacy of the speaker's instruction or encouragement to "dolly" in order to be part of the competition, which she ends up winning.[24] Robin Bernstein presents this history as an example of Daisy Turner's "performance of resistance" (228) to expectations of racial servitude represented by the doll Dinah, which is a useful lens for viewing Daisy Turner's interruption of her teacher's instructions. However, framing Daisy Turner's actions through the lens of *temporal agency* enables us to see further aspects of the time-based dimension of her interruption and of her own poetic composition in crafting a present that she chooses to give voice to through her rejection of the racially instructed past.

Thus, temporal agency is a lens that allows for the emphasizing of young people's initiative, ideas, and purposes in relation to time, beyond their resistance to adult imperatives. Such re-centering of young people's "own" temporal priorities (to use Daisy Turner's word) is important for developing a fuller conception of youth agency. Thinking in terms of temporal agency brings to light young people's exertion of control over time, which can involve shaping time in ways that might work against or outside standard timelines and trajectories.

Remaking and Transforming Time: Dynamic Temporality

Young people can plan, speak, and act in ways that demonstrate the originality and strength of their temporal ideas and commitments. Sophie Kivlehan, one of the youth plaintiffs in the *Juliana v. United States* climate lawsuit discussed in the opening of this chapter, expresses the need for young people to take climate action now, to "take ownership of our future" in the present. This remaking of time or temporal sequence—in this case, transposing the future into the present in order to act on it—is an example of what I term *dynamic temporality*. Since the standard Western temporal narrative, structured according to a developmental model, views children as temporary, moving on a timeline, and for the future, "dynamic temporality" is a method of practicing temporal agency by manipulating taken-for-granted cultural representations of time as irreversible, forward-moving, steady, and linearly progressive. Dynamic temporality is evident in a young person's stretching out of the present, as Emma González did in holding the March for Our Lives audience in long minutes of silence; in repeating the present, as Thandiwe Abdullah did in taking her audience twice through "every single day" that black and brown youth face gun violence; or in a young poet's poetic representation that subverts the order or priority of past, present, and future. Dynamic temporality can operate at the level of lived experience or at the level of imaginative representations of time. Recognizing dynamic temporality requires a conception of temporalities and childhoods that makes room for young people's alternative trajectories alongside their use of developmental chronologies. While I do not claim either that young people exclusively use dynamic temporality or that dynamic temporality is practiced only by young people, it is one distinctive manifestation of children's temporal agency that young people can use.[25]

Concepts that help us explore young people's ideas of time and change can describe the perspectives that young people have on their lives in and over time that may not align with adult-derived models. Dynamic temporality is one such approach to temporality that can help account for young people's temporal perspectives in everyday interactions and in their own formulations.[26] Dynamic temporality is not a prescriptive concept; it can be used to make generalizations about children that are open-ended, that refute a singular notion of "child time," and that allow for potential commonalities alongside differences among children's ideas and experiences. Conceptual language that enables us to better recognize and track young people's temporal perspectives can contribute to theorizations of agency that are formulated through awareness of how young people shape and understand their lives in time.

Complicating our understanding of temporality is crucial for theorizing children's agency and subjectivity. A developmental approach that positions young people at fixed points along a trajectory of human growth marking progressive incremental change toward adulthood—where full personhood resides—has been dominant throughout the nineteenth, twentieth, and into the twenty-first century.[27] Yet change need not be seen solely as a unidirectional continuum, since it can encompass narratives of and across growing up, growing down, or "growing sideways," in Kathryn Bond Stockton's term. Stockton's idea of "growing sideways" (11), derived from renderings of "the queerness of children" (2) in twentieth-century literature and film, "suggests that the width of a person's experience or ideas, their motives or their motions, may pertain at any age, bringing 'adults' and 'children' into lateral contact of surprising sorts" (11). Work on queer temporalities by Stockton and other scholars, including Lee Edelman and Jack Halberstam, helps bracket normative temporalities, such as that of normative "childhood" and "a middle-class logic of reproductive temporality" (Halberstam 4), and opens up space for alternative modes and models of childhoods and temporalities. Michelle M. Wright ("Queer Temporalities") speaks of the importance of centering plural notions of temporalities intersecting with such factors as race, gender, and sexualities—and, I would add, age—in our theorizing and our consumption of scholarship, including considering a "diversity of queer identities" given differently "marginalized and/or disempowered" queer lives (289).[28]

Dimensions of social-political power (including age) can increase the felt need or urgency for temporal control in artistic work. Homi Bhabha writes of critical-theoretical efforts that "attempt to interrupt the Western discourses of modernity" (241) and open up temporal options for agency for the subjects of racism and other forms of oppression. The insertion of what Bhabha terms the "time-lag of postcolonial modernity" into the "linear, progressive time of modernity" (253) can produce "a structure for the representation of subaltern and postcolonial agency" (237); specifically, he posits a rewriting of the past toward the future—a "projective past" (252)—in order to better represent complexities of time and agency that accompany cultures of human power and difference.[29] In chapters 2 and 5, I write about how young black poets exerted control over timescales and expanded temporal possibilities for crafting poetic accounts of racialized histories, practices, and imaginaries.

Because children are relegated to the beginning of the lifespan's trajectory and, at least in contemporary Western contexts, their daily lives are regulated by adult-controlled temporal practices, children may have more at stake in reimagining temporal order in their artistic work than do adults. Pierre Bourdieu usefully connects temporality and practice in linking the rhythm of people's daily activity to a "logic of practice." In practice, people use time flexibly, in contrast to the rigidity of clock and calendar, as Bourdieu writes: "like the map which substitutes the homogeneous, continuous space of geometry for the discontinuous, patchy space of practical pathways, the calendar substitutes a linear, homogeneous, continuous time for practical time, which is made up of islands of incommensurable duration, each with its own rhythm, a time that races or drags, depending on what one is doing" (84). This "practical time" involves "play[ing] strategically with time" (81) across rhythm and tempo. Yet for Bourdieu, the temporality involved in practice is linear and irreversible, whereas I argue that children can choose to avoid or subvert temporal directionality in their artistic engagements by, for example, pulling the future into the present, or sending the past into the future.

Children's Temporal Standpoints

Complex ideas in young people's creative work that may fly under the radar of adults include youth identity, conceptualizations of childhood and adulthood, and the ways in which youth envision and grapple with temporality through their identities as young people. Children's ideas and experiences of time connect to their sense of their age-related social status as children. I use the term *children's temporal standpoints* to convey children's understandings of their temporal agency—their agency in relation to time—as children, which involves agency at the levels of social role (or youth identity) and action, in this case by writing and by potentially also crafting representations of youth agency. "Children's temporal standpoints" are important given that children's sense of childhood as a social position contributes to our understanding of the social world (as Mayall and James ["Giving Voice"] have stated) and of connections between youth and temporality.

Delineating children's temporal standpoints has a further political purpose in facilitating adults' recognition of young people's agency and insight, which can help reform our age-based power structures. Myra Bluebond-Langner has discussed "the child's role in the initiation and maintenance of social order" (5), a form of social agency that can involve children's participation in understanding and maintaining the social roles of child and adult, and that may often be, as in her research, outside of adults' awareness. Drawing from feminist standpoint theory, such as Sandra Harding's argument for the importance of "observations and theory that start out from, that look at the world from the perspective of women's lives" (124), Berry Mayall takes up a related idea in advocating for "child standpoints" (176) that incorporate children's perspectives on their lives and conditions as children for what they reveal about the social order and can contribute toward its re-envisioning. As Mayall states, the notion of standpoint remains to be fully developed in the field of childhood studies. Allison James, in her constructively critical discussion, has argued that adults' "giving voice to children is not simply or only about letting children speak; it is about exploring the unique contribution to our understanding of and theorizing about the social world that children's perspectives can provide" ("Giving Voice" 262).

Like other forms of social and cultural identity, youth is not fixed in meaning, but requires active positioning. Stuart Hall has theorized identity as "never complete, always in process, and always constituted within, not outside, representation" (222). As Hall reminds us, acts of representation always implicate identity positions: "Practices of representation always implicate the positions from which we speak or write—the positions of *enunciation*" (222). If it is surprising to think about childhood or youth as a category of identity, this is because the ideology of developmentalism, parading under the guise of a "natural" view of childhood as biological immaturity, has obscured the fact that youth is a contested position with shifting social meanings that young people must negotiate. Children's social identities and positions as children, which transpire in and over time, are aspects of their daily lives that help structure their sense of themselves, other people, and their societies. Considering how young people engage with their identities as children alongside other social identities and their lived experience offers a means of thinking about what constitutes children's perspectives.[30]

To discuss children's social identity as children depends on recognition of children's agency in using, resisting, and remaking the category of "child" and other age-related categories. Kimberlé Crenshaw, legal scholar and early theorist of Critical Race Theory, reminds us that "there is unequal power, but there is nonetheless some degree of agency that people can and do exert in the politics of naming. And it is important to note that identity continues to be a site of resistance for members of different subordinated groups" (1297). Age-related categories should be considered alongside other types of social-political power, and in doing so Crenshaw's concept of "intersectionality" helps us to consider how power operates differentially in children's lives in conjunction with other social identities, "to account," in Crenshaw's words, "for multiple grounds of identity when considering how the social world is constructed" (1245).

Child status has long been fraught for children of color in the United States, with the continuing incidence of tragic murders of black children at the hands of civilians or police—Emmett Till, Tamir Rice, Trayvon

Martin, among so many others—often accomplished in part through erasure of the protection of child status. Recent work is accumulating that documents how black children have been and still are often denied the protection afforded by being seen as children by instead being judged to be older than their actual age (Rebecca Epstein et al.; Philip Atiba Goff et al.). Jamilia J. Blake and colleagues use the term "adultification" to encompass the stereotyping attitude by adults "to overestimate children's stated age, viewing them as less innocent and more mature than their same-age counterparts" (119), which is prevalent in relation to black children and puts them at greater risk than white children of the same age in terms of criminal justice, school discipline, and child welfare systems; and Epstein and colleagues issue a call to action to conduct more research on this phenomenon. Further, Priscilla A. Ocen argues that black girls historically and currently inhabit a "liminal childhood" (1598) that denies them adequate protection from sexual violence and exploitation. It is worth noting that in the late 1960s, as I discuss in chapter 5, a group of black and Latinx young people in New York City named the publication resulting from their out-of-school writing workshop *The Voice of the Children*, thus staking their claim to childhood and to writing *as children*.

Accounting for plural childhoods is necessary for an inclusive notion of young people's temporal agency, in order to think about how varied and multiple temporalities intersect with individual subjectivities, identities, and historical realities. The prevalent conceptual model of children has moved from a focus on single case studies during the "child study" movement in the nineteenth century,[31] to a twentieth-century "child" constructed through psychological research practices to represent a generalized child,[32] to sociological and critical psychological viewpoints—"the new social studies of childhood" (James, Jenks, and Prout 217)—that have moved away from a singular "child" (typically white, male, and middle class, as in Robert Louis Stevenson's *A Child's Garden of Verses*) toward a plural vision of childhoods that can encompass a multiplicity of experiences, perspectives, and ideas.[33] Such a plural vision can account for the imaginative space created by each young writer in living her specific life *as* a young person.

Conceptual Problems of Youth Authorship

Age is built into our central generic terms. The term "literature" assumes an adult author addressing adults, and the term "children's literature" assumes an adult author addressing children.[34] I must resort to the awkward terms "youth-authored poems," "youth-produced poetry," or "poetry written by young poets" to refer to poetry written by children. I use the terms "children," "youth," and "young people" interchangeably to refer to people younger than eighteen years, which is the definition of "child" used by the United Nations Convention on the Rights of the Child ("Convention"). While certainly there are important distinctions between, say, elementary school–aged children and adolescents, what matters for the purposes of this project is that these identities are defined in contrast to adult identity, and that these people—individually and collectively—are denied the social, cultural, and political power of adults in twentieth- and twenty-first-century Western societies. Without the cultural authority of authorship, young writers are not enabled to fully claim the agency that they express through crafting their ideas in written form. Lucia Hodgson has discussed how scholarship on Phillis Wheatley, "particularly research concerned with recuperating the poet's agency, has characterized her as an adult woman rather than a girl child" (664), even though Wheatley published her first poem at about the age of fourteen, achieved renown for her elegy for George Whitefield at about sixteen, and published her collection *Poems on Various Subjects, Religious and Moral* in 1773 at the age of eighteen or nineteen.[35] Adults continue to play a pivotal role in recognizing, or not recognizing, young authors' writing *as work produced by youth*.

Another mode of questioning and discounting young people's authorship involves adults' exaggerated concern about the extent of adult mediation in the production of youth-authored texts. Janna Nadler discusses literary publishing as "an adult-controlled institution that authorizes and regulates most reading and writing" and does not readily accord value to texts written by youth (413). I have frequently received questions from reviewers, audiences, and college students that reveal that adult readers are often compelled to inquire about how young writers' poems were shaped by adults: what prompts or editorial suggestions were given by adult teachers or editors; what poems by adults were read as inspiration or models;

how parents, teachers, or editors might have helped shape the words on the page.[36] I do not believe that these questions need to be answered in order to read and appreciate poems written by children. Indeed, too often these questions can't be answered. Recent anthologies published in the United States may contain work from decades earlier (e.g., Nye's *Salting the Ocean*), or the teaching poets might not be identified (e.g., WritersCorps) or are deceased (e.g., Lyne, *Ten-Second Rainshowers*). There are anthologies of youth-written poems that do include writing prompts (e.g., WritersCorps, *Tell the World*), and youth poetry programs that publish pedagogical guides (e.g., Weiss and Herndon, *Brave New Voices*), as well as scholarship on youth poetry that discusses pedagogical practices (e.g., Jocson, *Youth Poets*). The fact that adults often raise questions about adults' influence on children's writing reflects their assumptions that young writers are apprentices who need to be tutored by adults. Many adult poets show their work to colleagues, mentors, or editors, yet adults reading poems written by adult poets do not typically pose similar questions about others' influence, guidance, or editorial assistance. Adult readers by and large assume that adult poets are independent and capable, and that young poets are dependent apprentices who are only partially capable.

Young writers could be more directly involved in collecting, curating, and editing the work of other young poets. Roger Hart's "ladder of children's participation" (41), initially developed to think about young people's involvement with adults in community development projects, is a useful model for thinking about young writers' level of participation in adult-facilitated or collaborative projects between adults and children.[37] The rungs on the ladder indicate "degrees of participation" (41), with the lowest rungs indicating degrees of nonparticipation such as "tokenism" (42), which can characterize projects in which children have their work included and seem aware of a project "but in fact have little or no choice about the subject or the style of communicating it, or no time to formulate their own opinions" (41). Higher rungs, by contrast, indicate "genuine participation" (42) that maximizes individual children's choice to participate and, to varying degrees, children's engagement in leadership roles. While published anthologies of writing by children often do not convey sufficient information about the process of the selection and organization of the work to fully determine the level of children's participation, one can apply different judgments about the level of children's participation to different aspects of a project. For instance, the innovative writing workshop The Voice of the Children (the focus of chapter 5) produced a mimeographed weekly publication with young writers exercising leadership positions, which reflects a higher level of children's participation than the print anthology *THE VOICE of the Children*, which involved adult editors June Jordan and Terri Bush making editorial selections from the weekly publication (Terri Bush, personal interview).[38]

Typically, when adult editors publish work by young poets, age status is rigidly enforced, with most anthologies printing each young poet's age or grade (school year) alongside or beneath the poet's name on the page where the poem appears (e.g., Brewbaker and Hyland; Lyne, *Ten-Second Rainshowers*). Very few anthologies—Nye's *Salting the Ocean* is a rare exception—allow young people's poetry to be reproduced free from specific age expectations. Further, young poets are not generally given credit for a level of literary craft that controls whether and how to transform personal experience. Adult readers of poetry by children often read a first-person speaker autobiographically, as the direct speech of the poet rather than as a literary representation constructed by the poet. For instance, Katie Roiphe's review of *Tell the World: Teen Poems from WritersCorps* begins with a dismissive claim that poetry "lends itself to the fierce dramas and false clarities" of adolescence and concludes by stating that in reading poetry by young poets, "one gets the sense of reading someone's journal, glimpsing a private universe," as if the poem is no more than a transcription of a young writer's diary. This mode of reading flattens the complexity that inheres in the poetic speakers that young poets construct.[39]

Lurking in the half shadows is a still unresolved debate about the possibilities, potential, and merits of poetry written by youth. The "poetry in the schools" movement blossomed in the United States in the 1970s, and Kenneth Koch among others saw his role as not so much teaching children to write poetry but getting out of the way and "permitting the children to discover something they already have," given that, as he asserted, "Children have a natural talent for writing poetry" (29). On the other hand, Myra Cohn Livingston, also writing in the 1970s and 1980s, claimed that run-of-the-mill poetry by children "flouts the tradition of poetry as a crafted work" (37); she believed strongly that instruction is necessary to "develop children's potential" (289) to be poets in the future and that "to publish [poems by children] as poetry does no particular good for children" (29). In his essay "Can Children's Poetry Matter?" on poetry written by adults for young audiences, Richard Flynn points out prevalent contradictions in pedagogies that devalue both children and poetry, which helps us discern that both Koch and Livingston view young poets' work through the prism of adult temporal values: either for their nostalgic effects on adult readers (Koch) or as apprentice tasks for children's futures (Livingston). Yet even these viewpoints are multifaceted, since Koch wrote of the "contemporaneity and relevance, both in subject and in tone" (34) of poetry written by children as texts to inspire other young poets, and Livingston wrote that young people are capable of writing "real poetry" (271) with instruction, such as in June Jordan's writing workshops (the subject of chapter 5), about which Jordan herself wrote that children "consume and they incorporate, they experiment, and they master" poetic craft (Jordan, " 'The Voice of the Children' Saturday Workshop Diaries" 146).[40]

Even when children produce creative works, their presentation can be delimited and contained by the categorization practices of adult editors, publishers, or archivists. Some of the anthologies I mention have been classified as "school verse" on their copyright pages, according to the Library of Congress subject headings (e.g., Nye's *Salting the Ocean* and Pawlak et al.'s *When We Were Countries*). "School verse" obviously relegates young poets to the institutional location of school regardless of whether the poems were actually written in a school context, and carries a temporal resonance of valuing youth-written poems for the past of school days. Angela Sorby discusses nineteenth-century American adult poets' figuration of the past as a child and the prevalent expectation for children to perform poetry in the schoolroom in ways that positioned them "as conservators not just of a personal but also of collective—local and national—versions of the past" (186).

The most available and sanctioned lens through which adult critics think about writing by youth is that of "juvenilia," which, like "school verse," retains young writers in the past. There is burgeoning interest in juvenilia in English-language literatures, as seen in Christine Alexander and Juliet McMaster's valuable edited volume *The Child Writer from Austen to Woolf* and the more recent collection *Home and Away: The Place of the*

Child Writer, edited by David Owen and Lesley Peterson. Alexander is the current editor of Juvenilia Press, founded by McMaster, which publishes "scholarly editions of early writings by children and adolescents (up to the approximate age of twenty) [that] provide a window on the writer's development and engaging glimpses of the young genius at work," as the press website indicates. Thus far, in publishing juvenilia by such adult writers as George Eliot, Louisa May Alcott, and Margaret Atwood, this approach grants children's writing visibility because of the stature of the authors' work as adults, though Juvenilia Press does publish the work of a few young writers who did not go on to publish as adults, such as Iris Vaughan and Opal Whiteley. In examining the work of young writers who became established adult writers, scholars of juvenilia typically discuss the youthful writing as a prelude or preparation for the older writing (e.g., Victor Neufeldt's "The Child Is Parent to the Author: Branwell Bronte"). However, juvenilia scholars' comparisons of younger and older writing by the same author do sometimes value features of the "youthful writings" (Owen and Peterson, "Introduction" xvii), as in the case of Jane Austen.[41]

Alexander and McMaster acknowledge that current approaches to juvenilia are a starting point and usefully highlight that children's writings have value in and of themselves and that scholars could "examine childhood writings as a body of literature, almost a genre, in their own right" ("Introduction" 3).[42] Alexander begins the second half of her recent essay, "In Search of Juvenilia," by asking "What Is the Way Forward for Literary Juvenilia Studies?" (15); and she first reviews approaches already taken—comparing a writer's juvenilia to the same writer's adult works, editing newly discovered or rediscovered works of juvenilia, or considering the value of juvenilia for genre studies—and then invites broadening the focus of juvenilia studies beyond affluent middle-class white children (primarily in the United Kingdom) who had the leisure to write, and beyond young writers who "became" canonical adult authors. Alexander advocates considering a broader range of young writers (across class, race, gender, family context, education, and geographic location) whether or not they continued writing into adulthood, and asks whether there are "young writers who feel a shared social identity as youthful authors" (18). Anna Redcay thinks across a range of "child-authored" (iv) Anglo-American texts published in the 1920s and 1930s to explore how "young authors negotiate concepts of childhood" (6) and contribute to otherwise adult-framed discourses of childhood. Laurie Langbauer demonstrates how some of the British Romantic poets in the late eighteenth and early nineteenth century maintained and recognized each other's identity as young writers, and were recognized in reviews as young poets.[43] Finally, Victoria Ford Smith brings to light examples of "child collaborators" (240) with adults who, as young artists and writers in the nineteenth and early twentieth century, demonstrate the active roles that children played in producing literature and culture as well as "in shaping discourses about childhood" (259). In helping to rewrite literary history, Smith's work "challenges definitions of authorship and paradigms of childhood that collectively eclipse the role young people play in children's literature and culture" (240) and suggests the value of collaborative models in considering children's cultural contributions.

How do texts written by children circulate? In the nineteenth- and early twentieth-century United States and United Kingdom, they typically circulated domestically, as with family newspapers created by the Stephen (Virginia Woolf's family)[44] and Alcott families, and self-produced books, such as the hundreds of small books created by two generations of the Hale children.[45] For the most part, texts co-constructed by siblings were confined to their family audience, or shared with friends.[46] As a child writer, finding an audience outside one's family is still a challenge. Adora Svitak, who published her first book at the age of seven, spoke at a 2010 TED conference about how she "wanted to get [her short stories] published" and was told "ironically" by one "large children's publisher" that they "didn't work with children"; Svitak muses about this strategy that "you're kind of alienating a large client there." One means of young writers' publication involves parents arranging or facilitating the publication of their children's work, as with Hilda Conkling's volume of poetry *Poems by a Little Girl*, published in 1920 when she was nine years old and dedicated to her mother, poet Grace Conkling.[47]

Another way that young poets can seize publication opportunities involves "passing" as an adult. Gwendolyn Brooks reported that her first poems were published at age eleven in a local newspaper, the *Hyde Parker*, because the adult editor was not aware of her age: "I sent them to the editor. He didn't know I was eleven, and just went ahead and published these four poems," which she found "Very encouraging!" (Hackney 158). Brooks's experience of "passing" as an adult exemplifies a child's expression of agency at the expense of the adult gatekeeper's knowledge. While young Brooks's actions resulted in publication in an adult-controlled venue, her agency as a young person was not recognized as such.

Collective composition among children is yet another approach to authority and audience. Joseph T. Thomas, Jr., writes about poetry jointly created by children on playgrounds, which he suggests belongs to the "rich poetic tradition" in the United States (40). Thomas rescues jump-rope rhymes, chants, and hand-clapping rhymes from the exclusive realm of folklore, and identifies them as "owned and reinvented by each new generation of children" (59–60). Thomas demonstrates that, since playground poems are "not monitored by [adult] authority figures" (41), they have been used to support children's purposes, including transforming and subverting adult norms and cultural references.

The surge of interest since the 1990s in spoken word poetry (also called slam poetry when performed in competitions) offers an interesting case of teen poets composing and performing, particularly for live audiences of other teens.[48] Ruth Kim considers spoken word poetry a liberatory practice for young people who are disenfranchised by social and political ideologies and practices, and writes about the value of spoken word poetry for youth as a form of "activism . . . toward decolonizing literacy" (404) from the "historical scripts and logic of heteropatriarchy, white supremacy, and settler colonialism" (403). Kim explores young people's involvement with the organization Youth Speaks in the San Francisco Bay Area, which describes its pedagogical approach in terms that highlight poetic expression as one of the "tools" young people can use "to take control of their lives": "By making the connection between poetry, spoken word, youth development and civic engagement, Youth Speaks aims to deconstruct dominant narratives in hopes of achieving a more inclusive, and active, culture. Believing that young people have the tools to take control of their lives through language, Youth Speaks encourages youth to express themselves using their own vernacular" (Youth Speaks, "Pedagogy"). Kim quotes one "former youth poet" speaking about the value of literacy for his own "freedom," specifically "the freedom to be in control" or to exercise agency, and thereby defining literacy "in his own terms: 'Literacy is so important. I never knew literacy could get at my soul. . . . What literacy does is, it allows you the freedom to be in control when you don't have the physical freedom'" (403).[49]

Similarly, Korina Jocson, in her study of "youth poets," discusses young people's reading and writing of poetry "as a form of critical literacy" (3) that young people can use to understand and imagine themselves in the context of their worlds, which is particularly important for young people of color in underresourced communities. Jocson calls for "improved and innovative pedagogies" (188) to use within and outside school settings to help support "youths' continued crafting of words as an invitation to enter everyday imagination" (188), such as the approach in a university-school partnership connected with Poetry for the People, the community-based poetry program developed in the 1990s by poet June Jordan. Antonio, a participant in Poetry for the People who went on to participate in Youth Speaks, reflects on the role of writing for his experience of his "individuality" and his "place in the world": " 'Writing has given me the vision to understand myself and my place in the world. I found people who shared similar experiences and simultaneously, I experienced my individuality' " (Jocson 143).[50]

The dominant means of publication for young poets in the late twentieth- and early twenty-first-century United States have been journals or anthologies assembled by teachers, writing programs, writing contests, and editors of literary publications.[51] In writing about her experience editing *Teen Ink*, a journal of teen writing, Elissa Gershowitz notes, "Many of our submissions arrived in packets of classroom work, adding another layer to the creative process. In some cases the authors were highly aware of their dual audience of adults and peers, which is reflected in their writing" (40). Published poems by young people, whether or not they are generated in classrooms, are typically mediated by the pedagogical or editorial attention of adults, and thus could be said to have an audience of young people and adults, the "dual audience" to which Gershowitz refers.

Juliet McMaster ("Adults' Literature") believes that a young writer is often writing for an audience of adults and is "not trying to produce 'children's literature' (whatever that is). She has her eye on the Canon" (281) in order to be "an author with authority among authors" (296). Thus, according to McMaster, child writers could be said to write "adults' literature" (282), literature for an adult audience, which may include children. Her evidence rests on work such as Daisy Ashford's *The Young Visiters*, written when Ashford was nine years old, published in 1919, and subsequently adapted for the stage and screen. *The Young Visiters* follows conventions and plot elements of adult fiction and has exclusively adult characters in its twelve chapters, yet, as the title suggests, preserves what McMaster calls "dicey spelling" ("Adults' Literature" 282).[52] In fact, McMaster suggests that the misspellings—a kind of authentication of young authorship for adult audiences—in a tale of romance and social striving ensures its interest for adult readers: "Of course much of our pleasure in *The Young Visiters* derives from what is probably a rather prurient delight in this degree of sexual knowingness from a nine-year-old, especially as the dicey spelling keeps reminding us of her tender age" ("Adults' Literature" 282).[53] Alexander ("Defining and Representing Literary Juvenilia") explains that spelling "is usually a straightforward consideration in editing an adult-authored work but . . . can be contentious for juvenilia" (87), and describes how in the manuscript for Jane Austen's *Love and Freindship*, written when the author was fourteen, Austen misspells "freindship" on the title page but spells it correctly throughout the rest of the manuscript, and yet the misspelling is retained in almost all editions of the work. The "contentious" nature of spelling errors in publishing juvenilia, as both McMaster and Alexander ("Defining and Representing Literary Juvenilia") discuss, can be understood to reflect how adult editors and publishers help to produce and reinforce a childishness in youth-written texts, which can be at odds with young writers' efforts to contribute to "the Canon" (McMaster, "Adults' Literature" 281).

Publishers' and editors' decisions to preserve idiosyncratic spelling in publishing work by young writers can also help shape how child-authored texts participate in cultural-political projects. *Poems by Kali*, written when Kali Grosvenor was six and seven years old and published in 1970 when she was eight, contains many poems that forefront black identity, and was widely read by adults and children in African American communities when it appeared, as Katharine Capshaw discusses. Capshaw sees the publisher's preservation of conspicuous misspellings in many of the poems as indicative of positioning Kali, through use of black vernacular speech, as "the authentic representative of blackness" and as a voice not yet shaped by white-dominated values: "As the authentic representative of blackness, Kali was required to use a language that demonstrated her commitment to the common people. In addition, authenticity demanded a voice untrammeled by white education" (173). Yet adult Kali Grosvenor explained to Capshaw that, as a child, she objected to publishing these misspellings: "'the publisher published the poems exactly as I had written them. . . . [T]hat was *so* disappointing to little me. But they talked to me about that and I saw they were going to do what they wanted to do. To get through that I calmed myself and imagined the poems were sort of 'dialect' poems of a kid'" (Capshaw 172). At the time of her book's publication, Grosvenor clearly recognized the limits of her "authority" given that the publishers "were going to do what they wanted to do." Grosvenor remembers that, when she was "little me," she tried to console herself by thinking of the misspellings as indicative of "kid" speech, as valuable for their identification with her child status ("little me") and with her identity as a child writer ("'dialect' poems of a kid"). We don't know how young Kali Grosvenor's sense of herself as a "kid" intersected with her identification as a black child, but her comments as an adult suggest that despite her political engagement with blackness evident in many of her poems, she viewed the question of misspelling in common with other child authors as a mark of childishness she was hoping to shed as part of her achievement as a published writer. This example illustrates the complexities of conflicting orientations that young poets and adults sometimes have to editing and publishing practices, and the importance and validity of young writers' own goals and preferences related to the presentation of their work in the time of their youth.

Young Poets Writing Lyric Times

Gwendolyn Brooks, one of the foremost American poets of childhood, thought about time and childhood across her poetic career. Born in 1917, Brooks wrote poetry from the age of seven, began publishing in her teens, was the first African American to win a Pulitzer Prize in 1950 for her second book of poetry (*Annie Allen*), and continued to write for adult and young audiences until her death in 2000. Brooks's early poems reveal interesting continuity with her adult interest in time and temporality as means of representing the subjectivity of her characters.[54] In the first volume of Brooks's autobiography, *Report from Part One*, she includes a poem she wrote in her youth titled "The Busy Clock." Brooks describes finding the poem in notebooks she kept in the late 1920s, from age eleven on, and she refers to these early poems as "Careful rhymes" and "Lofty meditations" (*Report* 55).

> Clock, clock, tell the time,
> Tell the time to me.
> Magic, patient instrument,
> That is never free.
>
> Tick, tock, busy clock!
> You've no time to play!
> Bustling men and women
> Need you all the day.[55]

When I asked my undergraduate students whether they thought Brooks had written this poem as an adult or as a child, most thought at first glance that she had written it as an adult. They were impressed by the poem's use of rhyme, rhythm, and alliteration, and this level of poetic craft suggested to them adult-like knowledge and artistry. A few students thought these same features could indicate that Brooks had written the poem as a child, since it conformed dutifully to basic ideas about how to write a poem. One student argued that by referencing the importance of "play," the poem put forth a youth-oriented priority, and another expanded on this theme to say that "no time to play" results from adult "men and women" using the clock's time for their own purposes. Yet another student noticed the speaker's direct address to the clock as a friend or comrade, which could suggest a young writer who identifies with the clock. For young Brooks, thinking about time and the clock in relation to youth involves thinking about agency and freedom, since the clock is beholden to the "Bustling" adults' priorities and is "never free" to pursue its own interests.

Most striking about Brooks's "The Busy Clock" is its concern with the clock as a form of being. Young Brooks imagines, with empathy and immediacy, the life of a clock in an extended present ("all the day"), and that extended present—the "all the day" that resonates with "never free" in concluding the final lines of each of the poem's stanzas—is the temporal canvas on which young Brooks paints her speaker's alliance with the clock.[56] Young Brooks's temporal choices convey her valuation of the present for constituting and experiencing oneself, whereas for adults, from the Romantic tradition onward, the past and future have been important benchmarks for the self.[57]

Literary representations of time are thus imbued with personal and cultural values concerning age, subjectivity, and experience. In twentieth- and twenty-first-century European American societies, children are typically positioned as the objects of adults' ideas and representations of time, or as instruments that serve adults' projects, rather than as subjects of their own time. We might say that for these adults, children are clocks: adults look to them, measure their lives by them, and impose their priorities on them. Young Gwendolyn Brooks's poem "The Busy Clock" uses and resists this dominant cultural trope of children as clocks and suggests the value of poems written by children as sources of their ideas about subjectivity and agency in relation to time, as well as the potency of temporal representations as means of crafting these ideas in poetic form.

Temporal agency—agency in relation to time—is a central component of the agency that young poets practice both in terms of the poetic representations they create and the agency they claim in constructing these representations. The linguistic and grammatical choices, poetic devices, and temporal representations in poems by young people serve as the prime evidence for agency within this project: young poets' particular methods of parsing past, present, and future; the relations they establish between child or adult characters and temporality; the connections they draw between age and action; and the strategies they employ for delineating daily clocks and calendars. Most of the poems I explore in *Time for Childhoods* are written in the first person, and I follow literary critical convention in referring to "the speaker," rather than the young poet, as the constructed voice of the poem. My intention is not to conflate the young poets' lived experience with that of their poetic speakers (though their work is certainly influenced by their own temporal standpoints) but to explore how young poets' constructions of temporal representations reflect their skill at figuring time and crafting temporal worlds, and reveal their practice of temporal agency.

I explore two other youth-written poems in this section in order to demonstrate and deepen my method of engagement with temporality in poetry. These next two poems—both from Sandford Lyne's anthologies—figure youth temporal standpoints. Elizabeth Thompson's lyrical, evocative poem "Different Worlds" begins mysteriously without announcing or explaining what the "Different Worlds" are that the poem eventually reveals as age positions or life epochs. "Different Worlds" launches from the culturally available idea that it is not possible to inhabit or to see one's childhood and adulthood simultaneously. However, Thompson's poem quietly subverts even the available dilemmas of agency, temporality, and childhood by having her young speaker imaginatively claim agency over the temporal and spatial relations of the age positions of her life.

Thompson's young speaker demonstrates her temporal standpoint in being able to yoke the mutually exclusive worlds of childhood and adulthood:

> Different worlds,
> one in leaf,
> one in flame.
> It seemed that one world
> was holding me back
> from the other.
> But not that day.
> Off in the distance
> I could see adulthood.

Thompson initially places the "Different worlds" in a single landscape of natural, elemental images, "one in leaf, / one in flame," lines whose sonic resonance derives in part from the letters in "leaf" being contained within "flame." These opening lines are rhythmically resonant, repetitive two-beat lines, which launch the poem with imagistic clarity and rhythmic directness. The thematic problem of the poem is how the "Different worlds" of age status interact, and whether it is possible to see oneself at different temporal epochs at the same time. This nine-line poem is structured thematically in three tercets (without spatial divisions) that differ in tone and temporal emphasis: the first tercet is tenseless, the second is in the past progressive, and the third involves a particular construction of the past. The central drama of the poem is the interplay between the second and third tercets. In the second tercet, the self is placed in a passive role, caught between one world and the next—with "me" trapped in the middle between "one world" and "the other"—in an ongoing past. In the third tercet, the self takes an active role in a direct statement of action that concludes the poem with the line "I could see adulthood," where "I" is in a strong position anchoring the left margin.

The conceit of Thompson's "Different Worlds" is that on a particular day in the past, the speaker was able to glimpse the future age epoch of adulthood. In the final tercet, the poet chooses not to use the simple past

(I saw adulthood) but instead crafts a complex temporal landscape that hinges on a particular temporal location, "that day," in which a traversing of worlds was possible. Thompson opens up the past tense through a spatial metaphor—"Off in the distance"—that conjures a future that is visible if not yet reachable, in which "I could"—that is, was able or had the capacity to—"see adulthood." Thompson positions her young speaker as a child seeing her adulthood at a distance that she can fathom, though the age positions are still considered "Different worlds" in this both/and perspective.[58] Thus, Thompson uses figuration to depict her young speaker as powerful enough to imagine herself in the same temporal landscape as her future adulthood, a complex feat of language, imagery, and temporal agency.

Thompson's "Different Worlds" appears in an anthology compiled by poet and educator Sandford Lyne titled *Soft Hay Will Catch You: Poems by Young People*. In his introduction, Lyne writes about his teaching in terms he borrows from his description of the approach that his mother, a schoolteacher, took with him, as "the guardian and supplier of means and opportunities"; the children in his workshops "did the rest" (xiii). Lyne situates the range of his engagement "as a visiting poet" in primary and secondary schools in the United States from 1983 to 2004 with children who were "from a variety of racial, ethnic, religious, and socioeconomic backgrounds" and who "lived in urban, suburban, and rural areas" (*Ten-Second Rainshowers* 11). While Lyne's anthologies do not describe his pedagogical approach in detail, he does mention the elements of "safe and sensible starting places, a few guidelines (for example, don't try to rhyme), and the 'fairy dust' of attention and praise" (*Ten-Second Rainshowers* 11). In framing the relation of the adult "visiting poet" to the children in his classes, Lyne writes about his experience as an eight-year-old child in his backyard with his father, who "put into my hands a small, boy-sized shovel" and suggested he dig "for buried treasure" (*Ten-Second Rainshowers* 9) around their yard, each time revealing a coin that his father had surreptitiously placed there for Lyne to dig up. "A few years into my teaching," writes Lyne, "I realized that my father's invention was a universal way to reach out to young people. 'Try this,' I say, introducing an approach to making a poem. 'Dig here. Maybe this will have something for you.' The treasure found is always more than the treasure buried. The implement used is a soft lead pencil. Everywhere I look, I see the garden" (*Ten-Second Rainshowers* 13).

Notice that the shovel, the "implement used" to find the treasure, is in the child's hands, and the adult is merely suggesting where to dig. The adult is a consultant, providing tools and suggestions about where and sometimes how to use them. The child does the digging.[59]

Whereas Elizabeth Thompson's poem "Different Worlds" ends on "adulthood," Jennifer Edwards's poem "Masters"—from Lyne's first anthology of poems by young people titled *Ten-Second Rainshowers*—ends on "childhood" in its figuration of young speakers' temporal standpoints. Edwards's "Masters" presents a plural voice, a consistent "We" of child protagonists throughout the poem. The poem opens with an image of practiced and drilled regimentation of children's movement as they "march," and suggests that perhaps this orderliness does not belong to earthly children, who are behaving "like angels."

> We march out of the classroom
> like angels in front of the teacher,
> but when we get outside onto
> the soft earth we run and yell
> and fight and scream.
> We are no longer angels.
> We are masters at childhood.

The poem's third line ushers in a shift in space and time from classroom and hallway to "when we get outside," where "the soft earth" accommodates changes in the children's physical activity and voices. Although the present tense of the poem does not alter, once "outside," the collective child speakers themselves have altered ("We are no longer angels") and claim a new present that is for themselves and not for or "in front of" adults. Thus, "when" introduces a temporal and spatial shift that occasions differences in the children's actions and identities, whereby they act as children for themselves.

The last line of "Masters" indicates a transformed identity—in contrast to the simile "like angels"—that suggests the performance of childhood and a keen awareness of context. There are at least two ways to read the line "We are masters at childhood," one of which suggests that running, yelling, fighting, and screaming constitutes "childhood": to do those actions is to perform childhood. Research in sociology and anthropology by Myra Bluebond-Langner, Nancy Mandell, and William Corsaro has begun to outline how children use their social knowledge "in order to act like children," in the words of Mandell (436). Among recent discussions of childhood as performance, Robin Bernstein explores the notion of children "as experts in the scripts of children's culture, as virtuoso performers" of childhood in their everyday lives (28) who can express agency by following or resisting particular culturally "scripted" performances of childhood (240).[60] An alternative reading of the final line of "Masters" is that knowing to "run and yell / and fight and scream" only outside school and not in a classroom or school hallway is to be one of the "masters at childhood." In this reading, exercising agency as a child, being one of the "masters at childhood," involves making use of one's knowledge of adults' expectations for and tolerance of children's actions across temporal and spatial contexts.

One clever—even arch—aspect of "Masters" is the resonance that the title "Masters" has by the poem's conclusion, which involves subverting expected power dynamics. The poem's final line proclaims that the children are "masters" rather than the teachers, yet rather than masters *of* children they are "masters at childhood." This is a brilliant manipulation of power-inflected rhetorical reference that conveys childhood identity and solidarity (emphasized also by the repetition of "We" at the start of three of the poem's lines), appropriation of power (accentuated by the consistency of the children's subject position in the poem's syntax), and the performance of childhood (with the conspicuous use of the term "childhood" referring to the state or position of being a child), which indicates Edwards's skill in crafting young speakers' temporal standpoints.

Poetry written by children can offer temporal ideas, dynamics, and trajectories that articulate possibilities for youth-identified speakers and draw from young poets' own standpoints. Both Elizabeth Thompson's "Different Worlds" and Jennifer Edwards's "Masters" represent poetic speakers with explicit youth identities who position their ideas in relation to the social position of "childhood" or "adulthood." While indicated prominently beneath the poets' names in Sandford Lyne's anthologies are the school grades of the poets—Edwards was in sixth grade (age eleven or twelve) when she wrote "Masters," and Thompson was in fifth grade (age ten or eleven) when she wrote "Different Worlds"—not focusing on that precise information arguably opens up wider interpretive possibilities for adult readers by side-stepping age-related ideologies. The notion of children's temporal standpoints expands possibilities for lyric poetry's representation and remaking of temporal realities.

In "A Poetics, of Sorts," poet Bin Ramke writes, "Poetry is about what all physical things—including human beings—are about: the refusal to be something else; it is about the dignity of being" (158). In the same essay, Ramke mentions the "sorting" that poems accomplish: "A poem is a system for sorting" (157), both in terms of sorting within poems—"putting words and sounds and commas and semicolons and whatever comes to hand into groups with connections" (157)—and sorting across poems into genres. It usually goes without saying that poems written by children are sorted out of the genre of poetry, and are instead considered to be writing practice, homework assignments, examples of adults' teaching, or illustrations of "childlike" thinking. Not works of art, not claims for "the dignity of being." In *Time for Childhoods*, I sort poems written by children into the genre of poetry. Young poets' writing of time is a form of agency hiding in plain sight, given that temporal words and terms are such a common element of languages and literatures. This temporal agency remains hidden because recognizing young people's crafting of poetic times requires granting them authority as poets, as creative shapers of time, and as artists who apply the experiences and knowledges of their youth temporal standpoints. In order to recognize this agency, adult readers must set aside common ideologies of children and childhood as "less" knowledgeable, experienced, and worth listening to; and as useful only in relation to adult priorities rather than for children's own times.

Literary scholars continue to engage with time and temporality as central elements of lyric poetry. David Baker has written that "the subject of time infiltrates the lyric genre" (236) even in poems that are not ostensibly "about time," since Baker argues that "time provides the subject, the story, and the style of lyric poetry" (239). While the subgenre of lyric poetry is difficult to define (and indeed "lyric" is now often used to characterize poetry in general, as Virginia Jackson discusses),[61] it is the most relevant poetic subgenre for this discussion of young poets precisely because of two contested elements: its focus on "telling" time and its typical framing through the singular voice or perspective of a poetic "speaker." Baker further writes, "Poetry is about the varieties of measuring, telling, and thinking about time" (242), and I would add that young poets can be contributors to establishing and exploring these "varieties." Particularly important for consideration of young poets is that lyric poetry invites the reshaping of time through its "temporal engine" (Baker 239) of verb tense and other means of making time happen within poems. Though many theorists of lyric poetry locate a singular lyric timescape, young poets can open up and expand lyric temporality through their impulse to remake and transform time.

Contemporary theorists of the lyric differ in their adherence to a uniform temporality and in the extent of their focus on the present as a time frame. In Jonathan Culler's view, "the lyric present" (243) is a key dimension of lyric poetry and is made possible by the "ritualistic" (131) elements—rhythmic and sonic patterns, lyric address—that characterize lyric poetry and "serve as instructions for performance" (7). For Culler, a lyric poem's "special temporality of the lyric present" (243) inheres in the "event" of the poem itself that enacts "a moment of time that is repeated every time the poem is read" (295). While Culler's view of a uniform lyric tense centers the present, Sharon Cameron's idea of "Lyric Time" (the title of her 1979 book on Emily Dickinson) focuses on a kind of timelessness, a "lyric compression of temporality" (241)—"collapsing" (260) temporal distinctions in order to "present sequence as if it were a unity" (241) or "stall time to a stasis" (260)—in the service of a "collapsing of eternity into immortality" (260), which is a preoccupation with death that I suggest can be, at particular cultural-historical locations, more relevant to adults than to children.[62]

In contrast to a temporal uniformity of lyric poetry proposed by Culler's "lyric present" and Cameron's lyric "timelessness," Helen Vendler's reading of lyric poetry allows for the interplay of multiple temporalities.[63] Vendler uses this strategy in discussing Emily Dickinson's "invention of poetic temporal structures that mimic the structure of life as she at any moment conceives it" (*Poets Thinking* 64), from an early "chromatic" (66) rendering of each temporal notch in a sequential scale to temporal revisions such as reducing sequence to key moments, figuring temporal oscillation without end, or holding contrasting temporalities within a single poem. Though, like Culler, Vendler refers to the present—the "here and now" of lyric—it is as a foundation from which poets can launch to other temporalities: a lyric poem "may speak about the there and then, but it speaks about them from the here and now" (*Poems, Poets, Poetry* xl). Reading for temporal flexibility, as in Vendler's reading of Dickinson, can account for a plurality of lyric times both within and across poets' projects.

I reframe the "here and now" of lyric poetry as a temporal groundedness, a poet's confidence in lyric time–making through her willingness to invent, to constrain or expand, to stay the course or uproot the foundation. The confidence to build a time machine according to one's own specifications is central to the lyric impulse. The lyric poet makes time happen through such elements as patterns of syntax, rhythm, and verb tense. I am interested in how young poets are "doing time" in their poems: how they use language, sound, space, and pattern to make their poetic time machines that call us to wind them through our reading. Young poets, through the variety and fluency of their temporal inventions, help establish plural lyric times.

In order to do justice to the work of young poets, complicating the idea of lyric poetry as a representation of poets' subjective experience is necessary in addition to rethinking lyric temporality. Culler rejects views of the lyric poem as an expression of a poet's subjectivity and as an utterance of a fictional speaker, because he believes neither model illuminates "what the poem itself is doing" that "compel[s] our attention in the first place" (350). Yet many lyric poems fit Vendler's description of a poem as "a fictive speech by an imagined speaker" (*Poems, Poets, Poetry* iii),[64] and in so doing, construct temporality as part of the making of perspective. Thinking of a poem as "fictive speech" by a speaker who doesn't necessarily align with the poet's subjectivity—indeed the speaker's identity, including age, may or may not be "socially marked" (Vendler, *Poems, Poets, Poetry* iv)—allows for readings that don't pin an age on the poet or the poetic speaker. Lyric poems need not commit to a specific identity or age of a speaker, even if they are in the first person. Indeed, Annie Finch's idea of "decentering the lyric self" (100) offers a way to expand the notion of the poetic speaker beyond an individual bounded "self." The opportunity for young poets to step into or out of specific age positions, or to craft a speaker who is age-ambiguous or of indeterminate age, is particularly important given that cultural bias about the development of "maturity" limits consideration of young people's ability and power as thinkers, as cultural makers, and as persons.

In *Time for Childhoods*, I look to see how young poets sort time, which is after all—given their fixed location in the age-based category of childhood—the primary reason for their exclusion from literary culture. Within a selection of poems written by people under the age of eighteen in the later decades of the twentieth- and early twenty-first-century United States, I explore how young poets assert their own value, perspectives, and capability by sorting time itself on the mutable canvas of their poem writing. How do young poets craft temporal landscapes, or timescapes? Does the past always precede the present then the future, or can the present invite the past into the future? Do young poets center speakers who are young, old, or ageless? Is temporality necessarily standardized or free to be remade, singular or plural?

I start from the premise that there is no uniform "child time" to be found in reading poems written by young people, but instead there are varied reimaginings of temporality or multiple lyric times that young poets write. I examine young poets' temporal structuring of action, use of common temporal markers, charting of temporal metaphors and trajectories, shifting or playing with verb tense, and reference to age or life phases. My interest is in learning about the range of young poets' approaches to representing temporality as a dominant component of their making of poetic worlds. Thinking about the age position of poets and young poets' crafting of the age standpoints of poetic speakers contributes to our understanding of lyric poetry.

Young poets, rather than taking time as an unproblematic given or fixed timeline, work with time as a pliable medium that they can shape and reshape, which can involve manipulating time to suit one's own purposes and projects. Young poets are not unique in crafting innovative temporal representations, but they have access to thinking flexibly about temporal experiences and trajectories in ways that reflect their knowledge and experiences *as young* and as such add new dimensions to lyric time. Poetry written by young poets reveals young people's complex imagined temporalities—their temporal standpoints—that can enrich our sense of the possibilities of lyric time in relation to human subjectivity.

Children can participate in temporalities that are particular to their status as young people as well as in temporalities shared with adults, which may shift across racial, cultural, and historical locations. In African American literature, as Daylanne English makes clear, time is a medium for representing contestations of power: "time, understood both ontologically and materially, has always been a fundamental theme in African American literature, one that has worked to explore and expose the lived experience of race-bound justice in the United States" (*Each Hour Redeem* 22). In her study of representations of time in African American literature from Phillis Wheatley onward, English explores the centrality of "Tropes of timekeeping" (23) in relation to "racialized injustice" (3) given that time and justice, "although often imagined to be standard and uniform—are actually contingent and unevenly available" (*Each Hour Redeem* 24). English is careful to acknowledge how African American persons and African American literature participate *both* in differential *and* dominant or mainstream temporalities in American society given that "social and economic formations continue to shape time in different ways for different individuals, different groups, different regions, and different aesthetic traditions" (*Each Hour Redeem* 24).[65] In her recent essay "Race, Writing, and Time," English convincingly argues that temporal analysis of African American literary texts and the experiences of African Americans should not be understood "always in relation to whiteness and understood always in terms of departure from a norm" (227) but can be seen in terms of distinctive meanings, forms, or patterns.[66] English thus refers to "*distinctiveness* rather than *difference*" (227, emphasis in original) in her thinking about "the intersection of race and time" ("Race, Writing, and Time" 227). Similarly, I argue that "time for childhoods" is distinctive but not limited to being defined in relation to an adult norm.

Young poets may be aware of dominant temporal perspectives, or temporal ideologies, and can choose to make use of and even alter them for their own projects. William Carlos Williams includes in his autobiography his "first poem" which "was born like a bolt out of the blue" in his late teens (*Autobiography* 47):

> A black, black cloud
> flew over the sun
> driven by fierce flying
> rain.[67]

As an adult writing his autobiography, Williams notices the impossible causation involved in this poem—"How could the clouds be driven by the rain?"—yet nonetheless, he writes, "joy remained. From that moment I was a poet" (*Autobiography* 47). Young Williams is not troubled by reverse causation, by the clouds being driven across the sky by the rain. Perhaps his ability to suspend the facts of natural causation—the expected chronology—is part of what enables him to seize control of language as a poet at a young age. Young people's temporal standpoints can make use of dominant temporal ideologies while also offering new configurations.

In *Time for Childhoods*, I focus on poems that were produced and/or made public within projects initiated, sponsored, or facilitated by adults, yet I foreground young poets' artistry and consider how young poets represent the agency of their poetic characters and claim temporal agency through temporal representation and through the act of writing itself. Conversations about youth agency are often limited by considerations of constraints on young people's action. This project acknowledges the role of adults *and* takes seriously the artistic and temporal agency that young people practice, and the imagined worlds that they write into existence through their temporal standpoints. Thus, I make use of contexts of adult mediation in order to bring into relief young poets' agency.

Reading Youth-Written Poems in Adult-Mediated Projects

In presenting a series of case studies in *Time for Childhoods*, I focus on poetry written by people under the age of eighteen in the United States from the mid-twentieth to early twenty-first century. In order to usefully complicate questions of youth agency, I focus on poetry that reached public audiences through projects that involved adults in facilitating, selecting, publishing, or promoting the poems. I begin and end the series of case studies by considering projects associated with Gwendolyn Brooks and June Jordan, who, as committed and innovative advocates for young poets, chart the directions of what is possible. Although in both of those cases I focus on projects during the 1960s and 1970s (and, for Brooks, into the 1980s), Brooks and Jordan continued their youth advocacy throughout the rest of their lives (and died within two years of each other at the turn of the twenty-first century). Framing the book in this way serves to honor the depth of Brooks's and Jordan's engagements with young people, their commitment to young poets of color, the model they each offer for thinking about how adults can support young poets, and their recognition of the importance of considering time for childhoods.[68]

In a climate of persistent and enduring racial oppression in the United States, Brooks and Jordan reflect the pioneering role black women poets have taken in the mid- to late twentieth- century in supporting young people (Clarke). Robin D. G. Kelley writes that radical black feminism "redefined the source of theory. It expanded the definition of who constitutes a theorist, the voice of authority speaking for black women, to include poets, blues singers, storytellers, painters, mothers, preachers, and teachers" (154). Kelley mentions June Jordan as one such radical black feminist, and in order to encompass Jordan's vision of freedom, we must add "children" to that list of artists and authorities. Jordan and Brooks each enfolded children into their vision of poets and poetry and worked throughout their lives to enact that vision. Brooks even noted that her interest in youth surpassed her interest in writing: "All my life is not writing. My greatest interest is being involved with young people" (Watkins).

Gwendolyn Brooks and June Jordan each came to poetry during their childhoods. As mentioned previously, Gwendolyn Brooks published her first poems at the age of eleven in a newspaper, the *Hyde Parker*, without the editor knowing her age. June Jordan describes in her autobiography *Soldier: A Poet's Childhood* that after she unexpectedly won a poetry contest in elementary school, she realized she could use poetry as currency and began writing poems "for my friends in need of an 'I Like You' or 'I Don't Like You' or 'I Don't Like You Anymore' poem" (*Soldier* 208) in exchange for "pocket money" (Jordan, "Interview" 144). Even without earning money or a place in an adult-focused publication, young people practice agency in and through poetry. Poetry writing is a form of currency that young people can create, use, and bring into the world, and it has value whether or not it is published, read, or performed in public, or is otherwise accessible to wider audiences. My focus is on youth-written poetry that did reach public audiences, and through projects facilitated by adults, because these projects bring questions of youth agency even further into focus. I explore young poets' representations of time and temporality because they magnify the ideas and practices of agency that young poets create and implement. Since childhood is a time-based phase of life, and prevalent ideologies of childhood value children in terms of the past or future or a timeless childhood (James and Prout), theorization of youth agency can benefit from exploring and advocating for the importance of young people's perspectives on temporality, or time for childhoods.

I focus in chapter 2 on Gwendolyn Brooks's multifaceted engagement with and advocacy for young poets and her use of her public success as an adult poet to support young poets through the sponsorship of contests and workshops. The heart of the chapter draws from archival research I conducted at the Gwendolyn Brooks Papers in The Bancroft Library at the University of California at Berkeley, which enabled me to recover and explore poems written by young poets who entered contests sponsored by Brooks from the early 1960s into the 1980s in relation to thematic questions of figuring entrapment by time, age, and racial injustice; life, death, and the trading of poetic visions; and temporal contrast and self-making. In addition, I discuss Brooks's advice manuals for "young poets" and "very young poets" published in the 1980s, and I conclude the chapter by considering a selection of young people's letters to Brooks for their perspectives on Brooks's poetry, public persona, and efforts on behalf of youth.

While in chapter 2 I consider how Brooks positions herself as an adult in her acts of bringing poetry by young poets to public audiences, in chapter 3 I think about Naomi Shihab Nye's editorial decisions in assembling the anthology *Salting the Ocean: 100 Poems by Young Poets* from across her long career teaching poetry in schools. I focus on exploring the multiple and sometimes contrasting strategies used by a sample of the young poets in figuring temporality in their poems. In crafting representations of time, these young poets make use of dynamic temporality in creatively manipulating temporal registers as a means of asserting agency. Primarily through shifts in verb tense, the young poets I discuss present speakers who are located in time, yet also step outside time to reflect on or manipulate aspects of temporality.

In chapter 4, I apply recent scholarship on children's rights in examining a recently launched series of annual anthologies of youth-written poetry published by *Rattle*, an adult-produced literary magazine, as a context for young people's participation in literary production. Children's rights discourse helps underscore young people's right to participate in literary practices as writers rather than solely as consumers of adults' literary productions. Yet even so, children's right to expression is framed largely in terms of children's right of access to information produced by others, rather than their right to create knowledge, art, or other cultural forms. Once again, a developmental conception of children as objects of adults' activities has hampered recognizing youth as cultural innovators, original thinkers, and makers of art. In analyzing a selection of poems from the inaugural *Rattle Young Poets Anthology*, I examine how these young poets craft poems that explore the conditionality of knowledge and self, and the poetic use of temporal control. Correspondence with parents of some of the young poets contributes to my discussion of young poets' agency in relation to adults' involvement in transcribing, presenting, and promoting youth-written poetry.

In the final case study in chapter 5, I discuss The Voice of the Children, an innovative long-term writing workshop co-facilitated by June Jordan and Terri Bush from the late 1960s through the early 1970s. The Voice of the Children workshop is striking for its longevity, for the ways in which Jordan (a black poet) and Bush (a white educator) nurtured the group of black and Latinx children yet opened opportunities for youth leadership, and for its role as a platform for young poets of color to write about racial oppression and injustice during the tumultuous time in which they lived. My consideration of published accounts of the workshop written by Jordan, Bush, and Vanessa Howard, one of the young participants, is augmented by a personal interview I conducted with Terri Bush and archival research I carried out at the June Jordan Papers in the Radcliffe Institute's Schlesinger Library, and is situated in the context of Jordan's other writings and projects. In reading a selection of poems from the workshop's book-length anthology *THE VOICE of the Children*, I explore how these young poets demonstrate temporal agency in the face of racial injustice by crafting the present in relation to the past and future of racial oppression, and by practicing a temporal fluency in creating varied lyric temporalities.

How can young poets be further involved in collecting, curating, and editing the work of other young poets? Gwendolyn Brooks advocates for such youth involvement in her suggestion that teachers "Let the children create a poetry magazine for the class" that includes the work of classmates, and that is managed and edited by the young people ("Poetry and the Educating of Children"). While such efforts are sorely needed within schools, how might they move beyond school settings? Might there be youth-controlled spaces or collaborative spaces with adults where young people's goals, priorities, and aesthetic judgments more directly shape the projects? What could these projects look like, what funding sources could support them, and how could they reach public audiences?[69]

In claiming authority as writers, young poets express agency, and assert their intentions and actions in the context of available forms, structures, and institutions. We might consider young poets as theorists making art through their conceptions of youth and temporality, and their standpoints as young people in time, as long as we also retain and respect the poetic artistry through which these ideas are constructed. Through their literary inventions, young poets can move beyond culturally available ideas about the value of children and childhood, as well as about temporality itself. Poetry is a site in which young writers claim their full personhood: not their potential or their promise but their actual personhood in the present-time of their lives as young people.

What does *time for childhoods* enable and what new worlds can it envision? Through their poetic innovations, young poets can alter expected chronologies and grant authority to the knowledge of child speakers. By subverting children's typical position as the past or future potential of adulthood, young poets open a temporal space that enables them to chart trajectories that can engage with new possible realities. Perhaps children are always doing so, but their acts of remaking temporality in their everyday lives are often unrecognized or unacknowledged by adults. Young people understand time too well in terms that matter to them, and they practice a temporal logic that depends on their own conceptions and agency yet may seem incoherent or opaque to adults. How do young poets envision temporalities and trajectories, and use temporal language to imaginatively shape chronologies? How do they position their child speakers in relation to time or the clock: are their speakers at the mercy of time, or masters of time, or allies of the clock? Do young poets always align themselves with a perspective of a young speaker and do they implicitly or explicitly identify their speakers by age? In what ways do young poets' embodiments of youth intersect with other important social identities such as race? How do young poets use temporal means in figuring and challenging racial oppression and age-based injustice? What do representations of time by young writers reveal about how young authors can conceptualize or represent youth agency or contestations over power? How do young writers express agency through their acts of writing and of seeking an audience or publication?

A Note Regarding Consent and Reprinting Poems by Young Poets

In carrying out this project, I have taken on some of the constraints I highlight regarding young poets' consent to be included in the outcome (e.g., anthologies, readings, archives) of adult-facilitated poetry projects. In the case of older published anthologies, I relied on the fact that adult editors (e.g., Nye [*Salting the Ocean*] in chapter 3) indicated when they made an effort to contact formerly young poets to procure their consent to have their poems included, although in other cases (e.g., Lyne [*Soft Hay* and *Ten-Second Rainshowers*] discussed earlier in this chapter), it was not clear whether such consent was sought. With the most recent project I discuss

(*Rattle Young Poets Anthology* in chapter 4), I worked with the current editor to procure consent for inclusion of young poets' poems, yet in corresponding with the young people's parents it was not always evident whether the young poets themselves or solely their parents issued consent, and I was unable to contact the person whose words appear in the title of that chapter since the editor did not have her current contact information. I chose to use this quotation—"My sole desire is to move someone through poetry, and allow for my voice to be heard"—despite the irony of lacking explicit consent for reprinting it here, because it so well illustrates the challenging circumstances we currently inhabit. In the case of archival or previously published work from projects associated with Gwendolyn Brooks and June Jordan, I was successful in reaching some formerly young poets, but not others. The formerly young poets and parents of currently young poets who responded to my queries were consistently supportive of this project and of the value of paying attention to and respecting the work of young poets. Also important to note here is the paradox of exploring young poets' agency through a thematic focus on temporality that I, as an adult, have imposed. Thus, at the heart of this study of young poets' agency is the difficulty of full engagement with the young poets' consent to have their work included and discussed in this context, and a decision to proceed with my adult-driven purpose.

CHAPTER 2

"to bloom in its own time"

Gwendolyn Brooks and the
Poetic Vision of
Very Young Poets

"I am a little Black girl TRAPPED": Young Poets on
Racial Entrapment in the Present

IN APRIL 1986, Gwendolyn Brooks was invited to join other women poets—among them Adrienne Rich, Toi Derricotte, Denise Levertov, and Sharon Olds—to commemorate the centenary of Emily Dickinson's death at a joint reading at Seton Hall University, a "Celebration of Emily Dickinson and American Women's Poetry" (Horner). As transcripts and audio recordings reveal, most of the invited poets read poems by Emily Dickinson in addition to reading their own poems, but Gwendolyn Brooks did not.[1] Instead, she opened her reading with a poem written by Aurelia Davidson at the age of twelve. In addition to Brooks's radical act of substituting the young Davidson for Dickinson, her introduction to Davidson's poem is notable: "Well, the first woman-oriented poem I want to read, or at least it was written by a woman, although a woman of twelve, not myself, Aurelia Davidson, entered this poem in my . . . Illinois poet laureate competition in Chicago. . . . And I had to give this poem a prize because I felt it was such a clear note of warmth-oriented and honesty-oriented poetry. She called her poem 'Trapped'" ("Emily & I Are Absolutely Different").[2] I find fascinating Brooks's approach to introducing Aurelia Davidson and her poem—a 1980 prizewinner in a

48

contest Brooks had initiated as Illinois poet laureate—for the ways that she navigates questions of gender and age.[3] Brooks claims for Davidson status as a woman, but as "a woman of twelve," thus entwining gender and age status in elevating Davidson's status to a female adult role. I think she does so out of her respect for Davidson's poem and its ideas and craft, and as part of her strategy to include Davidson among the adult women poets whose work is being read at this event, but another explanation is that Brooks relates herself to Davidson directly—Davidson is "not myself," not Brooks.

After reading Davidson's poem, Brooks announced to the audience that she wished she had written it herself. Brooks told the audience, "I would like to think that all of our little black women would subscribe to that and I told Aurelia, 'Aurelia, I wish I had written that poem'" (Brooks, "Emily & I Are Absolutely Different"). The phrase "our little black women" has an additional element of racial solidarity interwoven with gender solidarity, and the same paradoxical girl/woman fusion as the phrase "a woman of twelve." Brooks uses her position as an established adult black female poet to elevate a young black female poet to adult status by her introduction, by substituting Davidson's poem for a poem by Emily Dickinson, by bringing Davidson's poem alongside the poems by adult women at the Seton Hall event, and by paying Davidson the ultimate compliment in announcing that she wished she had written the poem herself. Alongside her deeply respectful treatment of Aurelia Davidson's poem are attributions—"warmth-oriented and honesty-oriented poetry"—that can be seen as conveying potentially limiting adult assumptions about youth as straightforward and transparent.[4] The strength of Brooks's denial that the poem is "written by a woman, a woman of twelve, not myself," along with her statement that she wished she had written the poem, suggest an identification with this young poet that, I argue, is grounded in respect for Davidson's poem as a work of literature, as well as Brooks's own history as a poet who achieved some recognition at a young age.[5]

I learned of this history after I had found "Trapped" by Aurelia Davidson written in Brooks's hand on a piece of thick notepaper decorated with the logo of the Amtrak train line in the Gwendolyn Brooks archive in The Bancroft Library at the University of California at Berkeley. Brooks's careful notation on the notepaper that Davidson is an "Ill[inois] Poet Laureate prizewinner" who is "age 12" from "Chicago, Illinois" suggests that Brooks was on a train journey to an out-of-state event.[6] Davidson's "Trapped" is a striking exploration of a first-person speaker navigating being trapped by racial oppression.

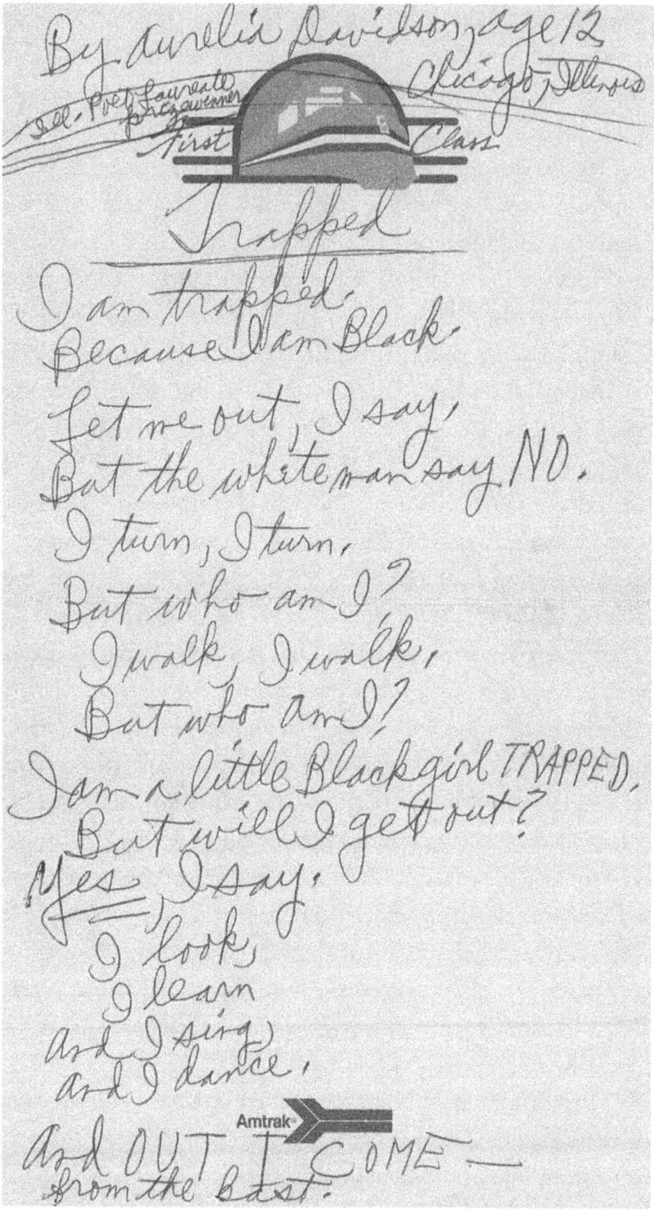

By Aurelia Davidson, age 12

Chicago, Illinois

to: Poet Laureate Gwendolyn
First Class

Trapped

I am trapped,
Because I am Black.
Let me out, I say,
But the white man say NO.
I turn, I turn,
But who am I?
I walk, I walk,
But who am I?
I am a little Black girl TRAPPED.
But will I get out?
Yes, I say.
I look,
I learn
And I sing,
And I dance,
And OUT I COME —
from the East.

FIGURE 1. Aurelia Davidson, "Trapped." Gwendolyn Brooks Papers, BANC MSS 2001/83 z, box 11, folder 32. Courtesy of The Bancroft Library, University of California, Berkeley.

I am trapped
Because I am Black.
Let me out, I say,
But the white man say NO.
I turn, I turn,
But who am I?
I walk, I walk,
But who am I?
I am a little Black girl TRAPPED.
But will I get out?
<u>Yes</u>, I say.
I look,
I learn
And I sing,
And I dance.
And OUT I COME—
from the past.[7]

The speaker's search for escape from her state of entrapment is the poem's thematic heart, and along the way she names the source of her entrapment as "the white man." The poet conveys her speaker's negotiation of this predicament by multiple assertions of identity and a figuring of entrapment and emergence through the poem's architecture and use of pronouns and verbs. While grounded in the present ("I am trapped"), the speaker calls on the future ("will I get out?") and refers to "the past" of racial oppression from which she will emerge.

Aurelia Davidson has her speaker question her identity explicitly and multiply across the poem. The initial couplet announces her speaker's identity—and the reason for her entrapment—as "Black," yet after this confident claim, she twice asks a presumably rhetorical question—"But who am I?"—which occasions repeated reference to actions—"I turn, I turn," "I walk, I walk"—that suggest a metaphorical wandering or perhaps a spinning of her wheels. Davidson's speaker then identifies her intersectional position in relation to race, age, and gender in a way that reverses the syntactical order of her initial self-introduction: rather than "I am trapped / Because I am Black" she states "I am a little Black girl TRAPPED." The strength of this extended assertion of identity—in which her identity as a black female child precedes the situation of being trapped—highlights the contrast between the poem's first half, where the speaker begins in a more passive role as the object of denial of permission by "the white man," and the poem's second half, where the speaker's more direct action and confident assertion ("<u>Yes</u>, I say") assure her freedom.

Davidson's control over temporality helps construct the conditions of her speaker's escape. The line at the exact center of the poem in which Davidson names her speaker's intersectional identity—"I am a little Black girl TRAPPED"—leverages shifts in temporality. Before that point, the poem's tense adheres to a drawn-out present. The speaker's direct appeal for liberation is denied, by "the white man" who "say NO," and the poet figures entrapment through extending the present of repetitive action. After that central line, which in breaking free of the poem's short-line structure prefigures the poem's conclusion, Davidson has her speaker question the future, engage in varied activity, and emerge "from the past." What occasions her emergence is in part suggested by the alteration of verbs; rather than being stuck repeatedly turning and walking, the speaker shifts her activities: "I look, / I learn / And I sing, / And I dance." These graceful and joyous acts could be seen as children's acts, and thus it is the speaker's own actions *as a child* that make possible her liberation from entrapment. This range of her actions prompts an ability to escape the condition of entrapment that has been the inheritance of the past; and one can view the last of these verbs—"dance"—as acting on the "past" through its off-rhyme. The poem's final lines—"And OUT I COME—/ from the past"—suggest an exuberance occasioned by the escape.[8]

Aurelia Davidson represents agency through the strength of her speaker's self-assertion. Despite the speaker's questioning of her identity in the poem's first half, Davidson maintains a determined focus on the first-person pronoun across the poem. "I" appears in each line of the poem except the two from which it is thematically excluded: "But the white man say NO" and "from the past" of racial oppression. The omission of "I" from the final line tempers the exuberance of the penultimate line, and is a sober acknowledgement that the speaker's freedom is hard-won from a past that has denied (and potentially continues to deny) it to her. Notable is the dynamic temporality that Davidson uses in drawing out the present tense of entrapment, and using her speaker's articulation of embodied agency and identity to question the future and rewrite the present in a way that turns it, by the end, into the past. Davidson's deployment of dynamic temporality is a bulwark against the moving target of racial injustice.

Yet in fact Davidson's speaker's escape from racist entrapment is multiply determined. The clear statement of racial logic that opens the poem—"I am trapped / Because I am Black"—suggests in its clarity of articulation that the speaker has the power not only to free herself from the limitations imposed by white anti-black racism but also to free blackness from the limiting lens of racist logic. Michelle M. Wright in *The Physics of Blackness* argues that an expansive idea of blackness is not possible through adhering to a "linear progress narrative" (4) that fixes blackness in a specific historic trajectory, but is enabled by what she terms "Epiphenomenal time" (4) that is grounded in "the current moment, or 'now'" (4) in which blackness is interpreted or defined. Locating oneself in the "now" of "Epiphenomenal time," according to Wright, frees one to discern "the full multidimensionality of Blackness" (146). In the poem's central line, Davidson accomplishes a temporal replacing in asserting her speaker's agency as grounded in the complexity of her intersectional identity. While the causal racial logic in the poem's opening two lines—"I am trapped / Because I am Black"—fixes blackness in the racist logic of "the white man," the intersectional blackness that comes to lead the speaker's identity (with "I am a little Black girl" preceding "TRAPPED") enables her, through the powerful grace of the final two lines, to confidently relegate the limiting view of blackness to "the past."

On the reverse side of the Amtrak notepaper on which "Trapped" appears is a second poem in Brooks's handwriting written by another young poet, Ebony Tillman, a 1978 Illinois Poet Laureate prizewinner. While Aurelia Davidson considers the present of racial oppression in relation to her speaker's future and past, Ebony Tillman's untitled poem figures the present of racial and economic injustice in relation to the past. Both Davidson and Tillman use temporal contrast to illuminate and respond to racial or economic injustice. For both poets, poetry is a means of naming, describing, and remaking entrapment toward an embodied resolution.

Ebony Tillman's untitled poem appears twice in the Brooks archive—on plain white notepaper, again in Brooks's hand, as well as on the reverse side of the Amtrak notepaper from Aurelia Davidson's "Trapped"—so clearly Brooks was taken with this poem.

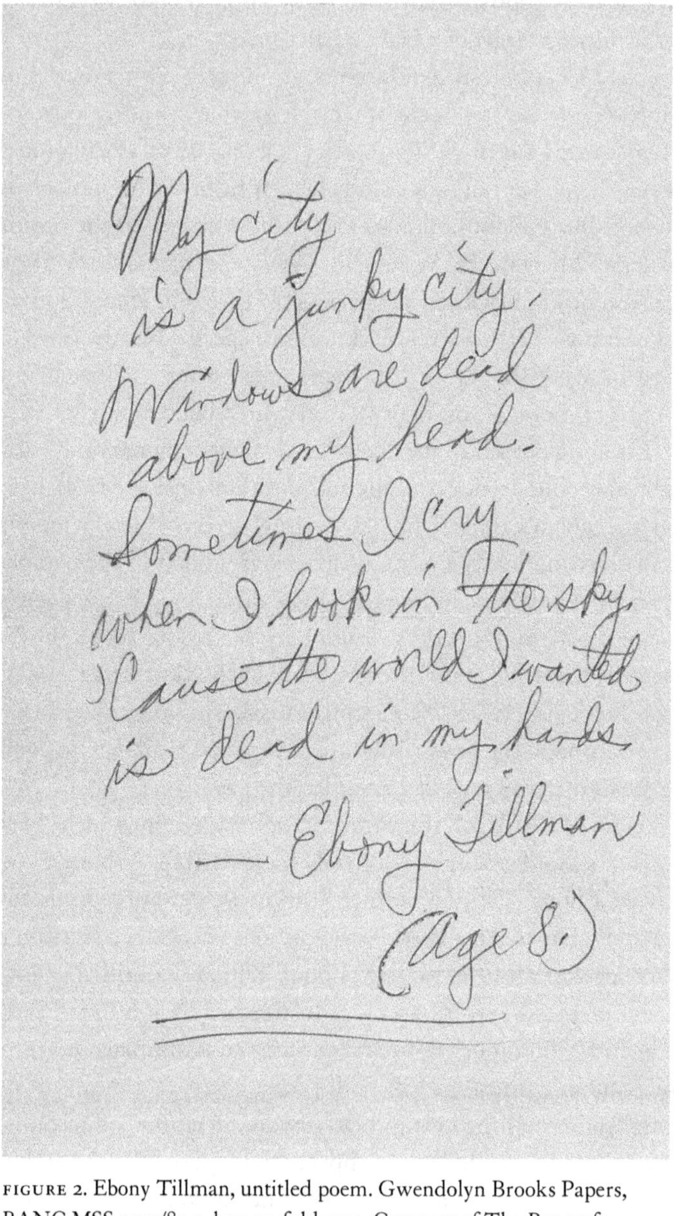

FIGURE 2. Ebony Tillman, untitled poem. Gwendolyn Brooks Papers, BANC MSS 2001/83 z, box 11, folder 32. Courtesy of The Bancroft Library, University of California, Berkeley.

My city
is a junky city.
Windows are dead
above my head.
Sometimes I cry
when I look in the sky.
'Cause the world I wanted
is dead in my hands.

Ebony Tillman's Chicago is not Carl Sandburg's "Windy City" (271) but her own self-designated "junky city" whose "dead" windows loom "above" her head, an image that depicts the domination of the speaker's present by the harsh urban world that rises above her. In this eight-line poem, powerful and direct in its tone, imagery, and rhythm, the first-person speaker is figured in embodied engagement with her surroundings. The lines "Windows are dead / above my head" use simple rhyme that reinforces the starkness of the contrast between the dead windows and the living child. The poem traces an arc of embodied movement in the speaker's looking up ("above my head," "when I look in the sky") and then looking down to her own hands.

There are three moves here. One has to do with size and scale: by the end of the poem, the imagined city has collapsed into the speaker's hands. In beginning with "My city" and ending with "my hands," the poem in its top-heavy structure suggests that the child speaker's body is initially overwhelmed by the looming landscape of urban decay. And yet the poem ends with an agentic image that leaves the embodied young speaker in control over the poetic landscape—"the world I wanted / is dead in my hands"—wherein the city of the speaker's past desires is contained, though lifeless, in her hands. The second move has to do with time and immediacy. Ebony Tillman contrasts the immediacy of her speaker's stark relation to the present world with the past world she "wanted" that is "dead." Her time is punctuated ("Sometimes") by her awareness of this loss. By the end of the poem, the speaker uses her potency to contain both urban death in the present and the death of her past desires. The world of her past unfulfilled desires, the "world I wanted," is now contained in the present, "is dead in my hands." The power of this concluding image is reinforced by a shift from the tight end-rhymes of the center two implicit couplets ("dead"/"head," "cry"/"sky") to the final implicit couplet's buried assonance ("wanted"/"hands"). Lastly, these first

two moves are knit together by decisions Tillman makes about animating
this poetic cityscape. She personifies the city of Chicago only to describe its
deadness. By the poem's conclusion, Chicago is transformed into the city of
her speaker's internal life—"the world I wanted"—that is "dead" and contained in her hands. The reader is left with the strength of those hands that
carry the narrative of the poem, and by extension, those young human hands
that have crafted the poem. Ebony Tillman has created a wrenching portrait of a first-person speaker poised between grim urban conditions and the
literal holding of her unfulfilled desires in a manner that concludes with a
focus on the speaker's capacity and physicality, her being in the present. Poet
Ebony Tillman has positioned the "hands" of her speaker as the repository,
the living vessel in the present for the dead desires from the past. Ultimately,
the speaker's agency in the concluding image of her capacious hands over-
powers the deadness of the city.

In "[My city]" and "Trapped," racial and economic oppression constitute a present world from which the young speakers ground themselves,
their hopes and longings, in relation to the past or future. Ebony Tillman's
speaker stands in the present acknowledging her physical containment
of the death of the world she desired in the past. Aurelia Davidson's
speaker questions her future until she affirms her escape by transforming the limitations of oppression from the present to the past. What is it
about these poems that might have caught Brooks's attention, aside from
poetic skill? One reason might be that both poems figure their speaker's
embodied agency in the present as a means of emergence from entrapment
by injustice: for Aurelia Davidson, entrapment by racial injustice, where
emergence is occasioned through the speaker's identification by age, gender, and race ("I am a little Black girl TRAPPED") and exuberant physical
action, and for Ebony Tillman, entrapment by racially linked economic
injustice, where emergence is occasioned through overpowering the dead
city by recognizing and imaginatively containing the death of her desired
world. Brooks referenced Tillman's "[My city]" directly at a public reading
in March 1985 at Southwest Virginia Community College in a discussion
of her sponsorship of the Illinois Poet Laureate Awards for young poets
(Barth). "Children are capable of surprising things at the ages of six, seven
and eight," said Brooks, with Tillman's poem presumably one of those
"surprising things" (Barth). In introducing Tillman's poem, Brooks explicitly referenced Tillman's economic circumstances, underscoring the theme

of economic injustice: "I gave a prize to a little black girl in Chicago who lived in a poor neighborhood. 'My city is a junky city. Windows are dead above my head . . .'" (Barth).

Tillman's "[My city]" and Davidson's "Trapped" each appears at least twice in the historical record in connection with Gwendolyn Brooks. Aurelia Davidson's poem was read by Brooks at the Seton Hall Dickinson commemoration, and copied by her hand presumably while on a train to another public event where she most likely also recited it. Brooks transcribed Ebony Tillman's poem twice by hand, indicated on both copies Tillman's age—"Age 8" (plain-paper version) and "wrote it when she was 8" (Amtrak notepaper version)—and read it in Virginia in addition to (or as?) her Amtrak destination. Thus, Brooks animated, celebrated, and preserved these poems by acts of recopying and bringing them into public spheres through her referencing and reading them. Just as significantly, these poems animated Brooks and her sense of herself as poet. Brooks's statement at the Emily Dickinson centenary reading that Aurelia Davidson was "a woman, a woman of twelve, not myself" is an indication that Brooks's invocation of young poets on the public stage was deeply tied to ideas about herself as a poet and her connection to young people.

"a poet laureate should do more than wear a crown—should be of service to the young": Brooks's "service" to Young Poets

At the height of her adult fame, Gwendolyn Brooks, arguably the foremost twentieth-century American poet "of childhood," whose lengthy career included publishing poetry as a child and as an adult—primarily for adults, but also for children—on themes of childhood, famously positioned herself as a young child when she referred to her political awakening as a black poet in the turbulent 1960s as "the kindergarten of my new consciousness" (*Report* 86). She credited the launch of this "kindergarten" to the 1967 Fisk University Writers' Conference in Nashville, Tennessee, with its theme "Black Writers and Human Rights" (Kent 196), where Brooks sensed "a general energy, an electricity, in look, walk, speech, *gesture* of the young blackness I saw all about me" (*Report* 84). In a 1973 conversation with Hoyt Fuller, Eugenia Collier, George Kent, and Dudley Randall, Brooks refers to "young people such as Don Lee" (later Haki Madhubuti) without whom "I wouldn't know what I do now about our time, our condition" (Fuller et al. 71): "I know that sounds incredible but my stupidity, my ignorance, were incredible. I hadn't read. That is one concrete thing that they did for me—they introduced me to reading I should know, that all of us should know. I hadn't even read *The Autobiography of Malcolm X* before I met them. I hope that puts to rest those rumors that I was an inspiration to these people, which is always being said here and there, and it's not so" (Fuller et al. 72). Here Brooks takes pains to emphasize her own "ignorance" and her growth in social and political knowledge due to the influence of these much younger poets, in part to dispel "rumors" that it was she who inspired them, though certainly that was at play as well. She doesn't admit the influence as bidirectional, perhaps from a desire to counter common cultural assumptions about the influence of established poets on younger writers.

References to Brooks's engagements with young poets typically encompass the "under-thirty group" (Kent 226), people in their twenties, such as Haki Madhubuti, whom Brooks met when he was a college student in 1967 in the workshop she ran for the Blackstone Rangers (Jabbour and Miller 127). Though Brooks is well known for her support of such young poets, less acknowledged, discussed, or celebrated are her engagements with "very young poets," to use the title of Brooks's 1983 poetry manual addressing people who might not count their age with double digits. In this chapter, I explore the scope of Brooks's advocacy for and involvement with people of elementary and high school age and explore a selection of poems written by young poets whom Brooks encountered, primarily through her sponsorship of contests.

Gwendolyn Brooks leveraged her own prominence as a poet, as the first African American to win a Pulitzer Prize (in 1950 for her second book, *Annie Allen*), and as the Illinois poet laureate for decades, to establish poetry contests for young people. While Brooks was already sponsoring contests for young poets in the early 1960s, after she was appointed Illinois poet laureate following Carl Sandburg's death in 1968, she launched a contest she called the "Illinois Poet Laureate Awards." This contest was initially for high school–aged poets from Illinois, but eventually Brooks opened it to elementary school–aged poets as well; as Illinois poet laureate, she maintained the contest for over thirty years until her death.[9] It's worth noting that Brooks didn't call her contest the "teen's" or "children's poetry awards," but she gave it the status of her own public recognition—she loaned it some of her own luster—in titling it the "Illinois Poet Laureate Awards."[10]

In 1969, not long after Brooks's appointment as Illinois poet laureate, a notice in the *Negro Digest* announced that she would award an "Illinois Poet Laureate's Award" in the spring of 1970 to high school students, two of whom who would share the $500 prize ("About writers and writing").[11] The notice continued, "Miss Brooks is the first poet laureate of Illinois to offer the prizes. Her reasons: 'First, a continuing interest in the health of poetry; and second, my belief that a poet laureate should do more than wear a crown—should be of service to the young'" and promote poetry in general ("About writers and writing" 97).[12] A few years after the high school contest was established, Brooks began giving awards for elementary school students' poems as well.[13] Eventually, the annual Illinois Poet Laureate Awards conferred ten prizes for elementary school–aged poets and ten prizes for high school–aged poets, who were invited to read their work at a ceremony at the University of Chicago.[14] Each year's winning poems were printed in an awards booklet, and Brooks turned down at least one offer to have a single year's poems published[15] because she hoped to produce an anthology integrating winning poems across the years.[16] Brooks referred to the young prizewinners of the Illinois Poet Laureate Awards as "my young poets," a phrase significant for its respectful reference to the writers as well as for the personal pronoun that indicates her feeling of connection and alliance with these writers ("Interview" 408).[17]

Many of the hundreds of poems written by young people preserved in the archive of the Gwendolyn Brooks Papers in The Bancroft Library at the University of California at Berkeley were submissions to the annual Illinois Poet Laureate contest that Brooks sponsored. In a 1983 mailgram to a prizewinner, Brooks's congratulations are accompanied by an invitation to read the winning poem at a celebratory event at the University of Chicago, "enjoy a university lunch with your family guests," and receive a "$50 check" (Brooks, "Mailgram").[18] The notice concludes "Proudly, Gwendolyn Brooks," which conveys how this prominent and revered adult poet addresses younger poets with an award of public recognition and also with her personal pride in each young poet's poetic accomplishment. Another form of her award announcement to young prizewinners delineates some of the specific sources of Brooks's pride in young writers: "I am proud of you, and I am proud to meet you. I appreciate your respect for poetry, and your interest in experimenting with language __ with sound and texture and manner" (Brooks, "Congratulatory note"). Brooks's appreciation of young poets' "respect for poetry" and "interest in experimenting with language" reflects her own respect for young people's engagement with poetry.

In addition to sponsoring writing contests, Gwendolyn Brooks's other activities with and for young and "very young" people included hosting reading and writing groups, visiting schools, giving public lectures, and writing poetry manuals. Most basically, Brooks valued and respected young and very young people, as well as the poetry they produced. In many of her speaking engagements, particularly when addressing teachers or young people, she made clear her championing of poetry written by youth, and she delineated clear ideas about how to foster children's poetic engagement and provide opportunities for young poets. In an undated set of handwritten notes from a lecture that seems aimed at a young audience, Brooks writes encouragingly about young people's involvement with poetry:

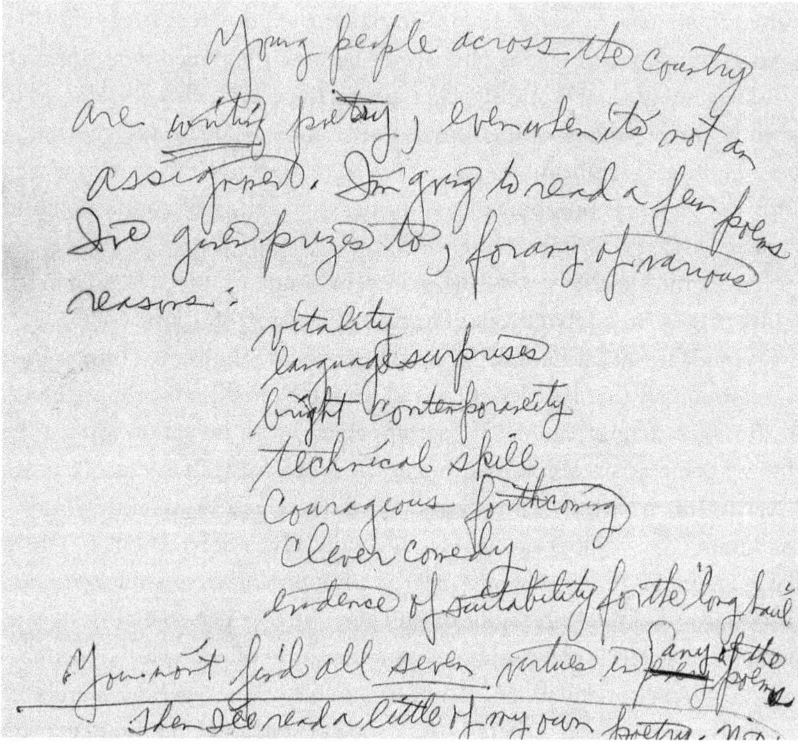

FIGURE 3. Gwendolyn Brooks, untitled lecture notes. Gwendolyn Brooks Papers, BANC MSS 2001/83 z, box 11, folder 32. Courtesy of The Bancroft Library, University of California, Berkeley.

Young people across the country are <u>writing</u> poetry, even when it's not an assignment. I'm going to read a few poems I've given prizes to, for any of various reasons:

> vitality
> language surprises
> bright contemporaneity
> technical skill
> courageous forthcoming
> clever comedy
> evidence of suitability for the "long haul"

You won't find all <u>seven</u> virtues in any of the poems.

Then I'll read a little of my own poetry.[19]

In this passage, Brooks articulates the features she looks for in judging young people's poems. This range of "virtues"—with the possible exception of the final one ("evidence of suitability for the 'long haul'")—does not seem to differ from the set of qualities Brooks would expect from a poem written by a person of any age: aliveness, freshness of language, relevance, skill, boldness, intelligent humor. Brooks's choice to recite poems written by young people prior to reading "a little of my own poetry"—as she did with Aurelia Davidson at the Dickinson centenary event—is an act that exemplifies a strategy she used repeatedly to introduce poetry written by young people into the public sphere by positioning it to literally precede and take time from recitation of her own poems.[20] In fact, Adrian Matejka recalls a poetry reading in which Brooks read more poems written by elementary school–aged people than by Brooks herself.

Brooks believed that young poets serve as crucial inspiration, sources, and audiences for each other. In handwritten notes she wrote for a November 1987 talk to educators titled "Poetry And The Educating of Children. How To Use Poetry With Students" at the Independent School Association of Central States (with a projected audience of 1,200 to 1,500 teachers from fifteen states), Brooks indicates the following elements as being of the highest priority:[21]

1. Introduce children to poetry by people <u>their</u> ages.
2. Invite them to write poetry.

She advises educators to "Introduce" children to poems written by people of "their ages" (with a double underscore), perhaps even in their first exposure to poetry. Further, she urges educators to explicitly "Invite" young people to write poetry so they will not merely serve as an audience for poetry written by adults. Thirty years later, Brooks's first point, in particular, is not often followed, judging from poems and curricular materials typically made available to children and teachers.[22]

Through her list of "How To Use Poetry With Students," Brooks makes clear her view that adults have an important role to play in helping children position themselves as authors and audiences for each other's work. Of the six items in Brooks's list, all but one—her third suggestion that teachers play recordings to students of adult poets reading their poems—concern positioning young people in active roles, even leadership roles, in relation to the writing, reciting, and publication of poetry. Item four in the list prompts teachers to sometimes relinquish their position as reciters of poems in classroom settings and "Encourage them to get up (not teacher all the time) and read aloud (poetry) to the class." Item five is a blueprint for a publishing venture that is much needed today in being youth-led, youth-curated, and youth-produced, with clearly delineated roles: "Let the children create a poetry magazine for the class—with elected editors, business manager, etc. It can be xeroxed, or multigraphed, etc. Contributors will be classmates."[23] Finally, Brooks encourages teachers to support young people in developing their own critical interpretations of poems (Brooks, "Poetry And The Educating of Children").

In the 1973 conversation with Hoyt Fuller and others, Brooks mentions an aspect of her motivation for reaching out to young people, who are "going to be . . . our black citizens of tomorrow": "It's important to remember, though, that the children are here and are going to be the citizens, our black citizens of tomorrow. So whatever we can do to help children is important. And it can be a very immediate and seemingly small thing" (Fuller et al. 71). In this interview, Brooks goes on to describe her plan "to corral the children in my block" into a "summer reading and writing club. . . . And I think that might be helpful in a small way. If it works, others may want to do the same thing" (71). The humility of her remarks is evident, as well as her casual suggestion that she is modeling a type of involvement that others might also take up. In a footnote, she mentions that although she did not "corral" all thirty children on her street, she "started a forum for the 18 highschoolers on the block. I kept it going four years" (70), which is one understated example of the variety of structures that Brooks invented, implemented, and sustained in order to engage with young people. Elsewhere she mentions that this "forum" of young people gave themselves the name "T.H.E.M.": "Trying Hard To Express Myself" (Brooks, "Interview" 409).

My selecting and writing about poems written by young people from Gwendolyn Brooks's archive was a strangely intimate process, particularly when young people's poems were copied in Brooks's hand or retyped, apparently by Brooks. I can find no other word than "encounter" to describe the situation among the young poets, Brooks, and myself that I navigated in my thinking about Brooks thinking about these young poets. It is obvious from archival evidence that in addition to her selection and/ or preservation of poems by young people, Brooks carefully curated the work of young poets: among the hundreds of poems in the archive are a subset that she selected excerpts from or recopied by hand or typewriter, talked about and recited at readings and lectures, folded and unfolded, read and reread. For the most part, the poems that I explore in this chapter are among those poems with which Brooks so engaged.[24] Given their well-worn condition and multiple appearances in the archive, these poems seem to have been touchstones for Brooks's thinking about young people and poetry, about poetic vision in general, and, given the themes of poems such as Aurelia Davidson's and Ebony Tillman's, about poetry in relation to racial and social-political injustice.[25] That these poems have come to light at all is, of course, evidence of Brooks's valuation of poetry written by young people.

After concluding this discussion of Brooks's advocacy for young poets, I return to reading youth-written poems that I found in the Gwendolyn Brooks Papers (in The Bancroft Library at the University of California at Berkeley) concerning the use of temporal strategies in themes of poetic vision, age and embodiment, and entrapment by age injustice. Toward the end of the chapter, I consider the two advice manuals that Brooks wrote for young poets: *Young Poets Primer* was addressed to middle and high school–aged poets and published in 1980 by Brooks's own imprint, Brooks Press; and *Very Young Poets* was addressed to elementary school–aged poets and published in 1983 by Third World Press. I end the chapter discussing a small selection from the hundreds of letters in the archive addressed to

Brooks from young people, which sometimes included poems written by the young people in tribute to this person who believed she "should do more than wear a crown—should be of service to the young" ("About writers and writing" 97).

Brooks began sponsoring poetry contests at individual elementary and high schools in the early 1960s.[26] In a 1971 interview with Ida Lewis, Brooks relates how her initial idea for a contest for young poets arose spontaneously when she was honored at Burnside Elementary School: "The school had given a program in my honor, and in my thank-you speech, I suddenly found myself saying, 'I'm going to sponsor a poetry contest here. Would you kids like to have a poetry contest?' 'Yeah!' 'I'll give you $100 for four prizes, and your teachers can be the judges'" (Lewis 63). During the 1963–64 school year, Brooks hosted poetry contests at Burnside and Cornell Elementary Schools, and though teachers served as judges,[27] Brooks marked up the winning poems in order to choose a selection to be typed.[28] In this set of curated poems from the early 1960s, Brooks's own attitude toward the authority of young poets can be discerned through her comment on one of the winning poems from Cornell Elementary School, "The Day of Thanks," which includes a footnote written by the poet, Ricardo Sims, a student in eighth grade (age thirteen or fourteen). In order to justify the rhyme of "fest" with "rest," Sims explains in a footnote that "fest" is a noun meaning "to feast (now obsolete)."[29] On Brooks's typed excerpts from the Cornell poems, she includes only the two lines of Ricardo Sims's poem that incorporate the footnoted reference, and she typed underneath: "(MR. SIMS DID NOT TRUST HIS TEACHERS AND HIMSELF INCLUDED THIS FOOTNOTE!)" (Cornell Excerpts). Through Brooks's formal, respectful reference to the poet as "MR. SIMS" and her emphatic, capitalized explanation with punctuation mark that he "DID NOT TRUST HIS TEACHERS" to recognize his correct usage of "fest," we glimpse Brooks's recognition of a young poet as a calculating writer who is aware that his adult audience is ready to critique his word usage.

Some of these early contest-winning poems were among those kept, copied, and savored by Brooks. In looking at a few of the poems from these early contests, I first consider two poems by one of the poets from Cornell Elementary School whose work became a touchstone for Brooks in thinking about her own poetics. I follow this with a discussion of poems by two young poets from Burnside Elementary School who figured age contrast and embodiment in arresting ways.

"Even when I die, I think I'd like to see": Moral Thirus's
Poetic Vision of the Final Temporal Juncture

My most surprising moment in the Brooks archive arose when I found a page of Brooks's handwritten notes discussing her poetics. Her well-known conception that "poetry is life distilled" long anchored her view of poetry (Bezner 124). In her interview of herself published in 1984 in *TriQuarterly*,[30] Brooks asks herself "What is a poet? What is poetry?" ("Interview" 408) and responds, "A poet is one who distils experience—strains experience" ("Interview" 409). She continues by referring to how she talks about this idea with children: "I keep telling children: 'Poetry comes out of life. What happened to you yesterday and last week and six years ago and ten minutes ago and what you surmise may happen tomorrow is poetry-in-the-rough. Strain it—distil—work the magic of carefully-chosen words upon it—and there's poetry'" ("Interview" 409). Here Brooks directly connects the heart of her poetic conception to her commitment to sharing those ideas with young people. She calls attention to the temporal span of children's experiences—what happened "yesterday and last week and six years ago and ten minutes ago and what you surmise may happen tomorrow"—as "poetry-in-the-rough" that they can "strain" and "distil" through "the magic of carefully-chosen words." Despite Brooks's evident concern for children even in the context of theorizing her lyric approach, I was nonetheless startled to find archival evidence that reveals Brooks allying with a young person in expanding this central aspect of her poetics.

In handwritten notes on the back of stationery from Hotel Continental in Washington, D.C. (dated 1968 according to Bancroft Library archivists), presumably for a talk she delivered in that city, Brooks also refers to poetry as "life distilled." These notes begin by referencing Carl Sandburg, "my predecessor as Poet Laureate of Illinois" and his "at least 38 exceptional definitions for poetry" of which she thought "the most memorable . . . is— 'Poetry is a synthesis of hyacinths and biscuits.'" Brooks then states and reflects on her own singular definition of poetry ("Carl Sandburg"):

> I rely on ONE definition: Poetry is <u>life</u> <u>distilled</u>.
> —Now, what <u>is</u> the life that is to be distilled? (I have a partial list.) Diamonds, rhinestones, dandelions, a rose, birth, abortions, garbage pails, riots, love, hate, peace, war, President Nixon, Malcolm X, gas stoves, alleys and boulevards and spilled blood, Champagne and lobster in the White House and chit'lins and beer in the horror-streets of Harlem. (I knew a 13 year old boy who felt that even <u>death</u> is a part of <u>distillable Life</u>! Said Moral Thirus:[31]

Who is Moral Thirus, I wanted to know, and what did he write? What could be more radical than an adult poet, in the prime of her career, publicly recognizing the significance of a thirteen-year-old person's poetic originality and depth in relation to her own poetics?[32] Somehow, this "13 year old boy" helped Brooks deepen her own view of what constitutes poetic subject matter—the contrasting currents of everyday life—and added to her conception of poetry so "that even <u>death</u> is a part of <u>distillable Life</u>!"

I came across two poems written by Moral Thirus in the Brooks archive in The Bancroft Library—"Death" and "Things"—in a different folder than the lecture notes quoted above, with both poems indicating that Moral Thirus was in eighth grade (age thirteen) at the time he submitted them. Given Brooks's reference in her lecture notes to Moral Thirus's ideas about death, I first assumed that she was referring to his poem "Death," and indeed the final stanza of the four-stanza poem "Death" seems quite pertinent:

> Death, to me, is a world forever bleak and black.
> To me, death can be a gun or the inevitable end to a track.
>
> You cannot shrug it off, or pretend that it isn't there,
> For as long as you shall live, it will follow you everywhere.
>
> To me, death can be a course changing all the lands and the nations
> Or death can be a blanket of blackness releasing you from
> Your trials and tribulations.
>
> Without death, and things that come with strife
> We would not know how to ever appreciate life.

In "Death," Moral Thirus figures death variously as "a world forever bleak and black," "a gun or the inevitable end to a track," and the tight end-rhymes reinforce the inevitability and finality of death, its hounding quality, for "it will follow you everywhere." The temporality is that of "the inevitable": the "forever" that follows you "as long as you shall live." In the penultimate stanza, the images of death are more capacious, complex, and conditional: death "can be a course changing all the lands and the nations," or "death can be a blanket of blackness releasing you from / Your trials and tribulations," and their alliterative unity lends formality and precision to these lines.

Interestingly, Moral Thirus's poem is a personal portrait of death. It is death "to me," a phrase that is repeated three times across the poem. Tracking pronouns across the stanzas reveals a movement from "me" to "you" to a combination of "me" and "you" to a final collective "We." Moral Thirus begins by making personal this portrait of death, "Death, to me, is"; moves in the second stanza to addressing "you" three times in a reminder of the ever-presence of death; and shifts in the penultimate stanza to including both "me" and "you." The final stanza accomplishes a united "We" in concluding with a clear statement about shared knowledge of appreciating life because of death. This concluding commentary on the importance of death for an appreciation of life is mentioned but not enacted, and thus as a poem "Death" ends on a rather flat note.

Despite its vague title, Moral Thirus's other poem, "Things," demonstrates a more nuanced approach and more accomplished poetic craft in moving beyond commentary on the ever-presence of death to a startling and graphic representation of the process of death in its immediacy, its poetic vision indeed expanding on Brooks's notion of poetry as "life distilled." The fact that there are two copies of "Things" in the Brooks archive at The Bancroft Library—in different typescripts and in different locations—suggests the poem's importance to Brooks, along with her reference to Moral Thirus by name in her lecture notes.[33] I believe that "Things" is the poem announced by the colon in Brooks's lecture notes on the reverse of the Hotel Continental stationery: "I knew a 13 year old boy who felt that even <u>death</u> is a part of<u> distillable Life</u>! Said Moral Thirus:"

I love to hear the many things that our world is made of
I love to hear a gypsy singing a tune of love.

I like to hear the birds and bees, singing and humming around me.
I like to hear the wind, singing a forlorn love song to the sea.

Even when I die, I think I'd like to see the thousands and
Thousands of insects, digging their way to me.

And even when I die, I know I'd like to hear
The insects or the parasites, munching on my ear.

Moral Thirus's poem "Things" begins as a poem of celebration and self-validation. We could consider it an ode to the "things" it invokes, yet it is even more an ode to the sensorial power of the self. The poem delineates the self's ability to value sound and sight, the self's knowledge of its valuation of participating along with the "things" of this world. The poem moves from benign to sublime in beginning with the rather innocuous lines "I love to hear the many things that our world is made of / I love to hear a gypsy singing a tune of love." The parallelism of the opening couplets establishes echoes across the objects that the speaker professes he "love[s]" and "like[s]" to "hear." These objects are rather typical referents of lyric: a love song, the "singing and humming" of the birds and bees, and the wind, "singing a forlorn love song to the sea."

Yet in its second half, "Things" takes an unexpected turn and presents a stunning set of images—through sight and sound—of death as "a part of distillable Life," in Brooks's phrase. As in the first half of the poem, Thirus uses repetition of opening phrases, yet repeats the phrase "Even when I die" across rather than within stanzas in a way that opens up across the two last stanzas and emphasizes no longer the self but the temporal juncture of death ("Even when I die," "And even when I die"). The final "And even when" offers in its "And," alongside the overlapping images that are first seen and then heard, a sense that there are differences with repetition. The "when" is of crucial importance here, for this poem turns on the immediacy of death, on what happens immediately during the transition from life to death, "when" one becomes host to strange sights, a strange music. One's body becomes an instrument for the work of "insects" and "parasites." Alongside the importance of the temporal word "when" is the poem's shift from the present tense to the conditional in the last two stanzas—"I think I'd like," "I know I'd like"—a sequence that grows in confidence.

In the retyped version of the poem (author's name handwritten), which is likely to have been retyped by Brooks herself with Moral Thirus's name written beneath the poem in Brooks's hand, the rhyme in the third stanza is unearthed by a shift in line breaks from the poem's appearance in the other typescript. The third couplet is made into a triplet in order to accentuate the rhyme of "see" with "me," which results in the same stanzaic structure—couplets with a penultimate triplet rhyming ABA—as Thirus's poem "Death."

> Even when I die, I think I'd like to see
> the thousands and thousands of insects,
> Digging their way to me.[34]

In the final two stanzas of "Things," the speaker's self is turned on its ear, as it were, into the ground. While the poem's first four lines begin with "I," the "I" in the initial lines of the last two stanzas stands behind the movement of time ("Even when I die"), and the self becomes the object of the insects' activity. The self remains a thinking and embodied subject: the words that conclude the initial lines in these final stanzas reveal the speaker as still contemplative, and still sensing ("I think I'd like to see," "I know I'd like to hear"). The final words of these stanzas, however, indicate the self only as acted-on—"me" and, finally, "my ear"—and eaten, the self at the extremity of its embodiment.

In terms of temporal innovation, Thirus in "Things" opens up the temporal juncture where life ends and death begins, and inserts sensorial living even at the extremity of life, in the act of dying. Thirus uses "when I die" as a portal onto the immediacy of the transition from life to death. In a situation typically seen as void of agency, when one is on the verge of death, Thirus figures a deepening of agency that involves "think[ing]" then "know[ing]" what one would "like to see" and "like to hear." He embeds a threefold first-person pronoun ("Even when *I* die, *I* think *I'd* like to see"; emphasis added) in this meditation depicting the self in an act of temporal agency while contemplating the moment of death. Thirus's strategy here uses dynamic temporality in stretching out the "when" of the moment of death in order to contemplate it.

Moral Thirus's "Things" is a transformative poem that poetically alters repulsive images and sounds (or at least images and sounds that were previously repulsive to this reader) into "things" of beauty. The encompassing poetic vision of Moral Thirus stood out to Brooks so strongly that she carried around his poem and referenced it, I believe read from it, at a public lecture in Washington, D.C., years after she encountered it in the Cornell Elementary School contest. I cannot recall another poet of Brooks's stature who publicly referenced an unpublished poem by a young person and made note of its congruence with—even addition to—her own poetics. In fact, it turns out that in 1972, a few years after the lecture notes referencing Moral Thirus, Brooks arranged for "Things" to be published by including it *within her autobiography*. Moral Thirus's poem "Things" appears in Brooks's autobiographical *Report from Part One*, in a final section of the first volume titled "Collage," which was originally excerpted in *Black World* in 1972 (Brooks, "Report from Part One: An Excerpt").[35] It was not lost on me that when I found a copy of this edition of *Black World* that includes Moral

Thirus's poem "Things," the brittle pages of the upper left corner of the periodical were partially eaten by bookworms.

In *Report from Part One*, after a discussion of change in which Brooks states that even what we think we know "was never the same from moment to moment, from second to second," she asks "What are the little black children doing"? (*Report* 207). She dismisses the dismissive reports of "Experts" that black children are "kicking or killing their teachers, collecting Beatle wax and buttons and bubble-gum, trampling lawns and forging new routes to indolence and demoralization" (207). Instead, writes Brooks, "They are writing poetry. Poetry is still in the world, and black children are colliding with some of it. They reach, touch lovely words and strong words with excitement and timid respect. They work hard to merit ownership" (207). Here "ownership" suggests Brooks's awareness that questions of agency and authority—whether black children "merit ownership" of words—are at stake in young people's encounters with poetry. Brooks goes on to delineate some of the currents of black children's involvement with poetry: their knowledge of "beauty" and "horror" (207), their sometime use of "platitudes a-plenty" (208), their capability of "exaltation and thought and emotion that do them honor" (208). And finally, she includes two poems by thirteen-year-old poets that engage with complex themes; the other poem—Lillian Myricks's "Freedom,"[36] which explores freedom in the context of African American history—is also from the 1964 Cornell Elementary School contest. Brooks introduces Moral Thirus's poem "Things" by referring to the capacity of some young poets "to reconcile death and humor"—"Some of them have found that it is possible to reconcile death and humor. Listen to Moral Thirus, thirteen at the time he entered a Cornell School poetry-writing contest of mine:" (208)—and this time, unlike in her archival lecture notes, her colon is definitely followed by the text of the poem "Things."[37]

In her lecture notes and her autobiography, Brooks carries the poem "Things" by young poet Moral Thirus squarely into her public work as an adult poet. Brooks works to elevate Thirus's poetic authority through referencing the relevance of his ideas to her own poetics, inviting his poem into her autobiographical text, and enjoining the audience of her lecture and the readers of her autobiography to "Listen to Moral Thirus." It is difficult to overstate how unusual—how politically radical—this act is in overturning typical age-based hierarchies of knowledge, influence, autonomy, and originality. As Brooks suggests through her admiration of this poem, "Things" enacts a stunning moment of passing from life into death, or dying into the still-living universe. Moral Thirus has crafted "<u>death</u> [as] a part of <u>distillable Life</u>" (Brooks, "Carl Sandburg").

While contemplating the moment of death may seem unusual for a young poet, young poets reflecting on even younger age positions may also surprise an adult audience. A couple of other poems that Brooks selected from the early 1960s elementary school contests look squarely at age and embodiment. In the next section, I look at two such poems that work with a temporal contrast between personal past and present not only to figure age distinctions but also to convey judgment about these distinctions.

"Baby Days" and "When I Was Small": Temporal Contrast in Young Poets' Making of Self

Because of the intersection of age and power in twentieth-century European American societies, it should not come as a surprise that older children may work to distinguish themselves from younger children. Sociolinguistic and sociological research on children's language for and perspectives on age categories reveals that children begin very early to differentiate between younger and older (Cook-Gumperz) and use age distinctions in remembering and thinking across the years of their lives (James "Life Times"). In this section, I consider two poems—both of which center age distinctions and their relevance to a speaker's present—that were written by elementary school–aged poets during Brooks's collaborations with Chicago schools in the early 1960s.

The poems I discuss in this section, "Baby Days" by Belinda[38] and "When I Was Small" by Karen Cox, are poems of retrospection on early childhood written by people of elementary-school age. These poems are linked in Brooks's records by appearing in a handcopied set of winning poems, most likely the handwriting of a teacher (Burnside "Primary Winners"), as well as in a typed set of winning poems from Burnside Elementary School apparently typed by Brooks (Burnside Poems).[39] The poems share an identical opening phrase—"When I was"—which immediately establishes the first-person speaker's contrast between personal past and present and suggests its implications for the self. Both poems prompt adult readers to recognize that very young writers can figure their speakers' embodied past in a dismissive tone toward that even younger embodiment.

"Baby Days," written by Belinda, identified on the poem as a student in first grade (age six or seven), is neatly structured in two undivided quatrains rhyming ABCB and contrasts the speaker's present attitude and activity with her life as a baby:

> When I was a baby
> I was fat and jolly.
> I used to sit and play
> All day with my dolly.
> Now that I'm older
> It doesn't mean a thing.
> I'd rather read
> Or even try to sing.

This poem begins jauntily enough with clarity of characterization ("fat and jolly") and end words that are straightforwardly associated with children (with easy rhymes "jolly" and "dolly"). The second quatrain, which begins "Now that I'm older," shifts to another register with end words that reinforce a different tonality of being "older," with an emphasis on the activities that the speaker can now accomplish ("read" and "try to sing"). The tone is established by the insouciant and distancing line, "It doesn't mean a thing," which indicates the speaker's ascription of value. The rhyme of "thing" with "sing," a simple rhyme yet with marked contrast in tone between the two words, expresses the less straightforward music of the speaker's "older" present self that she makes in her own fashion, as opposed to the singsong rhyme of the "baby" self in the first quatrain.

In "Baby Days," Belinda launches each quatrain with an age distinction (being "older" compared to "a baby") intersecting with a temporal distinction ("Now" versus "When I was") that carries with it a different way of using time. In the "older" speaker's "Now," time is segmented through engaging in different activities ("read / Or . . . sing") rather than playing ("sit and play") in an undifferentiated "All day" of babyhood. However, the age epochs themselves are constructed through a kind of reverse logic that positions the baby self in a discrete though extended habitual past tense and the older self in a less bounded epoch. "Baby Days" are a delimited period though described partly in a habitual past ("I used to") that stretches out those days, whereas being "older" involves an open-ended temporality of the simple present and conditional that is perhaps foreshortened. After the pivotal line "It doesn't mean a thing" with its disdainful tone, the line "I'd rather read," the shortest line in the poem with two beats instead of three, reinforces a sense of self-sufficiency in the altered temporal universe. In claiming the contraction "I'd," the speaker rejects the full word "would," the carrier of the third beat. The "older" speaker makes judgments and comparisons, emphasizes her choice of activities, and attempts activities knowing that success may be only partial ("Or even try to sing"). Thus, analysis of temporal syntax helps reveal the complex construction of this short lyric, in which figuration of time and age is interwoven in nuanced ways.

The implication of temporal contrast for the self is also a dominant strategy in "When I Was Small" by Karen Cox, who is identified on the poem as a student in fourth grade (age nine or ten); the poem received an honorable mention in the 1964 contest at Burnside School (Burnside "Primary Winners") and Karen Cox read her poem at the Burnside Poetry Contest reading, while Belinda, the youngest winner, did not read.[40] Another eight-line poem, "When I Was Small" is crafted into the "small" units of rhyming couplets:

> When I was small, very small,
> I had no teeth at all.
>
> I had a little nose
> And some curly little toes.
>
> I had no hair,
> My head was bare.
>
> That's how I looked when I was small.
> I don't think I looked very well at all!

As with "Baby Days," "When I Was Small" contrasts the first-person speaker's past self with the present self, here with a focus solely on appearance rather than on activity. The poem is a snapshot in which the past is described in the simple past, unlike the habitual past of "Baby Days." "When I Was Small" uses repetition ("small, very small"; "little," "little") to reinforce the diminutive size of the baby self, and calls attention to features that the baby body lacks ("no teeth at all," "I had no hair, / My head was bare"), without providing any compensatory features. Karen Cox's unsparing infant portrait conveys a sense of the indignity of those missing bodily features by means of descriptions that derive their potency through overemphasis ("no teeth at all") and through their cumulative effect.

In "When I Was Small," the present self is described only in terms of its

judgment of the past self ("I don't think I looked very well at all!"), a judgment that, after the poem contracts from trimeter to dimeter, stretches out
the lines with the final couplet's tetrameter. The final stanza accentuates the
distance between the past self and speaker's present perspective ("That's how
I looked"; "I don't think I looked"), which anchors the speaker in a reflective
and cognitive present. Karen Cox thus figures the distinction between the
past of being "small" and the speaker's present age through repetition of
words of diminution ("small," "little"), attention to diminutive or missing
features, and contrast between short lines and the extended lines of the final
couplet's reflective judgment.

   In both "Baby Days" and "When I Was Small," there is an attempt to
distance the first-person speaker from her age-defined past self through
a contrast between past and present that expresses a judgmental attitude
toward or even disdain for the baby past. In "Baby Days," Belinda writes,
"Now that I'm older / It doesn't mean a thing," and Karen Cox writes,
"I don't think I looked very well at all!" Babyhood is seen by these poets
as not fully deserving of respect, a theme that is established through the
use of temporal contrast between the past self of babyhood and the present
self of the older speaker, and judgment-based contrasts between action or
appearance. The disdain for infancy is an element of these young poets'
temporal standpoints, in contrast to adult poets' often Romantic idealiza-
tions of infancy of which Wordsworth's "Ode: Intimations of Immortality
from Recollections of Early Childhood" is perhaps best known.

   As a reader, I relish the temporal judgments of poets Karen Cox and
Belinda that offer portraits and valuations of infancy so different from the
adult standard. These poets claim an authority to pronounce judgment not
necessarily on infancy itself but certainly on their speakers' infant selves. In
the next section, I read a poem from a decade later that takes on age itself as
a structure of social and political power.

"a gardener does not grow a flower by a clock": Young Poet Janet Docka Figuring Entrapment by Time and Age

Children's agency can be mobilized through pushing back against the constraints of societal practices that segment the lifespan into age-based categories
differentially inflected with power, and temporal practices that impinge on
children's experiences (what Allison James and Alan Prout refer to as "time

of childhood" and "time in childhood," respectively). In this section, I look at a poem by Janet A. Docka, "I Am in a Trap," winner of an Illinois Poet Laureate prize in 1973, that critiques temporal ideologies of childhood and the arbitrariness of cultural ideas about age and temporal markers of adult status.[41]

In "I Am in a Trap," Janet Docka works with and against prevalent ideas about children's abilities, age transitions, metaphors of growth, and individual differences in patterns of growth. The temporal and age-based entrapment that Docka figures is reminiscent of Aurelia Davidson's poem "Trapped" discussed earlier in this chapter, and these poems converge in figuring a present that enables their poetic speakers to name constraints, including those produced by racism and/or age-based discrimination. Like forms of testimony, both of these poems of entrapment open with a short line that straightforwardly and boldly announces their entrapment: Davidson's poem begins "I am trapped," and Docka's poem begins "I am in a trap."

> I am in a trap,
> The bars of which are the portals of time,
> The Lock of which is society's idea.
> For in the eyes of the Law, I am but a child,
> Something which has no mind
> But can only eat, sleep and play,
> Until,
> At the age of eighteen,
> It is suddenly given the ability to think.
> But remember, a flower is like a child.
> And yet a gardener does not grow a flower by a clock,
> But allows it to bloom in its own time.
> And should one bloom earlier than the next,
> He marvels only at its beauty,
> And does not complain that it is off schedule and an upstart.
> And so if I should come into my glory a little sooner than the next,
> Wonder only at the beauty.
> Think of me not as being a mutation
> But only as being different.

"I Am in a Trap" describes the entrapment of its young speaker by "society's idea" about youth. While the "bars" of the trap are temporal, the "portals of time" (that determine age) whose "Lock" keeps them shut is a cultural construction of youth as immature. The speaker's self is diminished in being viewed "in the eyes of the Law" as "but a child, / Something," without status as a person, "which has no mind" but can only act, "eat, sleep and play." This temporal problem—being entrapped by "the portals of time" as interpreted by "the Law"—has a temporal solution that hinges on the word "Until," isolated on a line, when "At the age of eighteen, / It is suddenly given the ability to think." In this poem, age-based ideologies of childhood depersonalize a young person as "Something," as "It"; in fact, the "I" of the speaker appears only in the first four and last four lines of the poem, at its margins.

"I Am in a Trap" is a tightly-structured argument that turns at its central line, "But remember, a flower is like a child," with the problem of the "portals of time" described in the poem's first half, and the paradox of the flower/child/clock pursued in the poem's second half. In the simile that launches the second half of the poem, "But remember, a flower is like a child," Janet Docka compares a flower to a child rather than a child to a flower, a reversal of the common expected metaphor of a child as a maturing seed. In Janet Docka's simile, the figure of "child" ostensibly opens up other meanings of "flower," rather than vice versa. Yet the next line—"And yet a gardener does not grow a flower by a clock"—brings slippage between "child" and "clock," and the focus shifts to the temporal monitoring of a flower's growth. Here, adults become metaphoric gardeners who are cautioned against interposing an external clock into a flower's self-directed project of growth. The enlightened gardener "allows it to bloom in its own time."

Docka's poem advocates tolerance for variant schedules of growth and the "different" forms of "beauty" that result from individual rates of growth. Interestingly, the first-person speaker is not identified again as a "child" in the second half of the poem. Instead, emphasis is placed on her own timetable in which she "come[s] into my glory," inspiring the audience she addresses directly in the poem's concluding lines to "Wonder only at the beauty" and to "Think of me not as being a mutation / But only as being different." In this poem that so directly speaks back to dominant age ideologies and articulates its own alternative valuations, beauty and difference become the salient dimensions rather than age and position as child or adult. Janet Docka figures the clock to refer to the sequestration of people under the age of eighteen, who are metaphorically locked in a temporal prison. With its normative cultural expectations of uniformity and developmental prescriptiveness, the clock is opposed to a personal temporality, "its own time," that enables a young speaker to assert her own "beauty," even if it is "off schedule." Thematically, then, "I Am in a Trap" champions a more nuanced and differentiated temporality than age, and a temporality that already takes account of young people's agency ("its own time").

Janet Docka's "I Am in a Trap" appeared in a finely printed booklet of prizewinning poems from the 1973 Illinois Poet Laureate contest, which as the fourth annual contest was still open only to high school students. It was one of twenty poems Brooks selected, as she indicated in a brief prefatory note, "from hundreds submitted" ("Fourth Annual"). Along with widening her sponsorship of annual contests to include elementary school–aged youth, and her visits to schools and workshops with young people, Gwendolyn Brooks also worked to validate and encourage young people in writing poetry by addressing young poets directly in advice manuals. In the next section, I look at the qualities of Brooks's advice to "young" poets and "very young" poets in two separate advice manuals from the early 1980s.

"You are as important as they are": Brooks's Advice to Young and Very Young Poets

I think that poetry is that quality which enables us to see clearly light, joy, gaiety, sorrow, sadness. It is that quality which we need most in the world, because without it we would not really know what the world is.
—Nora Brooks Blakely

So responded Nora Brooks Blakely, when she was a "little girl of thirteen," to her mother Gwendolyn Brooks's question, "What do you think poetry is?" (Brooks, *Young Poet's Primer* 9). Nora's response focuses on poetry as a crucial means to "see clearly" the full range of human experience, as a shared resource (indicated by the plural pronouns "us" and "we"), and as a necessary practice to "really know what the world is." Brooks carefully documented Nora's definition of poetry, spoken on "February 9, 1965; at home" (9) and included it in *Young Poet's Primer*, a short volume addressed "chiefly to highschoolers and to college students" (3) that Brooks published in 1980 under her own imprint, Brooks Press, and that consists of ten pages of advice across thirty-three precepts. Brooks's solicitation, precise documentation, and use of young Nora Brooks Blakely's statement reflect Brooks's attitude of seriousness and respect toward young people's ideas about poetry and that is also evident in the two poetry manuals that Brooks published in the early 1980s for young audiences.[42]

Though Brooks's advice in *Young Poet's Primer* is detailed and teacherly, she addresses young people directly and positions young poets as capable and knowledgeable. One key aspect of her advice echoes Nora's definition of poetry by reminding young poets to "Write about what you know" (6), including experiences that prompt a range of emotions and ideas. Brooks encourages young poets to speak their own truth: "In writing your poem, tell the truth as you know it. Tell *your* truth. Don't try to sugar it up. Don't force your poem to be nice or proper or normal or happy if it does not want to be" (7). Although Brooks adopts an authoritative voice in *Young Poet's Primer*, her stance acknowledges young poets' sense of ownership over their own inner life, over their process of writing, and over the poems they write. For instance, in exhorting young poets to revise their work "as many times as necessary" (7), she writes, "Revise until you have secured for yourself a fresh, *new* poem, that says what you feel, think, suppose" (7). Brooks suggests that young poets may be innovators and inventors of form and may help to propel the future of poetry itself: "Poetry HAS a future! You MAY initiate new forms. You MAY create" (14). She also writes about the shifting and growing relation between a reader and a poem, thus envisioning young readers as potentially changing over time and in relation to specific poems: "a poem should mean different things to you, *for* you, at different times in your life. Its meanings should be free to shift or grow, even as yourself" (10).

Brooks begins one section with the question "What is Black poetry?" and then defines "Black poetry" to her young readers as "poetry written by Blacks, about Blacks, to Blacks" (12). She writes about the "urgencies" of black poetry in terms of its social and political purposes, and with regard to black community and "caring and curing": "Black poetry features the urgencies of Black unity, Black churning, Black exhilaration, Black caring and curing" (12). Other precepts assume that young people are active members of their communities with their own perceptions, observations, and opinions. For instance, in the twentieth precept Brooks encourages young people to write not just about "flowers and trees and springtime" (11) but about their own sense of the world around them: "write about what you see in the street, what you see in the newspapers" (11).

In 1983, a few years following the appearance of *Young Poet's Primer*, Brooks turned her attention to even younger, elementary school–aged poets in a slim volume published by Third World Press titled *Very Young Poets*. This volume is structured similarly to *Young Poet's Primer*, with twenty numbered precepts, along with eight of Brooks's own poems at the end of the volume, including "A Little Girl's Poem," "Computer," and "To Young Readers." However, the tone of *Very Young Poets* is quite different from that of *Young Poet's Primer* in its warmth and personal engagement. This is evident even in the differences between the single-page prefatory notes in each volume. The introduction to *Young Poet's Primer* is rather straightforward, even dry: "This little primer does not pretend to supply All You Need. You will need other books, with technical tables, analyses, philosophy. In visits to hundreds of schools and colleges, however, I have found that the enclosed ideas and impressions have proven useful" (unpaginated). In contrast, *Very Young Poets* begins with an enthusiastic, encouraging, and capitalized "DEDICATION TO ALL THE CHILDREN IN THE WORLD and TO CHILDREN WHO WANT TO WRITE POETRY" (unpaginated):

> Writing a poem is very exciting! You can actually put on paper what you think and feel.
>
> Be brave! On your paper, write what is true.
>
> Once, I met a young girl who was very anxious to be a writer. With shining eyes she said to me, "I WANT TO TELL PEOPLE THINGS!"
>
> Isn't that beautiful? And natural?
>
> "TO TELL PEOPLE THINGS."
>
> That is what YOU want to do!
>
> That is what you CAN do!

Both primers quote from young people's words. In *Young Poet's Primer*, Brooks includes thirteen-year-old Nora Brooks Blakely's definition of poetry, and in the dedication to *Very Young Poets* quoted above, Brooks quotes from and commends an idea spoken by a young person. Yet Brooks positions the "young girl" with "shining eyes" prominently at the opening of *Very Young Poets*, whereas Nora's statement about poetry is somewhat buried in *Young Poet's Primer*, which launches with Brooks locating her authority in her own experience visiting and speaking at schools. In the dedication to *Very Young Poets*, Brooks reports that this "young girl" who was "very anxious to be a writer" said to Brooks, "I WANT TO TELL PEOPLE THINGS!" Brooks's capitalization of this young person's words emphasizes, supports, and enhances the voice and authority of very young people who are seldom heard in our society and whose words are rarely repeated or respected.

In contrast to many of the precepts in *Young Poet's Primer*, the "LITTLE LESSONS" in *Very Young Poets* are brief and direct. The first one reads in its entirety, "Poems do not have to rhyme!" (1), which, as with *Young Poet's Primer*, underscores young writers' freedom to be their own arbiters of poetic convention. As with the volume to older young people, in *Very Young Poets*, Brooks focuses on young poets' knowledge, perceptions, and ideas, as in the second lesson: "In your poem, talk about what you know. Talk about what you think. Talk about what you feel. Talk about what you wonder" (2). Many of the lessons in *Very Young Poets* are similar in content to those in *Young Poet's Primer* but are expressed more concisely, as in the ninth lesson, "Poems do not have to be happy. Sometimes poems are sad. Sometimes *life* is sad" (9), and the tenth lesson, "Do not be afraid to say something NEW" (10).

What I find most powerful about *Very Young Poets* is the fifth lesson—"Be yourself. Do not imitate other poets. You are as important as they are" (5)—which is a radical statement that runs counter to conventional pedagogy and literary hierarchies. Notable is Brooks's respect for very young people as poets in the present, as indicated by the simple present tense of these three sentences that address very young poets directly, refer to them as "poets," and compare them to poets of all ages. While Brooks does not identify "they" as adult poets, the implication here is that "very young poets" are "as important" as poets of any age. Finally, the last lesson depicts the relation between a very young writer and poetry itself: "Remember that poetry is your Friend!" (20). Thus, in its framing, direct and engaging speech, and careful crafting of brief lessons, *Very Young Poets* establishes an immediacy in its relation with Brooks's young audience and suggests the type of warm connection that, by the early 1980s, she had already been working for decades to establish with her young fellow travelers.

"I looked at / Her as one who could be / Gazed upon": Young People Writing about Their Encounters with Gwendolyn Brooks

Young people, particularly in Illinois, had many opportunities to engage with Gwendolyn Brooks: through reading her work, attending public readings, submitting poems to her contests, working with her in reading or writing groups, or writing to her individually or as a school assignment. In this last section, I discuss writing by young people addressed directly to Brooks in the form of letters or poems. Most of the letters involve a curious combination of compulsoriness and initiative, as it is clear that many were written at the prompting of a teacher or other adult, yet they sometimes express a sense of encounter between the letter writer and Brooks that owes itself to the letter writer's engagement and ideas.

In the Brooks archive in The Bancroft Library, there are groups of letters dating from the 1960s through 1980s, sometimes accompanied by a letter from a teacher, that resulted from an entire class or grade responding to a visit or public reading by Brooks, or to her published poetry. While most of these are from young people in Illinois, there are also letters from elsewhere in the United States (e.g., Maryland, New Jersey, Pennsylvania). Letters and poems from young people detail the deep impression made on them by hearing Brooks read and talk about poetry at public events. Thinking about these encounters described in the words of elementary and high school–aged youth seems a fitting way to end this chapter focused on young poets and Gwendolyn Brooks.[43]

Some young poets wrote thank you notes to Brooks for receiving an Illinois Poet Laureate award. One set of correspondence that stands out is a pair of illustrated "thank you" cards written by two students from Chicago's Graham School in 1980 after they each won an Illinois Poet Laureate award. A card from Kenneth Davis is illustrated with a drawing of snow-capped mountains covered by clouds and trailing birds; inside the card, he writes, "What I liked most about the program was listening to the poems." He writes of his joy at winning the contest, which made him "very happy," and his even greater joy at getting to meet "the greatest poet of Illinois," which made him "very very happy." The cover of the second card, from Christine Vodicka, depicts a face with a speech bubble saying "WE Thank you" and includes a haiku she wrote "especially for you," titled "Mrs. Brooks," that describes Brooks's poems as moving "With the ease of a river":

> Her poetry flows forth
> With the ease of a river
> Going to its bed.

In her note, Christine Vodicka praises Brooks for her "good taste in poetry" and writes about her own conflicting emotions regarding the contest, her participation in the public reading, and her meeting Brooks in person—"I was so nervous about winning but so happy. I was scared to death when I read my poem. I was so glad to meet you, Mrs. Brooks"—that conveys a sense of the emotionally complex charge young poets could feel through their contact with Brooks and the contest she sponsored.

One key aspect that emerges from some of the letters is that Brooks played an important role for black children in particular, as a prominent black poet who gave serious attention to young people. In a packet dated December 16, 1969, following Brooks's visit to the Family Living Center in Chicago, a letter from Willie Marvel King, an eighth grade student at the time, makes this clear by invoking black nationalist identity ("It is amazing and so wonderful that a woman of our Black nation would be so generous with her talent") and ending the letter with an affirmation of black pride ("Black pride is here to stay!"). Other themes in Willie Marvel King's letter that are echoed generally across the letters from young people include commending the manner in which Brooks read her poems "with feeling" and genuineness, and conveying appreciation for Brooks's positioning of herself on the same level as young people: "I like the way you read poetry. You read all your poems with feeling and you act like your words are all in your heart. I like how you were your self, and did [not] try to be nobody else. You didn't try to put your self over us, like you were somebody much more." King's articulation of Brooks's respectful stance toward young people—"You didn't try to put your self over us"—is echoed across the letters to Brooks from children.

I conclude this discussion by looking at a few examples from a 1973 batch of letters kept in an envelope marked, apparently in Brooks's hand, "Tribute poems from the Eighth Grade Class of Mrs. Anna B. Heming, Countee Cullen School. (April, 1973)," following a class trip to a poetry reading Brooks gave at the University of Chicago. Brooks had seen these tributes; in her handwriting on teacher Anna Heming's cover letter she wrote, "Send them all bookmarks." Most of these texts are structured as poems with line breaks—Anna Heming wrote in her heartfelt letter to Brooks, "We hope it can be called poetry"—and many include young people's perceptions of Brooks reading her poems and its effects on them. Ricki Hullert's poem "Mrs. Brooks" ends with reference to the "good" feeling that resulted from hearing Brooks "talk about youth":

> Mrs. Brooks made me feel good
> the way she talk about youth
> Mrs. Brooks is very good poet

Hullert's reference to the effect on her of "the way" Brooks spoke about youth accords with Willie Marvel King's sentiment above regarding Brooks's positioning in relation to youth ("You didn't try to put your self over us"). Christel Hardman, in her poem titled "The Beautiful Words," writes about the deeply embodied process of listening to Brooks's poetry. For Hardman, "words go inside of" her, which is "a great pleasure":

> Her words didn't just go in,
> my ears, but in me,
> To have words go inside of,
> you is a great pleasure,
> Espeacially[44] when the words are,
> Of Love, Laughter, and beauty.

Most eloquent is Deborah Berry, who at the end of her poem titled "Gwendolyn Brooks" refers to Brooks's ability to understand "us," collective youth. I close this chapter with discussion of Berry's gracious lyric portrait of Brooks, "the / True poet," "a sleek little woman / Conversed in life distilled" who "made me feel secure." Berry captures the shifting tone of Brooks's manner of addressing her audience, from intentionally "somewhat / Funny" to "serious," from "displaying fierce / Emotions" to expressing "Flights of reality." Most interesting for this chapter is Berry's mode of writing about Gwendolyn Brooks in terms that suggest a moving encounter: "I looked at / Her as one who could be / Gazed upon." For Berry's speaker, this "True poet" enables her to have contact with her "brightest dreams" and "darkest nightmares" and "the things which can / Neither be seen or touched." In closing her poetic tribute to Gwendolyn Brooks, Deborah Berry's speaker aligns with collective youth in accentuating Brooks's ability to "Understand us":

> I could think of know[45]
> Other person who seems to
> Understand us, and the way
> Our feelings move.

CHAPTER 3

"My future doesn't know / ME"

Young Poets and Dynamic Temporality in
*Salting the Ocean: 100 Poems
by Young Poets*

NAOMI SHIHAB NYE has devoted much of her professional energy to young people through teaching, writing, and editing projects that include her work as a poet in the schools, numerous poetry volumes written or edited for young audiences, and her editing of the youth-authored poetry anthology *Salting the Ocean: 100 Poems by Young Poets*.[1] She has edited many adult-authored poetry collections for young audiences, including translated poems from the Middle East (*The Flag of Childhood: Poems from the Middle East*) and an inclusive international anthology, *This Same Sky: A Collection of Poems from Around the World*; and has written her own poetry collections across multiple aspects of the interests and identities of young audiences, such as gender (*A Maze Me: Poems for Girls*) and culture (*19 Varieties of Gazelle: Poems of the Middle East*). In *Salting the Ocean: 100 Poems by Young Poets*, Nye partnered with acclaimed artist Ashley Bryan, among whose many works for young audiences are books on African American poetry (*Ashley Bryan's ABC of African American Poetry*, and *Sail Away* with poems by Langston Hughes). With *Salting the Ocean*, Nye and Bryan created a vibrant anthology that presents a generous selection of poems written by young people during Nye's long career as a visiting poet in schools, along with Bryan's brilliant full-color paintings, many of which portray children engaging directly with poetry.

Bryan's illustrations on the front dust jacket cover are vivid depictions of small groups of children (of diverse gender and racial backgrounds) floating on a book-raft as they read poems, or traveling on a boat named "POETRY" as they read books labeled "ODE" or "HAIKU" over waves that spell "BALLAD," "QUATRAIN," "Lullaby," and "Couplet." The back cover depicts children bent over paper or notebooks on a carpet that spells "Emotion," "TIME," "Love," and "NATURE," with the letters of these and other thematic words molded to the contours of the children's bodies as they sprawl out, pen in hand, writing poems. The thematic integration of Bryan's artwork representing young people in the act of writing poems is but one example of editorial decisions by Nye and Bryan that position *Salting the Ocean* as an innovative and respectful presentation of poetry written by young people.

The progression across the front and back covers from reading poetry to writing poetry is accompanied by a poem on the back cover by young poet Cyndea L. Peacock (with her name listed below the poem) that is also included within the book:

> I touched
> the roughness
> of my wrinkled paper
> as I rumpled it
> in my hands.
>
> And remembered
> as I rubbed the edges—
> how life expands.[2]

Peacock's poem explores the process and materiality of writing through engaging with the physicality of paper, using repetition and parallel structure to link "my wrinkled paper" with "my hands." Poet Cyndea Peacock grounds her first-person speaker's action across a past tense ("I touched / ... / as I rumpled," "And remembered / as I rubbed") that through past action and remembering opens up an expanding present ("And remembered / ... how life expands"), with the present-tense final word "expands" rhyming with the first stanza's last word "hands." This is an apt depiction of the embodied agency of a poetic speaker remaking the past into a present that opens and extends possibilities.

Assembling a Poetry Anthology: Practices That
Preserve the Agency of Young Poets

Salting the Ocean: 100 Poems by Young Poets distinguishes itself through organization and formatting practices that recognize and respect the authority, agency, and artistry of young poets. These practices include: referring to young people in the title and framing of the book in respectful ways that emphasize their role as writers; including an index of poets' names, which supports their position as published authors; identifying poems only with each poet's name rather than also with their age or school grade; writing about the process of involvement with the young writers in a manner that balances the agency of the adult editor with that of the young poets; using quotations from young poets for thematic headings, and crediting the young poets in the book's front matter; crediting the poet by name whose poem appears on the back cover; and including an introduction to the anthology that, though written by an adult, frames the volume effectively without detracting from the young writers' positions as artists.

The subtitle of *Salting the Ocean*—*100 Poems by Young Poets*—honors the writers' status as poets who are young, unlike an alternative such as "100 Poems by Children," which instead emphasizes children who happen to have written poems. In the inside book jacket, Nye and Bryan highlight poets' names by first listing nine names, followed by this text: "There are 100 poems in this book by 100 poets who wrote their poems when they were in grades one through twelve. These poets are not famous." Here the writers are identified simply as "poets," and the text ends, "They could be you," indicating not that all young people are poets but that each young person "could be" a poet. Another feature that supports young poets' position as authors is the inclusion of an index by authors' names at the end of the volume, which is comparable to adult-authored anthologies but not often found in anthologies by young writers.

Identifying writers' ages is a contentious issue in presenting youth-written poetry. Most anthologies of poetry written by young people either list each poet's age on the same page as the poem, or use a book title that includes a phrase like "teen poets" or "high school poets" that references the writers' general age range. Of course, identifying poetry by the age of the poet at the time of composition would be a highly unusual literary practice with adult poets. One could say that this practice is part of what prevents youth-written poems from inhabiting an artistic present and future. By identifying youth-written poems with specific ages, we relegate them to a very specific point in the poets' pasts. Identifying poets by school grade (e.g., Lyne, *Ten-Second Rainshowers*) assigns poets to the role of student in an age-graded institutional context. Indeed, the Library of Congress designation for *Salting the Ocean* is "School verse" (iv).

Nye and Bryan follow a very respectful practice in *Salting the Ocean*, identifying poets as "young poets" in general terms, and giving information in the front matter about the age span of the poets from grades one through twelve (approximately six through eighteen years of age), but identifying individual poems only by each poet's name rather than anchoring them to a specific age or school grade. Nye's and Bryan's decision not to print individual children's ages or school grades in conjunction with their poems, especially across such a wide range of ages/grades, is a departure from conventional practices of anthologizing young poets' work, which most commonly include poets' ages alongside their poems. This decision helps afford legitimacy for the young poets through resisting cultural preoccupation with children's age, what Allison James and Alan Prout term adults' "insistent demand of children that their age be made public" (235). Not including the poets' specific ages also takes the poems out of reach of developmental explanations for their themes, language, and imagery. It is not possible for the reader to compare or judge the poems written by younger poets against the poems written by older poets in the volume.[3]

Inserted into the collection's index material are glimpses of Nye's work with young people. Nye relates a story of an elementary school–aged person calling a teacher (presumably Nye) on the phone after her visit to his class, in order to dictate a poem to her: "She says, 'Umm, why don't you just— write it down yourself and give it to me next week?' He says, 'I feel I need to say it into somebody's EAR. Or it won't come out right. There's nobody else at home over here.' So she writes down what he says. It's pretty great. She promises to give him a copy next week. Two hours later, her phone rings again. 'Do you have another piece of paper?'" (110). This vignette, offset in a text box on a page of the book's "Index to 100 Young Poets" (110) along with a half-dozen other such vignettes (also in the separate "Index to 100 Poems" 108), conveys some of the flavor of Nye's work with young people and her respect for the power of their initiative and creative productions. By referring to herself in the third person, Nye diminishes her authority somewhat and makes her position more equivalent to that of the unnamed student. This vignette also suggests the importance of an attentive audience and the temporal urgency that Nye recognizes can be part of the process of young poets' composition.

Salting the Ocean owes itself to Nye having saved "vast heaps" of youth-written poems from her work as poet in the schools. Nye is identified on the book's cover as the person who "Selected" the poems, and a prefatory note indicates that the poems "were selected from the vast heaps that [Nye] has saved from her classes over the past twenty-five years" as a visiting writer with children across "dozens of schools in small towns and cities" in the United States (v).[4] While Nye doesn't specify the precise regions where these young people lived, the note indicates that she has taught in "inner-city schools and far-flung rural locations" (v) in Texas, Maine, Wyoming, Oregon, California, Hawaii, and Alaska, locations that suggest she most likely encountered a diversity of young people across the dimensions of class, ethnicity, and race in the United States.[5] The fact that Nye "saved" these poems is some indication of her valuing of them. She dedicates the book *"To the poets, the champions, with love,"* as well as to her editor (v).

Nye organizes the anthology using section headings anchored in phrases composed by young people. The poems I discuss in this chapter appear in two of the four sections of *Salting the Ocean*—"'My Shadow is an Ant's Night': Thirty-two Poems about the Self and the Inner World" and "'Silence is like a Tractor Moving the Whole World': Twenty-five Poems about The Wide Imagination"—whose lyrical titles (preceding the colons) were composed by young poets and positioned by Nye in conversation with her explanatory subtitles. Nye describes in the front matter that "The section titles in this book are memorable lines that have stayed with me over the years" (iv), and she gives "Grateful acknowledgment" to the "young poets" (iv) Sam Sanford for "My Shadow is an Ant's Night" (vii) and Barbara Gonzales for "Silence is like a Tractor Moving the Whole World" (vii). While her use and crediting of the young authors of these phrases acknowledges the authority, agency, and artistry of the young poets, one could argue that omitting thematic subheadings (see, for example, *River of Words: Young Poets and Artists on the Nature of Things*, edited by Pamela Michael) leaves space for poems by young poets to speak for themselves on their own terms.[6]

The inclusion of introductions by adult editors to frame an anthology of young writers' work often serves to assert the agency of adults and "authorize" the value of young people's writing, and begs the question of why young writers themselves are not invited to introduce the work of other young poets.[7] One notable exception is the pairing of young poet Chinaka Hodge's foreword with Youth Speaks founder James Kass's "Introduction" to *My Words Consume Me: An Anthology of Youth Speaks Poets*; Hodge writes, "We are called Poet. . . . Our writing is urgent, created to save us" (ix), and Kass provides context for Youth Speaks as an organization and emphasizes poetry as one of the "spaces that allow young people to speak for themselves" (xii).[8] Nye pursues a meaningful strategy in *Salting the Ocean* through dividing her introduction into three sections directed at different audiences, starting with "To Anyone, and to a Couple in Nova Scotia," a couple who gave her a place to stay for a night in 1974, when she was twenty-two years old and just about to start as a "writer-in-the-schools" (ix), and handed her a copy of Kenneth Koch's book *Wishes, Lies, and Dreams*, which "heartened me immeasurably in those early working days" (x). In the next section of the introduction, "To Teachers, Librarians, Parents, and Other Friends Who May Pick Up This Book," Nye writes about her experience leading a poetry exercise for "Parents' Night" at her son's school and having a fellow parent introduce herself as having been a high school student when Nye visited her class years ago and they "heard poems, talked, wrote our own, read them out loud" (xi). This mother continued, "after you left, we kids missed that experience terribly. We realized we had never had a chance really to *listen* to one another before those poetry sessions, and now they were over. We'd been going to school for so long! Why didn't we get to hear one another's real voices and thoughts more often?" (xi).

Nye picks up on the importance of voice and advocates for its role in classrooms. She writes, "There may be nothing more 'basic' in education than gaining a sense of one's own voice" (xii). She articulates the value for young people of reading poems written by other young people as well as by older writers: "nothing is better than reading the work of our peers, as well as the work of older poets, to get us going in our particular terrain. A poem we love makes us want to write our own—hand to hand, map to map, contagious, delicious voices spinning us forward inside our cluttered, clattering lives" (xii). Nye's identification with young poets here—the repeated "us" and "our"—may derive from her own experience as a young poet, having "published poems since the age of seven" (ix). It may also speak to a goal of inclusion, of acknowledging the continuities and commonalities of writing no matter one's age. Of course, to do so elevates the status of young writers, as in the address of the final section of Nye's introduction, "To the Poets."

In her advice to (young) poets in the final section of her introduction, Nye calls attention to claiming time for oneself and to writing as a regular practice to deepen one's experience by attending, thinking, and making. She suggests to writers, "Start where you are" and "write a little bit every day [rather] than wait for a perfect empty day to come along" (xiii). Along with this pragmatic incremental approach, Nye encourages writers to respect the pace of their language and ideas: "Get in the habit of welcoming your own words, however slowly or quickly they come to you" (xiii). She distills her advice to poets to two words—"Basically, here's my advice: *take time*" (xiii)—that advise them to harness time for their own purposes, to use "A quiet minute, a pencil, a page" (xiii). Nye's address "To the Poets" is framed with her gratitude to them and their efforts, and her introduction ends with her acknowledgement of and thanks for the voices of the poets: "I wish you well and thank you for your wonderful voices" (xiv). On the facing page is another illustration by Bryan—this time of two children on a book-raft in the middle of a calm ocean, with one child beginning to write "Salting Th" while the other holds the "O" of the next word—which introduces the poems written by the (young) poets.

Salting the Ocean, Controlling Time

The book's title, *Salting the Ocean*, derives from an untitled poem in the volume by Bill Collins, in which a first-person speaker describes his disillusionment from his past belief that his mother "salted the whole ocean" prior to his going swimming:

> When I used to go to the beach
> my mother would take a saltshaker
> and make the water salty
>
> With great expertise
> she would taste, salt, taste
> and salt again
> five minutes or so
> until she decided it was right

Then I would go swimming
thinking my mother
salted the whole ocean
however large it was

I now know
my mother isn't responsible
for the salty ocean

It takes some of the fun
out of going to the beach

This poem's temporal narrative structure across its stanzas—from "When" to "Then" to "now"—leaves the speaker holding his present knowledge by the penultimate stanza: "I now know," albeit reluctantly, that "my mother isn't responsible / for the salty ocean." With the transformation from past "thinking" that "my mother / salted the whole ocean" to present "know[ing]" that she doesn't, the speaker admits, "It takes some of the fun / out of going to the beach." Yet by the poem's conclusion, it is clear, though not stated explicitly, that the poet himself is "responsible / for the salty ocean." Nye chooses as title for the book a phrase she derives from Collins's poem that conveys the agency of the young poet in the present act of writing, the potency of the young poet as manipulator of "the salty ocean." Strangely, though, Nye does not acknowledge Collins in the book's front matter, where she scrupulously acknowledges the young authors of the book's section titles.

While Collins moves from a standard "Then" to "now" in narrating his speaker's realization of the origin of "the salty ocean," other poets in the volume remake temporal order as a method of asserting temporal agency. In reading a subset of poems from *Salting the Ocean* that explicitly engage with time in relation to representations of experience, I draw attention to how these poets manipulate time, or practice *dynamic temporality*. While many poems in *Salting the Ocean* mark their figured experiences as taking place in the present or through a remembered past or imagined future, other poems use shifting verb tense to interweave images about the past, present, and future. These poems could be said to be both in time and out of time. They offer speakers who live in and through time, yet also step partially outside of temporal experience to comment, reflect on, or manipulate an aspect of temporality. Some of these poems use explicit temporal markers (such as the words "past," "present," "future," or "time"), while others engage with these themes without explicitly naming them. Poems that demonstrate dynamic temporality use a creative manipulation of temporal registers often evident primarily through patterns of verb tense in relation to content. While simple present tense is most commonly used in poems in *Salting the Ocean*, some poets combine present tense with other tenses, such as tenses that convey ongoing action (e.g., present and past progressive); this cross-temporal reference also occurs through crossing tense with content (e.g., referring to the future in present tense). Dynamic temporality can involve stretching out the present or past, yoking the future into the present, looping the past into the future through the present, or otherwise taking charge over time. These efforts involve exerting control over time in ways that aren't limited by standard trajectories or linear timelines. They are *dynamic* because they set in motion temporal action in creative and unexpected ways.

In the following analysis, I focus on pairs of poems from *Salting the Ocean* that highlight young poets' multiple points of engagement with time. These half dozen poems offer compelling and sometimes contrasting perspectives on themes of knowledge and futures, direct address to time, and racing against time. What they share in common is the poets' engagement with temporal representation to suit their poetic purposes in a manner that demonstrates creative manipulation of temporal registers. Poems by Christopher Viner and Leticia Gray consider time in relation to knowledge and, respectively, claim that the future does not know one's present self or question whether one's self can know the future while rooted in the present. Karen Luk and Martin Laureles directly address elements of time as characters in their poems and, respectively, question the travels and habits of free time or imagine a relationship to a personified past in order to incorporate it in the present. Poems by Alberto Santillana and Jamshid Afshar, Jr., are concerned with time and motion in relation to the self, and represent the self, respectively, as overrun by time or as able to outpace time. Despite these varied engagements, these young poets demonstrate a striking similarity in constructing poetic voices that enable them to imaginatively manipulate time. Young poets' use of dynamic temporality can be understood as exercising imaginative control over time, practicing flexibility in temporal arrangements, or moving beyond perceived limits of time in young people's lives.

"My future doesn't know / ME": Knowledge and Futures

The initial pair of poems that I discuss concerns whether and how the self can be known, and by whom, in the present and future. These poems speak from the present, yet they position the future as an unknowing, unknown, or possibly unknowable force. In contrast to adult-driven tropes of children "as" or "for" the future, Christopher Viner's "Anonymous" and Leticia Gray's "Patterns" present speakers who refer to a future that, at best, is at a remove from themselves, and perhaps even poses a threat to their subjectivity. Viner's poem depicts the future as not knowing the self, while Gray's poem depicts the self as not knowing the future.

In Christopher Viner's "Anonymous," the speaker claims that the future does not know him. He begins with a present self—"I am anonymous"— and refers to a future that is personal—"My future"—yet is positioned outside and without knowledge of the speaker's present self:

> I am anonymous.
> I am only known to a
> small group.
> The world doesn't know
> ME.
> My future doesn't know
> ME.
> Sometimes I am not known to my
> PARENTS.
> My insides don't know my outsides.
> I am only known to some things but not many.
> I AM ANONYMOUS.

The future is a putative agent here, capable of knowing or not knowing. The poem's speaker claims that the future, the world, and even sometimes his parents do not know what he experiences as himself. While the speaker does not deny a future, and in fact identifies a future that is his own ("My future"), he claims a voice for himself in spite of possible futures. Cross-temporal reference is used through referring to the future in present tense—"My future doesn't know" rather than "My future will not know." In so doing, the threat of his future's ignorance about him is brought into his present and perhaps thereby defanged.

A complex, layered notion of subjectivity emerges through Viner's poem. Lack of knowledge is attributed to external forces—the world, his future, and his parents (who, though "PARENTS" is capitalized, are positioned as the object rather than subject of a clause)—which Christopher Viner contrasts with the emphatic, outsized, capitalized ME. Yet he further complicates this view by stating, "My insides don't know my outsides," questioning the extent to which even self-knowledge is possible, and positing a spatially differentiated notion of self. This representation of subjectivity is centered in the present, but not integrated across temporal frames or bodily space. The poem proceeds through contrasts: small / large (evidenced through manipulating typeface and capitalization), "doesn't know" / "known," "insides" / "outsides," "some" / "many"; and it begins and ends with parallel statements: "I am anonymous" becomes by the end of the poem the uppercase emphatic "I AM ANONYMOUS," a claim of power and self-definition through the articulation of anonymity as a strength. To be "anonymous" is transformed by the end of the poem into a positive statement of self-knowledge and self-assertion, and a claim to be known "Sometimes" to "some" people. In Christopher Viner's "Anonymous," the future remains safely cushioned in the present.

Poet Leticia Gray also invokes the future in her poem "Patterns," and does so through playing with ideas about growth and knowledge. Even though Gray summons a natural image of growth with the metaphor of trees as a figure for "know[ing] how to grow," she undercuts typical notions of maturational or unidirectional change.

"Wherever I stand, I hear the trees petition."—William Stafford

I think of how the rain
is washing life away.

How do I know what life
has in store for me?

It is strange that I cannot
figure out the pattern.

The trees are so perfect,
they know how to grow.

"Patterns" begins with an epigraph from poet William Stafford that suggests the solitary speaker is thinking about her voice against the "petition" of a community of trees. Gray's poem presents a speaker who claims she does not know the future. The opening two lines of the poem ("I think of how the rain / is washing life away") depict rain as a force of present erosion—driving present life into gutters or down slopes—that complicates a simple view of natural change or the forward motion of time. Visually, the "I" moves down and across the hillside of the poem's first three stanzas, pushed further toward the right as its certainty erodes ("I think," "How do I know," "I cannot / figure out"). Verb tense shifts from the first stanza's use of present ("I think") and present progressive tense ("the rain / is washing life away") to asking about the future in the present tense ("How do I know" rather than "how will I know'), a cross-temporal reference that connects the speaker's present knowledge with her questions about the future.

The craft of "Patterns" involves the juxtaposition of its careful making with the speaker's questioning of her knowledge. The poem's central two stanzas present the speaker's questioning about herself and her future ("How do I know what life / has in store for me?") in relation to pattern ("It is strange that I cannot / figure out the pattern"). And the poem's concluding stanza suggests praise for the naturalness of pattern, which seems to echo the common maturational model of development and growth. A maturational (or organismic) metaphor for development—in which a child, given a supportive environment, is seen as expected to mature into a functioning adult from her unfolding biological capacity, "as a seed planted in favorable conditions is expected to unfold and mature into a tree" (Meacham 75)—is one of the most common conceptions of development across the history of academic psychology (Parke et al.). In "Patterns," the speaker attributes to trees knowledge about "how to grow," an understanding of process and purpose that the speaker claims not to have herself. Yet it is hard not to read this poem as implicitly questioning the certainty of adults' expectations for young people and of their formulations of predictive developmental patterns. In addition to the previous features I mentioned that constitute the poem's craft, "Patterns" is composed in a careful pattern of four couplets with mostly regular meter of three beats per line. Leticia Gray has artfully constructed a poem about a speaker not knowing her pattern through careful use of poetic patterns, and the poem can be understood to question the knowledge and value of pattern and perfection in relation to young people. If adult expectations lurk in the shadows, seeing children as potentially perfectible, or as failures when they do not develop into perfect adults, Leticia Gray's poem is an artful, polished rebuke.

Leticia Gray and Christopher Viner position speakers who use their present knowledge to question or challenge the future through means that include cross-temporal reference (e.g., referring to the future in present tense) indicative of dynamic temporality. Young poets can also use their poetic authority to address aspects of temporal reality directly within their poems. In the next section, I discuss two poems that deploy dynamic temporality and alter the frames of time through referring to "free time" or "the Past" as poetic characters who are directly addressed.

"Hey, free time": Direct Address to Time

In the next two poems I consider, elements of time—"free time" in Karen A. Luk's untitled poem, "the Past" in Martin Laureles's "Charm to Bring Back the Past"—become characters in the drama of each poem. The speakers of these poems engage directly with time through questions, pleas, or directives; and these poets take risks through positioning their speakers in very particular positions in relation to time. Rather than a young person as an object of time, or as a figure of the beginning of a linear narrative, the speakers in these poems are constructed as potent, imaginatively resourceful, and capable of altering temporal frames.

In her untitled poem, Karen A. Luk playfully explores ideas about "free time" and addresses "free time" directly by the end of the poem:

> Where does my free time go?
> Does it fly off like a shooting star?
> Take a trip to the Bahamas?
> What if I don't use it?
> Does it feel neglected?
> Or does it understand?
> Is it all-encompassing?
> Or know give-and-take?
> Does it keep an alarm?
> Is it always on time?
> Is free time shared by all of us?
> I want more.
> Hey, free time . . .
> You're late.

Luk's poem proceeds through a list of questions in which the speaker imagines the journeys that free time might take, wonders about free time's feelings if she doesn't "use it," and questions whether free time is "shared by all of us." An aspect of the poem's craft is the structuring of this set of questions about "free time" in a descending pattern: three questions about where it goes (when the speaker doesn't have access to it), three questions about what it feels (when the speaker doesn't use it all), two questions on its manner of engagement ("all-encompassing" versus reciprocal "give-and-take"), two questions about its own time-keeping ("Is it always on time?"), and a culminating question about whether "free time" is "shared by all of us." Notable about all of these questions is that "free time" is the grammatical subject or central referent. "Free time" is an agent who might take vacations, experience emotions, engage in control or reciprocity, and rely on an alarm clock.

The final lines of Luk's poem involve a shift to the speaker addressing "free time" directly. The turn begins with a declarative statement, "I want more." This statement of desire for more free time prompts the speaker to take a very active stance in the final two lines by addressing "free time" directly in a manner that commands attention and the power to scold: "Hey, free time . . . / You're late." By the end of the poem, all of which is in the present tense, the speaker claims a powerful position in relation to an aspect of time, and it is likely important that this aspect is "free time," an element that arguably many children may believe they should have control over.[9] Here, in a clever co-option of typical adult power to scold children over their use of free time, Luk enables her speaker to exercise the rhetorical power to scold "free time."

Finally, Martin Laureles's poem "Charm to Bring Back the Past" is a meditation on its speaker's relation to the past that proceeds through playing with temporal reference:

> I will risk my life to bring back the Past.
> I will order it at a restaurant.
> It will cost but it's worth it.
> I will invite it to my house and treat it
> as if it were my relative.
> If the Past feels bad, I feel bad.
> If the Past feels good, I feel good.
> Sometimes I feel further back in the Past
> than the Past itself.
> I wish the Past would come back
> so my older relatives would have those good times
> they told me they had.
> Please come back Past please come back.

For a poem focused on the past, "Charm" begins by making promises toward the future, opening with the line "I will risk my life to bring back the Past." The poem's first four lines are structured "I will . . . / I will . . . / It will . . . / I will . . . ," an insistent series of promises about the speaker's future actions. By its fourth line, the poem quietly startles the reader by referring to an anthropomorphized past, as a character who in the future will be invited to take up residence with the speaker "as if it were my relative." The speaker engages in a range of interesting interactions and feelings with regard to "the Past," which include the absurd ("I will order it at a restaurant"), the fellow-feeling ("If the Past feels bad, I feel bad"), and the mysterious ("Sometimes I feel further back in the Past / than the Past itself").

The freedom to subvert temporal order that Martin Laureles engages in is accomplished with a tone alternately playful and serious. Toward the end, the poem's tone becomes earnest when the speaker mentions a reason for wanting the past to return: "so my older relatives would have those good times / they told me they had." The speaker's motivation for transforming linear time thus derives from social relationships, in desiring that his elder relatives "would have" (in the conditional future), "those good times" that they specifically "told me" about (in the past). The poignancy of this motivation is accentuated by its not being revealed until the end of the poem, just prior to the incantatory final line "Please come back Past please come back," a repetitive, pleading direct address to the past whose lack of punctuation adds urgency, as does the omission of the expected article "the": the speaker in the end pleads directly with "Past" as if on a first-name basis. The poem subverts the powerless supplicating image of juvenile pleading through the poem's overall image of a speaker potent, courageous, and clever enough to reposition the past in the future for the sake of the present. Dynamic temporality is seen in "Charm to Bring Back the Past" in its shifting temporal registers, in moving from talking about the past in simple future tense ("I will risk my life to bring back the Past," a striking cross-temporality), to subjunctive mood, to simple present tense, to conditional mood, to simple past tense, to a final direct address to the past in present tense, demonstrating a striking complexity of temporal reference.

Already, this range of temporal manipulation in poems by Viner, Gray, Luk, and Laureles demonstrates varied projects and temporal strategies. Another mode of temporal engagement is explored in the next section, with two poems that position their embodied speakers in an actual race against time. Alberto Santillana and Jamshid Afshar, Jr., endow "time" with a physical agency, which accomplishes figuration that enables direct comparison between the capacity of the embodied speakers and time itself.

"where time is as fast as I am": Racing against Time

Poets who make use of dynamic temporality ostensibly feel imaginatively equal to the project of engaging directly with time or challenging conventional temporal frameworks. This can occur by positioning speakers in direct comparison to time, for better or worse. The two poems I explore in this section present contrasting visions of the capacity of the self in relation to time. Both poems figure their speakers in motion relative to time, the first through the poignancy of not being able to catch up, and the second through the power of outrunning time. The speaker in Alberto Santillana's untitled poem opens, "I feel like a puppy that / can't catch up," whereas in "Roller-Skate!" by Jamshid Afshar, Jr., the speaker claims, "time is as fast as I am." Both poets make use of dynamic temporality in constructing these literal races against time.

Alberto Santillana's poem presents a series of images that conveys a sense of being behind time and unable to catch up. Santillana positions "Time" itself as an actor whose "racing" speed contrasts with the stalled or insufficient speed of the poem's speaker:

> I feel like a puppy that
> can't catch up to his mother.
> Like a creek that runs fast
> but can't reach the ocean.
> Like a runner who stays all day
> in the starting line.
> My mind is like an empty box.
>
> Time like a racing car
> running at the speed of light.

Santillana's poem depicts the speaker as feeling "like a puppy," "Like a creek," and "Like a runner" who "can't catch up," "can't reach" the goal, or can't even start moving—all images of active subjects who are in motion or ready for motion (the runner at the "starting line") yet can't launch or go fast enough. These images contrast with the incongruous final image of the first stanza, "My mind is like an empty box," which suggests a mind that is depleted, without resources, or unknowable.

Yet another way of looking across the first stanza of Santillana's poem is to notice that the first two images involve the immature ("puppy") or component ("creek") in relation to the mature ("his mother") or source ("ocean"), whereas the second two images, the "runner who stays all day / in the starting line" and the "mind . . . like an empty box," have questionable potency yet are in possession of autonomy, and as such can stand and act autonomously rather than in relation to a more mature caretaking or more complete entity. "Time" in the final stanza is clearly in a different league, "running at the speed of light," yet the speaker toward the end of the first stanza has at least has made it to the "starting line." In the poem's final image, "Time" is "like a racing car / running at the speed of light," an image of elemental time as potent and swift, yet interestingly depicted through images of human-made (racing car) or human-like (running) motion. Though the poem has been in the present tense, this final image makes use of present progressive tense ("Time . . . / running at the speed of light"), a fitting representation of Time's mobility in relation to the speaker.

"Roller-Skate!" by Jamshid Afshar, Jr., shares the project of figuring temporal movement as a race between the human speaker and time, yet he grounds his poetic authorship in a temporal determinacy that contrasts with the temporal indeterminacy of Alberto Santillana's poem. While Santillana's poem does not locate its action rhetorically in time aside from its present tense, "Roller-Skate!" by Afshar, Jr., launches each of its stanzas with the repeated temporal phrase "When I roller-skate." "Roller-Skate!" depicts a speaker in motion articulating the power and resonance of motion and speed. That the action of the entire poem occurs "When I roller-skate" results in a provocative set of images about the action and meaning of moving in space and time:

> When I roller-skate
>   I feel life in a way
>   where time is as fast as I am.
>
> When I roller-skate
>   I feel power, like being
>   superior to the world.
>
> When I turn on my roller skates
>   it's like my life changing
>   as I grow older.
>
> When I roller-skate
>   I feel that loneliness
>   cannot catch me.

The opening stanza conveys a fullness and sufficiency in the speaker's sense of himself roller-skating. This image raises the young speaker to the level of elemental time; when he roller-skates, time must catch up to him, must reach his own speed in order to be "as fast as I am." Roller-skating as an image of "power" is explicit in the second stanza, where the speaker while roller-skating feels "superior to the world."

By the third stanza, Afshar, Jr., presents an intriguing image that fuses present action with change and aging. Here, the launch of action—"When I turn on my roller skates"—is embedded in the poem's only simile: "it's like my life changing / as I grow older." This simile opens multiple temporal possibilities: the more mundane interpretations are that roller-skating makes the speaker feel more grown up, or more in charge of his own movement and change. Yet a more compelling and multidimensional reading recognizes how Afshar, Jr., constructs his speaker as inhabiting multiple positions of temporal agency. In the moment of starting his roller skates, he moves into and through the act of "changing" to propel his life forward over time across age. The act of anticipating speeding ahead accentuates the speaker's sense of his life "changing / as I grow older," a phrase that is an interesting combination of future-oriented ("grow older") but not necessarily linear ("changing") terms. This effect is heightened through the use of the present progressive tense ("changing") whereas the rest of the poem is in the simple present tense. Within this pivotal penultimate stanza, the speaker is positioned as exercising agency in and over time at each of three temporal junctures: "When I turn," "my life changing," "as I grow older."

"Roller-Skate!" by Jamshid Afshar, Jr., traverses a temporal landscape in which the speaker takes different stances in relation to speed, motion, time, and age. The speaker inhabits a temporal landscape where time just happens to travel "as fast as I am," where his own speed is raw "power," where his swiftness propels him forward across the temporal lifespan, and, lastly, where he is able to outpace "loneliness" in the last stanza: "When I roller-skate / I feel that loneliness / cannot catch me." Notable is how this exploration of motion and time is particular to the speaker's age position; while not identified explicitly as a young person, the speaker is cognizant of his position in "the world" and thinks repeatedly about questions of power, age, and time.

One measure of the potency of "Roller-Skate!" is that the poem's final stanza seems to have inspired Naomi Shihab Nye herself to write a poem titled "The Rider" that responds to the image in "Roller-Skate!" of leaving loneliness behind but does not make use of images relating to time, power, and change that can be seen to relate specifically to the social position of Afshar, Jr., as a young person. Nye's poem begins "A boy told me / if he rollerskated fast enough / his loneliness couldn't catch up to him"; it centers on the activity frame of roller-skating itself and questions whether the ability to outpace loneliness "translates to bicycles." In Nye's poetic homage, the content of the idea by Afshar, Jr., is accorded respect and resonance, yet the medium of his telling ("A boy told me")—that it was conveyed through the young poet's original verse—and the artistry with which he does so, is not directly acknowledged. It is notable that Nye does not convey or pick up on those aspects of "Roller-Skate!" that are most relevant to youth agency: the elemental resonance of competing against time itself, or the connections between self-propelled motion and time, age, and the world.

Nye's poem "The Rider" has received a level of attention that "Roller-Skate!" has not received.[10] "The Rider" is included in Nye's collection *Fuel*, and has been anthologized in Paul Janeczko's compelling anthology of poems by adults for young readers, *The Place My Words Are Looking For*. Since the anthologizing of Nye's "The Rider" in *The Place My Words Are Looking For*, published in 1990, occurred a decade prior to the appearance of "Roller-Skate!" by Afshar, Jr., in *Salting the Ocean*, one could also see Nye's inclusion of "Roller-Skate!"—and even the impetus for creating *Salting the Ocean*—as a practice of respect for such poetry and a desire to bring young poets' work to light. One striking example of the lack of recognition accorded to "Roller-Skate!" by Afshar, Jr., involves the fact that Nye's "The Rider" is included in the project sponsored by poet Billy Collins during his tenure as U.S. poet laureate (2001–3), "Poetry 180," which promotes having "a student, a teacher, an administrator or a staff person" read aloud a poem a day to a high school community ("Poetry 180"). The project's set of 180 poems, as far as I can tell, does not include poems written by young people, and it is ironic that "Roller-Skate!" by Afshar, Jr.—the inspiration for Nye's "The Rider"—is not visible within Collins's project, whose goal is "making poetry an active part of the daily experience of American high school students" ("Poetry 180"). In contrast to the multiple appearances of "The Rider" in print (and in a number of online blogs and websites), the print life of "Roller-Skate!" is limited to *Salting the Ocean*, and the online attention the poem has received slights its artistry. In an online review of *Salting the Ocean*, "Roller-Skate!" was selected as the sole sample poem, yet seemingly due to the poem being framed around a "fun" activity: "Kids love to do fun activities such as roller-skating. What a great way to encourage poem writing by having them create a similar poem about something they love to do!"[11] These examples of adults' limited references to "Roller-Skate!" obscure the artistry of Jamshid Afshar, Jr., in figuring time, change, and age and in exercising artistic control over time. It is not sufficient to admire poems written by young people or even to publish them. We need to make and sustain the argument that young people deserve respect *as* artists, or prevailing cultural attitudes will continue to disregard, disrespect, or bury their poems.

In "Roller-Skate!" and the other poems I discussed from *Salting the Ocean*, time is an elemental force that these poets confront imaginatively through metaphoric engagement, direct address, and multiple temporal configurations. It is important to note that in these poems, chosen from among the one hundred poems included in Nye's and Bryan's anthology, the young poets crafted multiple and even contrasting views of time from one another. This demonstrates a central point in analyzing young poets' temporal engagements in lyric poetry: young people's ideas about time are not reducible to a unitary "child's perspective." The dynamic temporality evident in these poems involves different approaches to articulating temporal metaphors and sequences—questioning time, ordering it around, stretching it out, moving it in unpredictable ways, and subverting straightforward temporal linearity. While all of the poems use the present tense in some form, many of them shift between tenses or display cross-temporal reference in referring to a temporal epoch in an unexpected tense. The frequency and multiple modes of playing with verb tense illustrate some of the ways that young poets can manipulate tense as a central technique in repositioning poetic speakers imaginatively in relation to time; exploring alternative metaphors and trajectories; and challenging ideas about time, age, change, and childhood.

It makes sense that adults have a stake in linear timelines, as they always occupy the "mature" and "developed" outcome, the "fulfilled potential." Acts of claiming power over time, whether in creative productions or even in memory, integrate imaginative and working conceptual understanding of time and its significance for agency, self-experience, and social roles. For youth, the freedom to imagine across and through temporalities, and to alter or subvert linear time, enables them to inhabit a position of temporal power over their imagined lives and worlds.

CHAPTER 4

"My sole desire is to move someone through poetry, and allow for my voice to be heard"

Young Poets, Children's Rights, and the
Rattle Young Poets Anthology

ONE ELEMENT ABSENT from most anthologies that include poetry written by young people is a space that enables young poets to introduce their work or otherwise comment on their motivation, their poetics, or their engagement with poetry. Such a feature is included in the *Rattle Young Poets Anthology* (Green), a print anthology launched by the literary journal *Rattle* in 2014, in their concluding "Contributor Notes." Christell Victoria Roach's note begins by introducing herself as "a young artist who always knew I was such" (86)—she is identified as "Age 14" (64) on the page including her poem—and ends with the statement included in the title of this chapter: "My sole desire is to move someone through poetry, and allow for my voice to be heard" (86).[1] She invokes her "desire" to "move" an audience through her poetry and in so doing to enable her "voice to be heard." Roach's description of her "desire" to participate in literary practices in ways that make possible her own influence intersects with contemporary discourse on children's rights. Do children have the right to write and be taken seriously as writers? How does thinking about youth writing as a right provide leverage for thinking about youth agency? In this chapter, I read a selection of poems from the inaugural *Rattle Young Poets Anthology* and consider young poets' use of temporal control in relation to their poetic priorities and concerns, as well as the role of adult mediation in the context of young poets' right to participate in literary practices. I focus specifically on young people's rights to participation and expression and the relevance of those rights for the production, publication, and critical reception of poetry written by young people.

Christell Victoria Roach's words are strongly reminiscent of Article 12 of the United Nations Convention on the Rights of the Child (CRC), adopted in 1989, which "assure[s] to the child who is capable of forming his or her own views the right to express those views freely in all matters affecting the child, the views of the child being given due weight in accordance with the age and maturity of the child" ("Convention"). While this wording interposes developmental judgment in adults' assessment of "the age and maturity of the child," the Committee on the Rights of the Child—which meets regularly to monitor implementation of the CRC—subsequently clarified that age or verbal ability should not be a barrier, that adults should "presume that a child has the capacity to form her or his own views and recognize that she or he has the right to express them" (6), and that children's views are relevant beyond their own immediate concerns and "can enhance the quality of solutions" (8) on all manner of topics (Committee, "General Comment No. 12"). In other words, adults should presume that even the youngest children have ideas of their own, are capable of expressing them, and thereby can contribute to the cultural and political life of the societies in which they live. The United States remains the only United Nations member state that has not ratified the CRC, yet given the otherwise wide global acceptance and use of the CRC, it is nonetheless the starting point for contemporary considerations of children's rights, even within the United States. That said, it is important to build on critiques of the ethnocentrism embedded in the CRC, as articulated by Karl Hanson and Olga Nieuwenhuys ("Living Rights") and others.[2]

Children's right to participation—"The right of all children to be heard and taken seriously" (Committee, "General Comment No. 12" 3)—is considered a central principle of the CRC, and "participation" has become a broad term used in children's rights discourse to encapsulate processes of children's involvement in their social, political, and cultural worlds, and their right to have their involvement respected by adults.[3] While scholars, advocates, and practitioners continue to explore means of integrating young people's participation in public spheres such as youth councils, this discourse has only recently begun to be applied to considering children's right to participation in literary practices as writers, as I previously argued in an essay looking at Slade Morrison's collaboration with his mother Toni Morrison on two books for children—*The Big Box* and *The Book of Mean People*—that represent young characters' views of freedom and transactions over meaning (Conrad, "Children's Right to Write"). In 2014, the National Council of Teachers of English in the United States issued a statement titled "Beliefs about the Students' Right to Write" that refers not only to young people's right to express their ideas without censorship but also to their right to exercise control over their writing in school contexts: "students should, as much as possible, have choice and control over topics, forms, language, themes, and other aspects of their own writing while meeting course requirements." Integrating young writers into the practice of literature could serve as a type of "dialogic approach to participation" (300), as discussed by Robyn Fitzgerald and colleagues, which involves mutual recognition and respect between adults and children.

While the right to participation is the cornerstone of considering young people's right to involvement in producing literature, also important are the right "to participate fully in cultural and artistic life" ("Convention," Article 31) and the right to freedom of expression ("Convention," Article 13). Article 31 describes children's right of access to, participation in, and contribution to creative activities, and acknowledges that children's "spiritual, material, intellectual and emotional expressions of culture and the arts" might help transform their societies (Committee, "General Comment No. 17" 4). Article 13 outlines children's right to the "freedom to seek, receive and impart information and ideas of all kinds, regardless of frontiers, either orally, in writing or in print, in the form of art, or through any other media of the child's choice" ("Convention"), yet children's right to "impart" ideas receives arguably less emphasis in public and scholarly discussions than does children's access to ideas produced by others. Certainly age functions as a "frontier" in the production, publication, and critical reception of "children's literature." Aimed at children but authored by adults, children's literature according to a children's rights framework does not adequately respect or uphold the freedom of expression and right to cultural and artistic participation of young writers and of young (and older) audiences who would be interested in reading works by young writers.

Young authors lack authority, or the cultural, social, and political power of authorship, and are not enabled to fully claim the agency that they express through crafting their ideas in written form. As discussed in chapter 1, to refer to literature written by children,[4] I must work around available terms that refer to literature written by adults ("literature" and "children's literature") or position young writers in the past of adult writers ("juvenilia"). To use a clunky but serviceable term such as "youth-produced literature," I must assert young people's right to participate in the production of literary texts as youth in the present, not as future adults, and their right to have their texts considered for publication and read as contributions to cultural life worthy of serious reading and critical attention.

Recent approaches to children's rights have begun to position children's agency, experiences, and understanding of their rights closer to the center of investigation. As mentioned in chapter 1, Karl Hanson and Olga Nieuwenhuys discuss children's rights as "living rights" that take shape in relation to children's ideas and activities ("Living Rights" 8), which is a view of children's rights that presupposes children's agency. If we define agency as an individual's capacity for intention and action as shaped through familial and cultural practices, power relations, and institutional structures, then even the agency that young people express through the act of writing can be undermined if that writing is devalued and not admitted into public culture but kept in the private spheres of families and classrooms. In order to consider young people as cultural producers, as original thinkers and makers of ideas and texts, adults must recognize their agency, respect their productions, and acknowledge that young people bring unique perspectives because of their youth. In presenting "children's standpoints" (Mayall 177) on their lives as young people—which, as I discussed in chapter 1, is a term used by Berry Mayall, drawing from feminist standpoint theories (e.g., Harding), for children's perspectives on their experiences and conditions as children—youth-produced literature can strengthen our conception of children's rights as a "'living practice,' shaped by children's everyday concerns" in the words of Hanson and Nieuwenhuys ("Living Rights" 8).

Children's rights discourse can help articulate a view of young people as capable persons in their present lives rather than as preparing for their futures under the tutelage of and entertainment by adults, as Reynaert and colleagues discuss in their review of scholarship on children's rights in the twenty years following the adoption of the U.N. Convention on the Rights of the Child. Given that conventional Western ideas of autonomy interfere with adults' recognition of young people's literary artistry, as I discussed in chapter 1, a children's rights framework can aid in formulating a view of artistic agency that encompasses individuals' interdependence and embeddedness in social and cultural worlds. Seen in this light, adult mediation in children's productions, rather than eroding children's autonomy, is part of the background against which children's literary productions take shape.[5] While adult mediation can certainly be acknowledged, respect for innovative youth-produced texts as literature depends on recognition of young people's agency as writers and cultural producers.

"These are real poems": *Rattle Young Poets Anthology*

The inaugural *Rattle Young Poets Anthology*, published in 2014 and edited by Timothy Green, is a finely produced slim volume with a full-color illustration by adult artist David Navas on the front and back covers of a child sitting on a lower step of a staircase, bent over a thick book, writing. The apparently white girl sits to the side on a low step, the staircase rising above and behind her, its design suggestive of a wide ladder. The image appears to be a pixelated painting, so there is fuzziness to the child's face, body, and the staircase, though the child's hand and the pen are oddly clear and crisp. Interestingly, the image is reproduced in reverse on the back cover: on the front cover the child is right-handed, whereas on the back cover she is left-handed. The image conveys a sense of the privacy, isolation, and focus of the young writer, who is positioned on a low rung of the ladder/staircase, her red sweatshirt vivid against the green and brown background. The red sweatshirt recalls the cover image of a recent edition of Louise Fitzhugh's *Harriet the Spy*, whose title character is the prototypic fictional child writer in mid- to late-twentieth-century American children's literature. Although *Harriet the Spy* was exactly fifty years old when the *Rattle Young Poets Anthology* appeared, Harriet keeps alive the notion of child writer as perpetual spy, as outsider, a view of child writers whose purpose Juliet McMaster describes as "the child's urgent need for knowledge in the face of knowledge denied" ("What Daisy Knew" 52).

Produced by the editorial staff of the literary journal *Rattle*, the 2014 *Rattle Young Poets Anthology* presents sixty-two poems by sixty poets, and is the inaugural volume of an annual publication. In terms of children's rights, *Rattle* is providing an opportunity for young people to participate in public literary culture through its print volume and website, where poems by young poets appear alongside those of adult poets (though, unlike adult poets, they are identified by their age). The guidelines for submission to the inaugural anthology slice a particular quadrant of age: "The author of the poem must have been age 15 or younger when the poem was written, and 18 or younger when submitted" (Green 88). The poems included are thus written by poets aged fifteen or younger (the youngest is three years old), and submitted when they were, at the oldest, on the threshold of adulthood in the United States. Unlike anthologies in which a teacher serves as editorial gatekeeper (e.g., Nye's *Salting the Ocean*), the inaugural *Rattle* positions the parent or guardian as the mediating power, and in fact only a couple of the young poets refer in the Contributor Notes to the influence of a teacher or indicate that their poems originated as school assignments. Having the poems derive from home life rather than school life may give these young poets greater leeway on form, diction, and subject matter.[6]

Editor Timothy Green's introduction mentions the paucity of anthologies that present alternatives to the "children's poetry" written by adults for children. In envisioning "children themselves as poets," this anthology is "written in the other direction—*by* children *for* adults, as well as those their own age" ("Introduction" 5, emphasis in original). The *Rattle Young Poets Anthology* is thus oriented to an audience of young people and adults, and Green writes eloquently about how it can "help us see through the eyes of another" and learn "what it feels like to be young in the 21st century" ("Introduction" 5). Green indicates young poets' similarities to adult poets and aims to elevate their status as poets: "These may be kids, but they write about most of the things that adults do, and with a depth of understanding that deserves more respect than they're often given" ("Introduction" 5–6). However, in a manner that conveys the contradictions often at play in adults' presentations of young people's writing, Green refers to characteristics he finds particular to young poets—"They write with a natural spontaneity that adults can only hope to achieve" ("Introduction" 5)—that bear resemblance to common Western assumptions about childhood discussed by Perry Nodelman and Mavis Reimer in their informed critical reading of children's literature, such as the notion that there is "a direct connection between childlike thinking, imagination, fantasy, and creativity" (Nodelman and Reimer 87). Yet overall, Green challenges readers' expectations of an anthology of poetry by children, stating that the *Rattle Young Poets Anthology* "is not a cute collection hoping to win your adoration" but that "These are real poems, by talented authors, with important stories to share" ("Introduction" 6).

While the title of the *Rattle Young Poets Anthology* refers respectfully to the writers as "young poets," its treatment of young poets' agency is paradoxical in identifying each poem by the specific age of the poet at the time of composition. Each poet's age is tucked into the upper outside corner of the first page of each poem, in bold font, an element that of course differs from anthologies of poetry by adults. Though childhood is a social position defined by age, it is important to ask whether young writers have a right to the artistic integrity of their work that precludes identifying it by their specific age. Indeed, the developmental belief that age is a metric of maturity is a component of the Convention on the Rights of the Child.[7] Including poets' specific ages invites developmental comparisons and reinforces adults' age-related ideologies, such as the belief that young writers' competence must be precocious—before their time—or that limitations in young writers' poems are proof of children's insufficiency, incompetence, or ignorance. Aside from invoking age and grappling with ideologies of childhood, the overall framing of the anthology is respectful of "young poets," refers to the poems in the anthology's introduction as "real poems, by talented authors" (6) and includes "Contributor Notes" that present the poets' responses to the question "Why do you like writing poetry?" (Green 81).

In the remainder of this chapter, I explore a selection of poems from the 2014 *Rattle Young Poets Anthology* with a focus on poets' temporal representations and their connections to questions of age, agency, and knowledge. I look first at a long poem by a very young poet in light of questions about the conditionality of knowledge and self, as well as the role of adult mediation. I then discuss two poems that are crafted by means of controlled temporal shifts that indicate each poet's skill in manipulating time to construct imagined worlds and act on the reader. Considering these texts written by youth to have literary merit furthers children's rights in acknowledging the importance of youth participation in cultural practices and the value of young people's perspectives on the temporalities that they imagine for themselves.

"Don't Worry, Mom, Don't Panic": Young Poets and
the Conditionality of Knowledge and Self

Philosopher Gareth Matthews relates the following anecdote (*Dialogues with Children* 113):

> Steve, exactly three years old, watched his father eat a banana.
> "You don't like bananas, do you, Steve?" said Steve's father.
> "No," replied Steve. "If you were me, you wouldn't like bananas either."
> Steve paused to reflect. "Then," he added after a minute, "Who would be the daddy?"

Matthews indicates that this type of "philosophical thinking" (116) by a very young child is unexpected according to standard developmental psychology. Steve is grappling with "counterfactual conditionals" (114), exploring the logic of "If you were me," if Steve's father "were" Steve. Matthews finds this notable not only because Steve is using the correct subjunctive form of *to be*, but because he is imaginatively trading selves, roles, and desires.

Cailena Bickell, at four years old, similarly uses the correct subjunctive form of *to be* in the beginning of her extended poem "Don't Worry, Mom, Don't Panic":

> If I made up a poem,
> I would call it:
> "Don't Worry, Mom, Don't Panic."
>
> And,
> If I were you,
> I would slide down a rainbow.
> If I were you,
> Mom,
> I'd get a bunk bed,
> So I wouldn't have to sleep with Dad.
>
> And,
> If I'm me,
> I'll marry a girl.
> Because boys are always being funny with the jokes,
> Jokes, jokes, jokes,
> All the time.

Like, I know Dad is tricking me,
When he says Aunty Kim doesn't have a heart.
'Cause Aunty Kim loves me
More than anything
In the whole world
And that takes a big heart.
Only bad guys don't have hearts.

Don't worry, Mom,
Don't worry about bad guys,
'Cause Dad is big, and he helps crying people,
And he shoots coyotes that get over the fence to eat us.
Too bad he's too big for the school bus.

I love Dad 'cause he's my dad,
All mine,
And Chloe's,
But she's a baby,
So it's OK to share with her.

And Mom is always like:
"Here's my card,
I'll do some work for you.
I write stories about horses,
And roosters,
And kids,
And work."
But not Elmo,
Never Elmo.

I'm too little,
But too little is not too bad.

And, Mom?
Be careful.
Don't talk to seagulls.
They eat garbage and their breath is stinky.

You don't have to be brave all the time, Mom.
Here,
Hold my hand.
Do you feel better now?

I love you, Mom.
Don't worry, I watch out for birds.
You are the banana in my eye;
You are my best Momma.
And Dad is a hero,
And everybody shouts,
"Yay, Freddy!"

I don't need to go to school today,
I know everything, now.
Oh, but
Mom, Mom, Mom, Mom, Mom,
I don't know anything yet.

But,
Someday,
I'll be a doctor.
And I'll say,
"Uh oh, Mom.
There's a beetle in your boob.
DON'T PANIC."

In this first-person poem of seventy-one lines across thirteen stanzas, the first stanza poses the possibility of making a poem based on the poet's knowledge that poems typically have titles. A poem is a "made up" thing that needs or deserves naming, and the poem's speaker enfolds her mother in the center of a double-phrased reassurance, "Don't Worry, Mom, Don't Panic" (10). The work of this poem involves role reversal in which the speaker adopts a caretaking stance toward her mother. While the second stanza's advice about the parents' sleeping arrangements raises the question of differential knowledge of adult and young readers and writers, the rest of the poem provides logical explanations for the speaker's beliefs and advice that even involves challenging adults' words (as in the fourth stanza, which begins "Like, I know Dad is tricking me . . ." 10). Arriving at this statement of knowledge is accomplished through a switch from the conditional future ("If I were you") to the present that occurs only after the speaker imagines herself as herself in the third stanza. The speaker takes the striking stance of posing the conditional possibility of being herself in the future: "And, / If I'm me, / I'll marry a girl" (10).

In the world of "Don't Worry, Mom, Don't Panic," there is no guarantee that you will be yourself in the future; it is one of the possibilities worth imagining. Yet doing so shifts the poem largely into the present tense, into what the speaker knows in her present reality. The poem remains in the present until the final stanza, where the tense shift (to future tense) is again propelled by a question of knowledge. In the penultimate stanza, the poet figures the complicated calculus of a child's knowledge (12):

> I don't need to go to school today,
> I know everything, now.
> Oh, but
> Mom, Mom, Mom, Mom, Mom,
> I don't know anything yet.

These lines are constructed by means of a contrast between "now" and "yet," between "everything" and "[not] anything," between the certainty of present knowledge and the awareness of not knowing what one will know in the future. I read this not as a matter of doing and undoing but as a weighing of different knowledges and a meta-awareness of what the speaker knows when.[8] It is a weighing of knowledges that tips itself toward the future in the last stanza, which carries resonance of humor or might be read as alluding to a medical concern. The final stanza begins "But, / Someday, / I'll be a doctor," with all the knowledge and authority that brings, the power to say and soothe: " 'There's a beetle in your boob. / DON'T PANIC' " (12).

What interests me is the poem's stance on the conditionality of knowledge and the conditionality of self in terms of social role and age. Cailena Bickell poses hypothetical alternatives to reality: the speaker as a poet, the speaker as her mother, the speaker as her future self, the speaker as a doctor reassuring her mother. Though the power of this conditionality is perhaps most evident in the speaker posing the conditional possibility of being herself in the future, the speaker also acknowledges her present identity as "too little" in the middle of the poem: "I'm too little, / But too little is not too bad" (11). In this pivotal two-line stanza, the speaker owns her identity *as* "too little" and reclaims her power to reassure in the rest of the poem, which ends with the loudly capitalized phrase "DON'T PANIC" that also concludes the title. In Cailena Bickell's poem, the flexible relation of the present to the future involves temporal knowledge that the poet deploys in crafting conditional selves. Young poets can take the voice of anyone they can imagine, including their present and future selves.

"Don't Worry, Mom, Don't Panic" uses a fluid conversational style in shaping its one-sided conversation addressed to the speaker's mother. Cailena Bickell's contributor note reads, "What's [poetry] again? I'm just good at talking" ("Contributor" 81). Along with her age of four, this note can raise the question of adult mediation in the construction of the poem, even suggesting the possibility that Cailena Bickell spoke the poem that was transcribed by her parent, which could prompt an adult reader to wonder about the poem's line breaks and stanza breaks. In fact, in corresponding with Cailena Bickell's mother for permission to reprint this poem, I learned from Katie Bickell that her daughter composed the poem in speech during a dinner-table conversation—"We were talking about poetry around the dinner table (I'm also a writer) when she began 'talking' this poem and I wrote her words down"—and Katie Bickell transcribed the poem by following her daughter's natural pauses in speech and imposing some of the line breaks.[9] Knowing this does not diminish my appreciation for the poem, whose conceptual, rhetorical, and linguistic inventions are Cailena Bickell's, while the line breaks and possibly stanza breaks could be viewed as co-constructions by Cailena Bickell and Katie Bickell. This example illustrates the relational context within which young poets may express their artistry. Interestingly, two years after the poem's creation, Cailena Bickell and her mother gave a joint reading of the poem at a "coffee house reading series," relates Katie Bickell, with Cailena "standing on a chair beside me so she could reach the microphone."[10] Learning to read deepened Cailena Bickell's engagement with her poem—at this public event, she read the stanzas she had circled while her mother read the remaining stanzas, and they jointly read the final line—and thus interacting with the written text was layered into the collaboration with her mother.

While poetry made[11] by very young poets can raise questions about adult mediation in transcription, contributor notes by other very young poets in the *Rattle Young Poets Anthology* specifically mention their engagement with writing or words. Ian Jasper Osborn, aged four, writes, "I like to write poetry because I can say anything that comes to my mind" (85). Aaron Fox, aged three, writes, "I love words, a lot of sounds that those guys talk" ("Contributor" 83). Here is Aaron Fox's poem, beginning with the title that runs into the poem's first line:

> *It's Raining*
>
> Today
> because someone
>
> turned on
> the sprinklers
>
> on
> top
>
> of
> the moon.

Aaron Fox uses visual effects in stretching out the form of the poem in the last two stanzas by isolating single words on lines like the long spray of the sprinklers falling from the moon to the earth. Yet the spatial trajectory of the poem works in reverse: the poem launches from the surface of the earth and reaches through that spray of words to the last words, "the moon." Thus in this elegant bidirectional pattern, the words move from earth to moon, and the rain moves from moon to earth.

The youngest poets whose work appears in the *Rattle Young Poets Anthology* think about writing and expression, about words and sounds, about the freedom to express "anything that comes to my mind" (Osborn 85). Writing is one means to articulate a conditionality of knowledge and self, to use language in order to craft imagined worlds, voices, and identities. While adult mediation might be part of the background out of which young poets' work is produced and published, that does not justify denying recognition of the knowledge, agency, and poetic craft that these writers claim.

"When People Leave This Earth": Temporal Control
in Poems by Young Writers

Two of the poems that I found most striking in the inaugural *Rattle Young Poets Anthology* demonstrate depth in young poets' control over temporal representation through working the past or future against the present. One eulogizes a murdered balloon, and the other envisions the deep future of Earth. "Eulogy for a Balloon" by Rose Foster and "When People Leave This Earth" by Theo Candlish are poems constructed in part through careful control over the representation of time. Both poets craft their poems with a striking final shift in tense that brings readers into the present, from the past in "Eulogy for a Balloon" and the future and conditional future in "When People Leave This Earth." Such temporal control indicates these young poets' ability to manipulate representations of time as part of exercising agency in directing a family ceremony or predicting a global future.

"Eulogy for a Balloon" uses control over temporality to achieve its poetic effects. Rose Foster follows the temporal convention of a eulogy in crafting a backward-looking narrative:

> A balloon once lived for a month
> and a little bit more
> until Daddy accidentally murdered him.
>
> But he is still in our hearts.
>
> He was brave to be pushed in the air.
> I remember when he made
> a little girl laugh so hard
> that she screamed.
>
> And this is true.
>
> He traveled with me upstairs
> and downstairs. His final trip was upstairs.
> I wish I could tell you all the adventures
> but the last adventure
> you can see
> ends here in this chilly sandbox
> with sandwiches.
>
> You may eat them.

Much of the poem alternates past with present in contrasting the past life of the balloon with the present voice of the eulogizing speaker. The tone of the poem engagingly interweaves the solemn form of eulogy with a tongue-in-cheek tone indicating that the lost loved one is a balloon who lived a month-long life until "Daddy accidentally murdered him." The contrast of past with present is accentuated through alternating multi-line stanzas that relay past information about the balloon's life (along with the present anchors "I remember," "I wish") with present-tense single-line stanzas. Yet in the penultimate stanza, the speaker brings the reader's attention firmly into the present with the most explicit sensory detail of the poem: "the last adventure / you can see / ends here in this chilly sandbox / with sandwiches." The final line, set off as its own stanza, most directly engages the reader through second-person address. The invitation to the reader to "eat" the sandwiches "in this chilly sandbox" echoes William Carlos Williams's poem "This Is Just to Say" with its speaker's confession of having eaten the cold plums in the icebox.

Rose Foster's drawing out of the final scene conveys a present-tense perceptual world more intimate and immediate than the rest of the poem. The poet makes those sandwiches in the "chilly sandbox" visible ("you can see"), tangible (through the sonic reverberations of "sandbox" and "sandwiches" at the end of successive lines), and available ("You may eat them") to the reader. While earlier in the poem, the poet is a life-giving force that animates the inanimate, by the end of the poem, it is the second-person "you," with whom the reader can so readily identify, who is offered an immediate perceptual reality, a taste of life. Thus, the work of this poem is to describe and commemorate the past and finally to yank the reader into the balloonless present.

Rose Foster was familiar with eulogy as form and with funeral as ceremony given her mother Shawna Foster's work as a minister, and, as Shawna Foster further related in e-mail correspondence, Rose recited "Eulogy for a Balloon" at a small funeral that Rose arranged for the "purple punching balloon that she won from a carnival." Rose Foster organized the funeral following her distress at her father's having "accidentally murdered" her balloon, the phrase she uses in "Eulogy for a Balloon" that perfectly expresses a combination of error and culpability. Rose Foster's writing and reciting of "Eulogy for a Balloon" was part of her orchestration of ceremony in which she assigned roles to adult family members, as she directed her mother "to call our friends to attend" and her father "to dig a gravesite in the sandbox and make sandwiches." Rose Foster thus used her poem as a leading element of her agency in redressing her distress within the context of her family. After reading an earlier version of this chapter, Shawna Foster wrote to me, "I appreciate you raising these questions and ethical perspectives. As a parent, I did not consider that my child should have a respected place in literature as a form of human expression." Here, Shawna Foster acknowledges the "ethical perspectives" involved in considering the respect that children's artistic productions deserve. Attention to her poem provided Rose Foster with another angle for action, in that reading an earlier version of this discussion a few years after the poem's publication prompted her to investigate further, as Shawna Foster indicates: "In reading this article and talking to me about it she realized that her dad popped it on purpose. We are now preparing for a trial. We are in search of a neutral party to serve as judge and she is gathering evidence."[12]

While Rose Foster's "Eulogy for a Balloon" works the balloon's past against an immediate present, Theo Candlish's "When People Leave This Earth" works the present against a future Earth that will not include humans:

> When people leave this earth
> Their buildings will crumble
> And the vines will creep in.
>
> Dogs will run and play wherever they like.
> Cats will hunt and poo on the carpets.
> Eagles will nest on the top floors,
> Soaring in the deserted concrete jungles.
>
> Tigers would go and lie
> In the meat section of the supermarket.
>
> The Earth is alive.
> The Earth is going back to the way it was.

As a poet, Theo Candlish is controller of worlds, coolly envisioning the movement of evolutionary time in imagining the deep future of the human species. The speaker, in a calm and collected tone, announces not *if* or *whether* people will "leave this earth," but *"When."* The poem thus announces itself as a temporal narrative from its first word, which indicates the certainty and matter-of-factness of the speaker's relation to these future events. One aspect of the poem's allure is that it is not clear whether the speaker identifies with the "people" or not. The other characters in the poem are nonhuman creatures—dogs, cats, eagles, and tigers—who, unlike the "people" who are displaced by the opening "When," each appears in a stronger position as the capitalized first word in a line. The images of animals on the loose in "deserted concrete jungles" are engaging, even humorous, or arch, particularly the tigers stretching out "In the meat section of the supermarket."

The entity pitted most directly against "people," as in the title of the poem, is "This Earth," or by the end of the poem, "The Earth." While the poem's opening positions "this earth" at the end of the first line as the object of people's leave-taking, by the last stanza "The Earth," capitalized and repeated in two successive end-stopped lines, anchors the left margin in dual statements of agency in the present. In this poem, the present occurs only in a future that is devoid of humans, yet it is a future that returns Earth to its past: "The Earth is going back to the way it was." The poem thus achieves its effect through a sophisticated manipulation of temporal registers: "When people leave this earth" (imagining a future temporality), "buildings will crumble" and "Cats will hunt and poo on the carpets" (in future tense), "Tigers would" (in conditional future) "lie / In the meat section of the supermarket," and when we reach the poem's conclusion, it is in a present tense—"The Earth is alive"—that has emerged seemingly in a future that the poem has already achieved. However, this statement of present truth, occurring ostensibly in the future, involves reclaiming the past: "The Earth is going back to the way it was."

Toni Morrison, in "The Future of Time: Literature and Diminished Expectations," contrasts the "diminished, already withered desire for a future" (170) evident in social and political commentary with the capacity for literature to imaginatively contemplate the future, "a future that will be shaped by those who have been pressed to the margins" (186). Surely a young poet, "pressed to the margins," is part of this literary company as he thinks across deep time and imagines a speaker who is identified not as a child or one of the "people" but as a calm seer of a future that returns to the unpeopled state of the past. In all, Theo Candlish has accomplished a brilliant temporal lyric.

I could say of "When People Leave This Earth" and "Eulogy for a Balloon" that they are provocative and well-composed poems; I have returned to them again and again, each time finding more of interest. I could also say that both of these poems were written by eight-year-old poets, which the corner tabs of the *Rattle Young Poets Anthology* so clearly advertise. A serious reading of these poems, which rests on recognition of the poets' agency and participation in literary practice, challenges our age-related ideologies about poetry and children, about children's literature and children's rights. Young writers' work conveys their standpoints as young people and can contribute to our conception and practice of children's rights.

The three poems centrally discussed in this chapter rely on temporal knowledge as a component of the poets' agency and artistry. Cailena Bickell uses a flexible relation between present and future hinged by meta-awareness of knowledge in order to imagine multiple conditional selves, and Rose Foster and Theo Candlish use their knowledge of death—the death of an anthropomorphized balloon or the demise of the human species—to work the future or past against the present for poetic effect. Temporality, while salient for poetry of childhood, is only one dimension that these poets use to stake a claim to poetry. The question that follows is whether adults who control access to literary publication and criticism will recognize young poets' right to do so.

In an interview with poet Henri Cole in the *Paris Review*, critic Helen Vendler articulates her view that a poem is "a score for performance by the reader, and that you become the speaking voice. You don't read or overhear the voice in the poem, you *are* the voice in the poem. You stand behind the words and speak them as your own" ("The Art of Criticism" 172). Are adult readers willing to stand behind the words written by children and speak them as their own, to accord them the respect due to literature? If we (as adults) grant young poets the right to have their work taken seriously in the public arena, the right "to be heard," we can allow ourselves to be moved by their poetry. Further, what effect does encountering youth-produced literature have on young readers, and how might this contribute to their understanding of their agency and their rights as children?

Theo Candlish's consideration of the future of Earth across deep time helps demonstrate the importance of young people's speaking to a range of issues, not just those that seem most directly related to their lives. The more constrained conception of young people's right to participation is conveyed in Article 12 of the Convention on the Rights of the Child, which "assure[s] to the child who is capable of forming his or her own views the right to express those views freely in all matters affecting the child." This framing of the right to participate in "matters affecting the child" was revisited in 2009 by the Committee on the Rights of the Child, which advocated for "a wide interpretation of matters affecting the child and children" that "helps to include children in the social processes of their community and society." The committee concluded, "States parties should carefully listen to children's views wherever their perspective can enhance the quality of solutions" ("General Comment No. 12" 8). This revision of the breadth of children's right to express their views better accounts for the value of children's standpoints on all manner of topics, including predicting the demise of human civilization. It sets the stage for young poets figuring the state of the "world" in light of environmental catastrophe, or, as in the next chapter, in contexts of political and racial injustice.

CHAPTER 5

"We Speak to Be Heard"

June Jordan, Terri Bush, and
The Voice of the Children

"IF THE CLUB was to be cut out then who would read my writing—who would pay attention to them?" So asks Miriam Lasanta in a brochure ("For the Children") designed to raise funds for The Voice of the Children, a writing workshop for children of color in Brooklyn, New York, that was already underway for a year and a half and would continue for another two and a half years, from 1967 to 1971. The young participants, identified in the brochure as "black and Puerto Rican youngsters," ranged in age across the years of the workshop from eleven to seventeen, with occasional participation by June Jordan's young son Christopher, who was nine years old when the workshop began. As the text of the brochure informs us, "A white teacher and a black writer"—educator Terri Bush and poet June Jordan—"stood with these children" as initiators, stewards, and co-facilitators of the workshop. June Jordan and Terri Bush met through the fledgling Teachers and Writers Collaborative, an organization founded in 1967 to support connections between professional writers and teachers of writing in the schools (Teachers and Writers Collaborative). The workshop met for a few months in Harlem, yet soon shifted to Brooklyn, closer to the homes of the children who attended Sands Junior High School in Fort Greene, where Terri Bush taught. For four years, from late fall 1967 until midsummer 1971, the group met on Saturdays at the Church of the Open Door and then at the Doctor White Community Center in Brooklyn "to rap, dance, snack, browse among the books lying around, and write their stories, poems, editorials, and jokes" (Jordan, "Afterword" 95).

According to Terri Bush, there were roughly fifteen children in the group at any one time, and approximately forty children who participated over the life of the workshop; a subset of these participated across all four years (Bush, personal interview). Their meetings eventually included Saturday afternoon fieldtrips to "the beach or museum or zoo, or to the park for a ball game" (Howard, "We Speak to Be Heard" 10–11), visits to poetry readings as audience members or as poets reading their work, and summer camps. Along the way, members of the workshop produced an in-house weekly newspaper, *The Voice of the Children*, and a quarterly publication "for subscribers" titled *Expand*, and Jordan and Bush co-edited an anthology of writing from the workshop titled *THE VOICE of the Children* published by Holt in 1970 (Jordan, "Afterword" 98). Over time, the older youth who remained part of the group took to calling themselves "The Council" and assumed leadership and mentoring roles in relation to younger children who subsequently joined the group (Bush, personal interview). Vanessa Howard, one of these long-time older members, writes of the group of children having "become a family, bonded not by blood, but by our inner needs: our need for speaking and for being heard" ("We Speak to Be Heard" 11).

In this chapter, I discuss a selection of the poems that emerged from this workshop (which the young participants eventually named The Voice of the Children) and were published in *THE VOICE of the Children* anthology. I begin by reading poems written by Michael Goode, Glen Thompson, and Christopher Meyer for the strategies they use in stretching out a present tense of racial violence and injustice. I then consider the approaches that Jordan and Bush used in supporting young people in The Voice of the Children workshop and the publications that resulted. I next turn to writing by workshop participant Vanessa Howard, who published a solo anthology of her poetry two years following the publication of *THE VOICE of the Children*, and who also wrote an essay discussing her sense of the workshop's value, and the importance of children writing and gaining an audience, "speaking not only for ourselves, but for all children who had not yet found a means of being heard" (Howard, "We Speak to Be Heard" 11). I look at a selection of Howard's poems and attend to her varied temporal strategies and the temporal fluency that she demonstrates, and end the chapter by discussing a poem by Eric Smith, a younger poet from The Voice of the Children workshop, whose work Howard championed. My focus is on understanding the roles of adults and youth in building and sustaining the poetic community of The Voice of the Children workshop, and on discerning how the young black poets on whom I focus figure time-scapes of racial violence and racial injustice, speak in and across multiple temporalities, and establish the present reality of their poetic vision.

"I will long remember this dark day": Elongating the Present of Racial Injustice

In a two-hour interview I conducted with Terri Bush at her apartment in Manhattan, she recounts how "a very dramatic event made us rather famous" in the spring of the first year of The Voice of the Children work-shop after the events of April 4, 1968.[1] On that evening, June Jordan was giving a poetry reading in Greenwich Village while some of the children, who at that time were eleven and twelve years old, were at Terri Bush's home nearby eating spaghetti. The television was on, and regular programming was interrupted with news of the assassination of Dr. Martin Luther King, Jr. As Bush recalls, the children were worried that further conflict could result and that they themselves could be endangered. "And then the kids said: 'We need some paper, Miss Bush, we need to write poems.' So we got paper and they wrote for a while," and then they started to make their way to the poetry reading. Terri Bush remembers people being "completely stunned" and "when we were walking a few blocks away to the church where the poetry reading was, a black man came up to these kids on the street and he said 'Children Children,' and they said, 'We know.'" At Jordan's poetry reading, the children resumed their own writing. Afterward, they encountered typical racial discrimination on the way back to Brooklyn: "The taxis wouldn't stop for us [Bush and her brother, who are white] as long as we were standing by these black children. So my brother went a block or so away and got a taxi and came back." Poem writing continued even in the cab ride back to Brooklyn, and one of the older girls, who "might have been 13, she was wearing a black leather jacket and she looked very tough. . . . She said to the taxi driver, 'Can you turn on the light in this cab? I'm writing a poem.' He turned it on!" (Bush, personal interview).

One of the poems that resulted, "April 4, 1968," by Michael Goode, was published in the *Village Voice* after Jordan and Bush sent the children's poems to Nat Hentoff, and the poem received "a tremendous response" that prompted donations for the workshop (Bush, personal interview).[2] As a result, Goode was invited to read his poem at his junior high school's memorial event for Dr. Martin Luther King, Jr. (Bush, personal interview). In the opening stanza of Goode's thirty-four-line poem, Dr. King is positioned as a singular heroic figure, already relegated to the past—"a great man once lived / a Negro man"—and Goode's speaker is forthright about naming the cause of his death in the second stanza: "but do you know what happened? / he was assasinated by a white man" (*THE VOICE of the Children* 56). Later in the poem, Goode emphasizes King's participation in a shared black community among other "black leaders," rather than singling out Dr. King as a unitary, irreplaceable figure. Terri Bush recounts the potency of Goode's depiction of Dr. King's murder "by a white man" in the Sands Junior High School principal's warning to Bush prior to the memorial event: "the principal of the school called me in and said 'if there's a riot in this school, Miss Bush, you and Michael Goode will be responsible for it.' How's that for the power of words?" (personal interview). Michael Goode, who was twelve years old at the time, uses direct address throughout the poem in ways that implicate the reader:

> war war
> why do god's children fight among each other
> like animals
> a great man once lived
> a Negro man
> his name was the Rev. Martin Luther King.
>
> but do you know what happened?
> he was assasinated by a white man.
> a man of such knowledge as he
> Martin Luther King
> a man of such courage
> to stand up and let a man hit him
> without hitting back

yes
that's courage
when you fight back of course you're brave
but do you think you yourself can stand up
and let someone beat you
without batting an eyelash
that takes courage.

shot him down
that's right
one of God's children

well you can count on a long hot summer
one of our black leaders has been killed
murdered
down into the gutter.

I will long remember this dark day.

it's funny it's so you can't even
walk out in the street anymore
some maniac might shoot you
in cold blood.

what kind of a world is this?

I don't know.

Goode's poem depicts Dr. King's murder as a shocking intrusion into the black community of which the speaker is a part, and which will have "long" effects. Toward the end of the poem, Goode repeats the modifier "long" in the initial lines of two successive stanzas (the second of which is a single-line stanza), which serves to extend the result and the memory of the unjust present into the future. This effect is amplified by emphasizing the depth of the violence through repetition ("killed," "murdered"), strategic line breaks, and movement "down." In this poem composed on the day of Dr. Martin Luther King, Jr.'s murder, Goode exerts control over its calendrical context in depicting that his speaker will "long remember this dark day" and forecasting the "long hot summer"—presumably of racial unrest—that he predicts will follow this alarming spring. Goode's speaker knows what this present means for the immediate future ("well you can count on a long hot summer") and he also knows that he will draw a mental through line from "this dark day"—the extended present of racial injustice and racist violence—into the more distant future ("I will long remember this dark day"). Thus, Goode crafts his speaker's confidence about the implications of the present for the future in a manner that draws out and deepens the resonance and significance of the present in its over-tones of temporal certainty layered with alarm. The tone of Goode's poem juxtaposes a resigned forbearance ("well you can count on") with shock at the protracted and brutal finality of the murder of Dr. King, who "has been killed / murdered / down into the gutter," with its set of phrases, empha-sized by line breaks, that focuses its vision relentlessly.

By the conclusion of "April 4, 1968," the present is both elongated *and* foreshortened to indicate the effects of racial injustice and violence. Along with predicting a "long hot summer," Goode's speaker acknowledges the implications of Dr. King's assassination for a constrained, perhaps fore-shortened present, where "you can't even / walk out in the street anymore" without the risk of being shot "in cold blood." The speaker's feeling of being targeted by danger is expressed through a second-person "you" that positions the reader also as under threat. Finally, Goode's speaker uses this disbelieving alarm to question the world and his knowledge of it ("what kind of a world is this? / I don't know"). Thus, in exerting agency in the face of tragedy, Michael Goode strategically deploys temporality and remakes temporal possibilities for life in a society rife with racial violence and injustice. In so doing, Goode recasts a stark reality as not simple and unidimensional but complex and contradictory, where temporal elonga-tion *and* foreshortening can co-exist.

After the publication of Goode's poem in the *Village Voice* prompted monetary contributions to support The Voice of the Children work-shop, Bush and Jordan asked the children what they wished to do with the resulting money. The young workshop participants said they wanted to spend more time together, so Bush and Jordan organized a two-week summer camp for them in Ohio. Later on, after receiving an advance from Holt for *THE VOICE of the Children* anthology, the group purchased a used Volkswagen bus for weekly fieldtrips, and the children received ten dollars for each poem published in the book (Bush, personal interview). Eventually, the young poets would give poetry readings on the radio or at university venues, and their work was published in a range of newspapers and magazines (including the *Village Voice* and the *New York Times*) in addition to anthologies (Adoff, *My Black Me*; Baron, *Here I Am!*), as well as their workshop's publications.

After reading the children's writing following one "Saturday Workshop" in 1968, Jordan reflected that "much of what the kids expressed today, in writing, amounts to an unanswerable indictment of the world that would term these children stupid, ugly, hopeless and wrong" ("'The Voice of the Children' Saturday Workshop Diaries" 143). One such "unanswerable indictment" of an unjust society was written by Jordan's son Christopher Meyer, who attended some of the workshops and is the youngest of the poets represented in *THE VOICE of the Children* anthology. At age nine, Christopher Meyer wrote an untitled poem re-placing history in his poetic critique of slavery:

> sitting on the dock
> I watch the ships come
> bringing shiploads of people in
> doomed to spend their lives
> in chains,
> the whip flickering about.
>
> A sharp crack of the whip brings me
> to my senses and
> getting up to my task of
> carrying loads of iron.
>
> As I go on I begin to stagger
> and the heat grows and I fall.
> The whip thrashes wildly
> but I am dead,
> dead to this world
> of hellish misery.[3]

Christopher Meyer crafts his poem of slavery in relation to the image, action, and temporal shape of "the whip," a metonymic figure of the raw power of slavery. The whip appears in each of the poem's three stanzas as an active force that conspicuously takes up space and time. The poem begins with the speaker in mid-action as an observer in repose in the present: "sitting on the dock / I watch the ships come." Terri Bush notes that the poem's opening line "sitting on the dock" most likely comes from the Otis Redding song of that name, since music was a regular accompaniment to the workshops (personal interview). The agentic position within the opening stanza quickly shifts to the ships and, by the end of the first stanza, to the whip, which has control over the future of the people "doomed to spend their lives / in chains." The second stanza launches with "A sharp crack of the whip," which comes to dominate the speaker's body in its present ongoing labor (indicated by gerunds "getting up" and "carrying"), yet the speaker retains sentience, retains control over "my senses." In the third and last stanza, the speaker is restored to the agent position at the opening ("As I go on"), yet "The whip" leads off the poem's final sentence in its seemingly uncontrolled action ("The whip thrashes wildly"). The poem ends on the implicit question of whether there is some kind of redemption or at least escape from injustice and brutality in death, and also whether one can place this redemption or escape in a particular time frame.

By the end of Meyer's poem, the speaker escapes the whip's power to pervert the present and future through a form of death that retains awareness. Though the speaker is overcome physically and dies in the present ("I am dead"), in being dead (rather than dying into the past) the speaker escapes the "hellish misery" that the whip has helped to create, and maintains sentience as the narrator of the poem's action. The present ongoing action (depicted both in simple present tense and in gerunds) is shared between the speaker and the whip, yet by the end of the final stanza, the "dead" speaker has escaped the thrashing of the whip and is able to designate the state of the "world / of hellish misery." The poem grants to the speaker an escape from the constraints of a present and a future (along with other "people . . . / doomed to spend their lives / in chains") that are bound by slavery, in order to inhabit and describe an alternative present in which awareness and clear-eyed judgment (of what constitutes "hellish misery") are retained. Although it is not evident whether this alternative present can be an embodied one, it is notable that the only "people" in the poem who have "lives" to "spend" are the people who are "doomed to spend their lives / in chains": they retain personhood, but they are enchained. Within this poem, Christopher Meyer practices an ethic of respect for people who are enslaved by representing them as retaining their personhood despite the brutal uncontrolled power of the whip of slavery. He does so by establishing an alternative present within the poem that withstands physical death and continues to assert the humanity of persons who are enslaved. The speaker is "dead to this world / of hellish misery," yet implicitly alive to himself, and alive to his vision of an alternative present free of chains, and beyond the reach of "the whip flickering about."

While Christopher Meyer depicts a speaker who dies into a present that he implicitly withstands, and Michael Goode both elongates and foreshortens the present of racial violence and injustice, Glen Thompson also alters the present in figuring racial "hatred," the tyranny of "power," and the state of the "world" in his poem "Hands":

> Hands of all nations
> stretching to pull one another together
> pushing and lifting
> the weight of hatred and greed,
>
> Hands, hands of all colors
> clasping each other in vain
> trying to pull together
> what's left of the world
>
> and suddenly . . .
>
> the hands are broken
> each finger broken
> by the hammer of greed and power
> and of hatred and blood
> and slowly the world breaks up,
> pieces float to nowhere
>
> the hands are gone
>   forever.[4]

In "Hands," Thompson uses a repetitive, anaphoric structure in which each stanza represents collective "hands," as a metonym for human cooperative effort, on either side of the determinative adverbial line "and suddenly . . ." In the initial stanzas, Thompson uses multiple present participles to depict the hands "of all nations" and "of all colors" as they engage in increasingly desperate actions: "stretching to pull one another together / pushing and lifting / the weight of hatred and greed" then "clasping each other in vain / trying to pull together / what's left of the world." The turn "suddenly" puts an end to these efforts since the hands have been "broken." The passive construction—"the hands are broken"—indicates that the hands have already been deprived of action, even though the phrase is in the present tense. Thompson's movement from active to passive across the poem thus complicates tense and results in a swift and irreversible shift between an active present and a passive and "broken" one. Nonetheless, Thompson depicts a present that moves "slowly" toward the world's end and the minimal final stanza that is diminished because "the hands"—humanity—"are gone / forever."

Michael Goode, Christopher Meyer, and Glen Thompson all end their poems by naming or questioning a racially unjust "world" of the present. Goode's poem ends by asking "what kind of a world is this?," Meyer's poem concludes by referring to "this world / Of hellish misery," and Thompson's poem ends by revealing that "the world breaks up, / pieces float to nowhere." Recall Theo Candlish's poem "When People Leave This Earth," discussed in the previous chapter, in which he imagines the deep future of "this earth," a future that does not include humans. Here, these young participants in The Voice of the Children workshop deploy time to figure the complexities of a racialized society and its implications for self, community, humanity, and the known world. Goode writes about the murder of Dr. Martin Luther King, Jr., by using the assassination's date as the poem's title and altering the standard calendar through both elongating and foreshortening the present to represent the effects of racial violence and racial injustice. Meyer crafts an alternative present in which people who are enslaved and die nonetheless retain their personhood. Thompson's portrait of hands alters the present from active to passive through a desperate struggle that is literally crushed by "the hammer of greed and power." Recognizing time *for* childhoods involves seeing how young poets engage strategically with time as an instrument of agency, in this case through depicting stark visions of humanity's self-destruction resulting from racism.

Michael Goode, Christopher Meyer, and Glen Thompson use their poetic skills to craft an ethic that counters racial oppression through a reimagined temporality. They use "poems [as] tools of power . . . to affirm the place of poetry in the struggle against social injustice," as poets Rita Dove and Marilyn Nelson have written about the work of many (adult) black poets (220). Goode, Meyer, and Thompson deploy temporal agency to reimagine conditions of power in ways that retain awareness of racial oppression, but open up or alter the fixity of the present to raise questions

(Goode's "what kind of a world is this?"), inhabit an alternative present that recognizes black personhood even in the most dire circumstances (Meyer's "I am dead, / dead to this world / of hellish misery"), or articulate the temporal and spatial result of racial "hatred and greed" in a disintegrating present (Thompson's "slowly the world breaks up"). The poems I discuss in this chapter (and those by Vanessa Howard that I discuss later on) were placed by Jordan and Bush either in the opening section of *THE VOICE of the Children* anthology titled "Politics" (Thompson's "Hands" and Howard's "The Last Riot") or in the central section titled "Blackness," which begins with Howard's "Monument in Black," ends with Goode's "April 4, 1968," and also includes Meyer's "[sitting on the dock]" and Howard's "The Question."[5] Jordan and Bush thus structure the anthology to convey the prominence of themes of racial politics and black identity.

"This book is a children's victory": *THE VOICE of the Children*

Terri Bush and June Jordan positioned The Voice of the Children workshop outside the bounds of institutional school culture, as Bush indicates during our interview: "And so the first idea was that it was *not* school. So here, you could walk around if you wanted to, we played music, we had books available, especially picture books and books of poetry, and the only rule we had was that you had to write something." Jordan and Bush thus offered multiple entry points (print poetry, music, poetry readings, art) for engaging with poetry and art, and did so in a way that introduced their relevance to racial and political identities and realities by bringing "an enormous variety of records and books" (Jordan, "'The Voice of the Children' Saturday Workshop Diaries" 142), including recordings by Billie Holliday, Dinah Washington, and Little Walter, and books ranging from collections by Gwendolyn Brooks and Langston Hughes to the *Pictorial History of the Negro in America* in order to accomplish "enablement: The encouragement of Black children to trust and then to express their own response to things" (Jordan, "The Voice of the Children" 29).

Jordan and Bush ascribe to the young writers the initiative for the idea of a regular publication and its title—*The Voice of the Children*—that promotes the young people's "Voice" and self-referentially indicates their age status ("Children"), although Jordan and Bush acknowledge their own facilitative roles throughout the tenure of the weekly workshop. Terri

Bush indicates that motivation for a weekly publication came in part from the children seeing their typed writings that Jordan and Bush would bring each Saturday from the previous Saturday's workshop: "that had a very dramatic impact on them because I think they'd never seen their own writing in typeface before. It looks more important, somehow, to an eleven year old, to see your words typewritten" (Bush, personal interview). Participant Vanessa Howard agreed, "We read our ideas in print, which made them more important and concrete" ("We Speak to Be Heard" 10). As the children looked at their "more important"–seeming typed writings, Bush recounts that "they would say 'we could make this into a paper,'" and the weekly publication launched in March 1968 (Jordan, "'The Voice of the

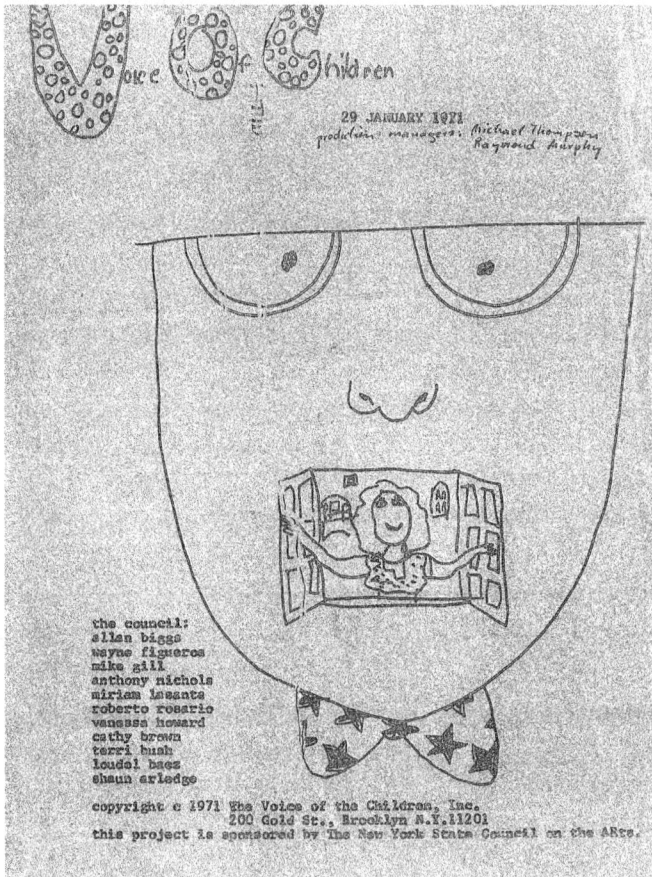

FIGURE 4. *The Voice of the Children*, cover of weekly publication, 29 January 1971. Copyright © 1971 The Voice of the Children, Inc.

Children' Saturday Workshop Diaries" 149) and continued until July 1971 (Bush, personal interview).

The title "The Voice of the Children" conveys the young participants' sense of purposefulness in facing audiences consisting at least partly of adults. They didn't call themselves "The Voice of the Teenagers": they stressed not their almost-adultness, not their adolescence, but their identity *as children* and as deserving of opportunities to write and to have their writing taken seriously. Jordan conveys the impression that the young people took the lead on the form and content of their writing, and requested specific assistance when they wanted it. Jordan explains, "Throughout, their writings have never been subjected to adult 'correction.' If requested by the children, the purpose of a paragraph might be described, or the use of quotation marks might be explained. Spelling errors were corrected, as an informal rule initiated by the writers. Spelling is one problem they want to solve; they want to avoid adult errors of understanding; they want people to receive the message, and no mistake about it" ("Afterword" 96). The young writers wanted their misspellings corrected "to avoid adult errors of understanding," that is, to prevent adults from misunderstanding them. Jordan is explicit that after the initial editions of the weekly "newspaper" (Jordan, "'The Voice of the Children' Saturday Workshop Diaries" 150) appeared, the children requested that their spelling be corrected for future editions: "the kids were very upset about typing errors, and very concerned to have their stuff reprinted in corrected form. There was a lot of asking about how to spell this and that, for instance. I have promised to arrange to have their work corrected before it appears in type" (151). Bush adds that "the children, spontaneously, became concerned about punctuation, stanzas, paragraphs, and form, generally. Questions about these aspects of serious writing were pursued by the children because they were determined to gain the respectful attention of a widening, partly adult readership" ("Introduction" 353). This is consistent with other youth writing projects in which young writers aspired to an adult-like form and audience and wanted their spelling to be corrected.[6]

The Voice of the Children workshop conveys the power and promise of these young writers in a community that nurtured and supported youth leadership and mentoring of younger children, and the caring, careful, and respectful approach of the adults involved in helping to build and sustain this community of young writers of color. Jordan wrote in her chronicle of the workshop's first year, published in a history of the Teachers and Writers Collaborative, that the children would elect the "newspaper staff" of the weekly publication, with roles including "Editor in Chief" and "News Managers" (Jordan, "'The Voice of the Children' Saturday Workshop Diaries" 149). However, for the 1970 anthology THE VOICE *of the Children* (featuring poems and short prose pieces by twenty-five of the workshop participants), the selections and organization were made by June Jordan and Terri Bush. As Bush describes in our interview, "June and I went through everything we had and we chose the ones that we thought were best, and we did the layout." Thus, there were opportunities for youth leadership and shared youth-adult decision making in some but not all aspects of the workshop.[7]

In framing the print anthology, Jordan and Bush chose to background their own role by using the title created by the young writers, THE VOICE [capitalized for emphasis] *of the Children*, and identifying the compilation on the title page as "collected by June Jordan and Terri Bush." The anthology opens with an interplay of the young and older participants, beginning with two facing pages of acknowledgments: the young poets write, "To the adults who have helped us" (iv), listing first Jordan and Bush; and on the opposite page is the "Acknowledgment" by Jordan and Bush, identified as "Directors" of "The Voice of the Children, Inc.," that begins, "This book is a children's victory supported by the continuing faith of many friends" (v).

While Jordan wrote an extended account of the context for the anthology's poems, she positioned it as an afterword so that the anthology begins with the young writers speaking for themselves.[8] Jordan's afterword begins by her contemplating adults' actions in relation to children: "It would be something fine if we could learn how to bless the lives of children. They are the people of new life. Children are the only people nobody can blame. They are the only ones always willing to make a start; they have no choice. Children are the ways the world begins again and again" ("Afterword" 93). Although Jordan's opening sentence positions adults as the subjects, it is through a collective adult "we" rather than a first-person "I"; while this could be attributed to her co-facilitation of the workshop with Terri Bush, elsewhere in the afterword it is clear that Jordan is using a collective "we" of adults. Jordan's hope for the "we" of her opening sentence is unusual for adults in hoping to "learn" from children rather than to teach them. In her upending of standard adult roles, Jordan explicitly identifies aspects of adult positions and adult-created institutions that constrain children's lives and voices. She writes in her afterword to *THE VOICE of the Children*, "in general, our children have no voice—that we will listen to. We force, we blank them into the bugle/bell regulated lineup of the Army/school, and we insist on silence" (93).[9] Notable is Jordan's collective pronoun of relation to the children, "our children," perhaps a reference to children in the United States, perhaps a more specific reference to children of color in writing as a poet of color.

Later on in her afterword, Jordan encourages adults to reflect on their own limiting of children's voices and freedom: "But even if we cannot learn to bless their lives (our future times), at least we can try to find out how we already curse and burden their experience: how we limit the wheeling of their inner eyes, how we terrify their trust, and how we condemn the raucous laughter of their natural love" ("Afterword" 94). Richard Flynn has written of Jordan's "rare understanding of both children's poetry and the poetics and politics of childhood" (Flynn, "Affirmative Acts" 123) across her writing, teaching, editorial, and activist engagements, and the intertwining of her private and public considerations of childhood whereby she "insists on a poetics that interrogates private notions of childhood through activist, public positions" (120). Indeed, Jordan has said, "Childhood is the first, inescapable political situation each of us has to negotiate" (Lee, n.p.). In her essay "Old Stories, New Lives," Jordan writes about the positions of adult and child as permeated with hierarchies of knowledge and power that interfere with children's own sense of the value of their ideas and feelings: "As a teacher it is invariably the fact that my primary challenge is, year after year, to convince our children that they know something we need to know, and that their own feelings are important, at least as important as those adult values they must struggle against and, somehow, survive, if they will ever be certified as legitimate human beings" (282).

As Jordan makes clear in her afterword to *THE VOICE of the Children* anthology, The Voice of the Children workshop was a space designed to counter school, given that "For Black and Puerto Rican teenagers, school is mostly a burial ground for joy and promise. School is where these poets and writers are often termed 'verbally deficient,' or worse" (95). Here, Jordan refutes a dominant institutional bias that belittles modes of literacy of black and brown youth, and instead she respects their linguistic productions as literary in referring to the young people as "these poets and writers." Rather than seeing them as "verbally deficient," Jordan again refers to the children as "poets and writers" (97) when she recounts the sites where they have been published and the radio and television stations on which they have read their work: "Now, the Voice of the Children has given poetry readings on WBAI, Channel 31, Channel 13, Channel 7, and at Hunter College, Queens College, and St. Marks in the Bowery. These poets and writers have been published in *The Village Voice, McCall's, UHURU, The New York Times, The Now Voices,* HERE I AM, SOULSCRIPT, and the list is very long" (97). Thus, while the twenty-five young writers represented in the anthology are introduced to readers through the book's title as "Children," by the end of the anthology they are recognized by a fellow poet as "poets and writers." In another act of solidarity that integrates writers across age status, Jordan lists herself (as the author of the afterword) along with the young writers in an "Index of Authors" (99). Jordan ends her afterword to *THE VOICE of the Children* by invoking these young poets as "people" as well as "children": "What really matters is *who*: the people who have put themselves up-and-down, on paper, ready for friends, and yes, getting themselves together" against "the indifferent, the inert," those who are not listening (98). Jordan keeps her sight on the "Who" of these young poets and their "new lives" in all of their complexity—"Who really matter are these young people: these new lives: original, furious, gentle, broken, lyrical, strong, and summoning" (98)—and she concludes her afterword by writing, "With all my heart I wish / the voices of these children / peace and power" (98). What emerges from this account is an adult poet who allied with an adult educator to make space for, hear, support, and promote the ideas and artistic creations and voices of young people.[10]

The striking ways that Jordan and Bush foreground the work of young poets become even clearer if one looks at another anthology of poetry by children that appeared in 1970.[11] Kenneth Koch's *Wishes, Lies, and Dreams: Teaching Poetry to Children* includes many examples of poems written by the elementary school–aged children in New York's P.S. (Public School) 61 with whom he worked as a visiting poet, yet the book's subtitle reveals that, unlike Jordan and Bush, Koch elevated his role as teacher. His extended introduction, titled "Teaching Children to Write Poetry," leads with a poem written by "Jeff Morley, Fifth Grade, P.S. 61," but Koch positions himself as the prime mover from the first sentence ("Last winter and the spring before that I taught poetry writing to children at P.S. 61 on East 12th Street between Avenue B and Avenue C in Manhattan" 1) and remains the subject of all sentences throughout that opening paragraph. Though he focuses on his own ideas for prompting children's poems ("It seemed I had stumbled onto a marvelous idea for children's poems" through the "I wish" prompt, 8), he stresses the important point that the children were very inspired by hearing poems produced by other children. Also inconsistent is the listing of the book's authors on the interior title page as "Kenneth Koch / and / The Students of P.S. 61 / in New York City," whereas the book's cover and spine present the author solely as "Kenneth Koch."[12] The intersection of gender and race in the contrast between Koch's (white male) and Jordan's (black female) demonstration of their political commitments in *how* they express their support for poetry by children is worth noting, as is the fact that cultural and educational institutions (such as the poets in the schools program funded by the National Endowment for the Arts) amplified Koch's approach.[13] Koch's book is currently available in print, having been reprinted in 1999 by Harper, yet Jordan and Bush's edited anthology, despite having received recognition at the time of its publication, including a Coretta Scott King Book Award "Author Honor" (American Library Association) and a Nancy Bloch Award for best children's book ("Vanessa Howard Speaks to Be Heard"), is today available only through libraries or used book sellers.[14]

Though both *THE VOICE of the Children* and *Wishes, Lies, and Dreams* were published at a politically charged time, one could say that Koch's approach, while its goals supported children crafting their own play with words and articulating their ideas and desires, safely accorded with ideas about children as imaginative and apolitical, whereas the workshop initiated and sustained by Jordan and Bush helped build a platform for children to name political realities, assert their perspectives about contemporary concerns, and claim space to critique unjust structures of power. The Voice of the Children workshop is consistent with Jordan's life work, which is infused with her awareness of the political contexts of children's lives and her commitment to counter injustice, and with her pedagogy that views education, in Jonathan Stalling's words, not as "a neutral accumulation of knowledge, but a foundational element in the formation of political agents" (Stalling 220).[15] Jordan's development of community-oriented poetry workshops would eventually result in the extensive and influential cross-age project Poetry for the People.[16]

June Jordan's defense of the value of poetry written by young people is also evident in another poetry project contemporaneous with The Voice of the Children workshop. In the same year as the publication of *THE VOICE of the Children*, a collection of poetry written by African American poets appeared, designed and selected by Jordan, titled *Soulscript: Afro-American Poetry*. *Soulscript* was innovative in including young and adult poets, such as

Gwendolyn Brooks, Langston Hughes, and Audre Lorde, and this collection
was reissued in 2004 as *Soulscript: A Collection of African American Poetry*.
Aimed at young readers, *Soulscript* includes the work of nine young poets,
five of whom are also represented in *THE VOICE of the Children* anthology (including Vanessa Howard, Michael Goode, and Glen Thompson).[17]
Archival correspondence between Jordan and editor Milton Meltzer reveals
that Jordan needed to defend the value of including an extended selection
of poetry written by a range of young poets as the first of the book's seven
sections;[18] in her careful reply to Melzer's query, Jordan writes, "Because they
are children, I feel that at least these many children, eleven, are necessary to
support my contention that children flow among the wellsprings of poetry
as much as any any adult." Jordan's repetition of "any" anchors her emphatic
argument for parity between children and adults in participating in poetry.
In the same letter, Jordan goes on to articulate the need for a larger number of
poems by children to "carry . . . testifying weight" given young writers' typical
underrepresentation: "If they were older, and more practiced, as artists, then
two or three would carry the same testifying weight. . . . I wish to hold for
all the poems of the children, as now presented. The less accomplished, by
professional standards, will testify to the ordinary, earnest talent of all youngsters to work towards a personal language of expression."[19] Here Jordan also
underscores the value of "the ordinary, earnest talent of all youngsters" to use
language in original ways to express their ideas and artistry.[20]

    In her introduction to *Soulscript*, Jordan embraces very young children
alongside adults in her view of poetry and human life: "People live a poem
every minute they spend in the world. Reaction, memory, and dream: these
are the springs of poetry. And a four-year-old flows among them as fully as
any adult" ("Introduction" xvi).[21] Later in the introduction, she expands on her
belief that young black poets are part of "the fabulous efflorescence of black
literary art" that deserves wide readership: "*Soulscript* opens with the poetry
written by black children ranging in age from twelve to eighteen. These
young poets, more or less accidentally known by me, should powerfully suggest the fabulous efflorescence of black literary art that we, Afro-American
and white, can enjoy and honor with our lives" ("Introduction" xix). Jordan
chooses to open *Soulscript* with a section dedicated to the work of young poets
as a means of honoring the work even as she keeps it in a separate age-bound
section. Both *Soulscript* and *THE VOICE of the Children* were radical acts of
witnessing, supporting, and honoring the work of young poets, specifically

young poets of color. In devoting an anthology solely to the children in The Voice of the Children workshop, Jordan and Bush proclaim that the book *THE VOICE of the Children* "is a children's victory" (v).

"Monument in Black" and "The Last Riot": Vanessa Howard's Temporal Fluency

In designing *THE VOICE of the Children* anthology, June Jordan and Terri Bush made the decision to position a text by one of the young workshop participants—"Vanessa Howard / age 14" (as the young writers' names and ages appear beneath each poem)—as the foreword. One of the two most prolific poets in *THE VOICE of the Children* anthology (the other was Michael Goode), Vanessa Howard was the only young poet from the workshop to subsequently produce a single-authored collection of poetry, titled *A Screaming Whisper* and published in 1972 by Holt, Rinehart (the publisher of *THE VOICE of the Children*) when she was seventeen years old. Reading across a selection of Howard's poems from *THE VOICE of the Children* anthology enables exploration of the varied temporal strategies she uses, in some cases to represent processes or outcomes of racial injustice and racial conflict. The result conveys a sense of the temporal fluency Howard practices in speaking with and across multiple temporalities.

Vanessa Howard wrote eight poems included in *THE VOICE of the Children* anthology, including the prose poem titled "Ghetto" that serves as the foreword to the volume. In positioning Howard's "Ghetto" as the anthology's foreword, Jordan and Bush follow this young black poet's authority in critiquing labels and assumptions about black children:

> Nine out of ten times when a person hears the word "ghetto" they think of Black people first of all. They think just about every Black child comes from a Ghetto with lots of brothers and sisters.
>
> Ghetto has become a definition meaning Black, garbage, slum areas. To me the word "ghetto" is just as bad as cursing.
>
> I think they put all Black people in a box marked "ghetto" which leaves them having no identity. They should let Black people be seen for themselves, not as one reflection on all.

"Ghetto" ends by critiquing the white supremacist hegemony ("they") that attempts to control the past and present of black subjects, and asserting a prescriptive alternative to a reductive racist lens that denies black persons' individuality: "They should let Black people be seen for themselves, not as one reflection on all." As the foreword to the anthology, Howard's "Ghetto" claims for plural "Black people" an authority over their own identities.

Howard's "Ghetto" connects thematically with her poems "The Question" and "Truly My Own," which speak to personal capacity, individuality, and the capaciousness of blackness. In "The Question," Howard's speaker questions whether one "must" alter one's form, one's embodiment, in order to experience life as human:

> Must I lay down and die to feel the Earth?
> Must I sprout wings and fly to smell the air?
> Must I grow fins to swim to sea?
>
> Must I be white to live in this humanity?
>
> I didn't die and felt the Earth.
> I didn't sprout wings and I smelt the air.
> I didn't grow fins and I swam the sea.
>
> So Black is all I'm gonna be.

"The Question" tests the temporal limits of identity and agency, and applies its own racial logic within the parameters of humanity. The opening questions are distilled to a central question of racial identity and personhood that stands alone as a one-line stanza: "Must I be white to live in this humanity?" The poem pursues a logical examination of racial possibility and existence through the initial questions beginning "Must I," the counterevidence (in past tense) beginning "I didn't" (in which the speaker reports, for example, being able to feel and sense the earth without bodily transformation), and the final resolution. "The Question" concludes with a line that conveys concise awareness of personal control over existence, embodiment, and identity in a present that moves forward into a future— "So Black is all I'm gonna be"—through a confident claim of positive black identity and a wide and inclusive "Black is all."

Howard's other poem that answers the "Ghetto" of the foreword is "Truly My Own," which valorizes individuality. "Truly My Own" begins with a speaker seeking to ground her own individual uniqueness, to "be seen for themselves" in the words of "The Ghetto":

> I think if I searched a thousand lands
> and twice the number in rainbows,
> I'd never find one human being
> who chose the things that I chose

The poem ends "for there is no one who thinks like me / for my dreams are truly my own." In this corrective to the reductive viewpoint referenced in "Ghetto," Howard's speaker owns the present of her individuality, knowing that, with "I'd never," she has control over a conditional future that won't undercut her individuality, and that leaves her confidently unique in her present desires: "for my dreams are truly my own."

The most widely reprinted of Howard's poems is "Monument in Black," a poem of reparation that claims memorialization for its speaker's family members; it is also included in Jordan's *Soulscript*, Arnold Adoff's 1974 edited collection *My Black Me: A Beginning Book of Black Poetry*, and Howard's solo collection *A Screaming Whisper*.[22] Howard describes the origin of the poem in an interview with *Scholastic Scope* youth magazine in 1973 ("Vanessa Howard: Young Author" 5):

> Once a group of us were going through a museum. There were all these statues of famous people. I didn't see any statues of black people. So I said, "Where are all the black heroes? Who are they?"
> I didn't know myself. So I wrote this poem. In it, I mention my grandfather, my parents, my brother. They were my heroes then.

From the lack of representation of "black heroes" at a museum, Howard constructs her own poetic monument to the people who were "my heroes then": "my grandfather, my parents, my brother." "Monument in Black" is structured in an imperative mood along with justifications that are framed in temporal terms. Its tone is one of quiet righteous confidence in claiming memorialization as a reparative act, and doing so by measuring unmeasurable, elemental timespans.

> Put my black father on the penny
> put his smile at me on the silver dime
> put my mother on the dollar
> for they've suffered for more than
> three eternities of time
> and all money couldn't repay

Make a monument of my grandfather
Let him stand in Washington
For he's suffered more than three light years
Standing idle in the dark,
hero of wars that weren't begun

Name a holiday for my brother
on a sunny peaceful and warm day
for he's fighting for freedom
he won't be granted
all my Black brothers in Vietnam
resting idle in unkept graves.

"Monument in Black" rests on the speaker's knowledge of the deep past of racial oppression and suffering, and her invocation of that deep past as a means of honoring and memorializing her family in the present. The poem's central project, which Howard reveals is autobiographical, is to memorialize the endurance of three generations of the speaker's family through a history of racial injustice that is measured through human suffering. The temporal dimensions of this suffering are figured as acts of endurance and as achievements. The speaker's father and mother have "suffered for more than / three eternities of time," and the speaker's grandfather has "suffered more than three light years." These timescales of suffering are beyond the human or the earthly; they are on the order of the greater universe—eternities, light years, in the plural.

The speaker organizes "Monument in Black" as a series of directives launching each of the three stanzas, in which she instructs the makers of currency, monuments, and calendars: "Put my black father on the penny," "Make a monument of my grandfather," and "Name a holiday for my brother." The measured insistence of these imperatives at the opening of each stanza is matched by the anaphoric repetition of "put" in the poem's opening three lines. The speaker uses references to the real embodiments of her family members to help give form to their memorial embodiments. Of her father, the speaker directs, "put his smile at me on the silver dime." Of her mother, the speaker enjoins, "put my mother on the dollar." Of her grandfather, the speaker urges, "Let him stand in Washington." While the speaker refers to the suffering of her parents and grandfather in the past tense ("they've suffered," "he's suffered"), only her brother—still engaged in the act of fighting ("he's fighting")—retains a present field of action while the memorializing involves naming a holiday after him. Yet the speaker sees this present action in relation to a predictable future, with her brother "fighting for freedom he won't be granted" along with a community of lost comrades ("resting idle" in an extended present) who have not been properly memorialized: "all my Black brothers in Vietnam / resting idle in unkept graves." In sum, "Monument in Black" achieves its title by placing the endurance, achievement, and heroic action of black subjects within timescales that are framed in the widest temporal dimensions of the universe.

This accomplished level of temporal command in Vanessa Howard's poetic craft is also evident in her poem "The Last Riot," a long poem that invokes, resists, and animates the finality of racial hatred through practicing temporal fluency in and across its two parts. While Glen Thompson in "Hands" manipulates an active into a passive present in depicting racial-political chaos, Howard crafts the first section of "The Last Riot" to anticipate the "coming of a racist fight" that by the end of the first section has already occurred, only for it to be suspended in the second section in a vivid and relentless present. Although most of "The Last Riot" is in the third person, it is nonetheless a poem of witness in which an embodied speaker appears at a pivotal point at the end of the first section, as sadness registers on the face of the speaker who gazes on the "ruins" of racial conflict: "I wipe these tears from my sad face / . . . And I look upon the midst of ruins / remains of the last riot."

I

Tension in the heat-filled night
The coming of a racist fight
When black and white will match their wits
And take this human race to bits
No more talking trying to care
No more tears and hurt and fear
One last fight to say who wins
But really this is where it ends
Black pushed up in a corner put in a box
Now they come out fighting with sticks and rocks
A cut of flesh a cry of pain

A ray of hope gone down the drain
The crash of glass shattered hate
discrimination met it's mate
All lives to be drowned in a pool of blood
Brought on by a hatred flood
Screams, fire, blood and death
Could have been stopped in one breath
by being kind to one another
by white saying you're my black brother
but it's too late they kept their pride
Now death shall sweep the countryside
I wipe these tears from my sad face
And so shall hatred do this race
All is gone and the night is desolate and quiet
And I look upon the midst of ruins
remains of the last riot

II

Hell, fire, bombs
Guns, screaming crying pain tears
Black white together
fighting killing
Babies stomped
Children bleeding screaming fearing
hurt pain
And then the Bombs
The last scream
The last cry of pain
The last tear
Last bleeding face
Last baby drops
Last riot
Last of the human race

In "The Last Riot," Howard crafts a brilliant exploration of temporal possibility in race relations and racial violence. She articulates a racial ethic of relation in referring to the "human race" at the opening and closing of the poem and to the possibility of imagining kinship between whites and blacks "by white saying you're my black brother," yet the "but" that follows this statement indicates that this possibility has been spent. The line "it's too late they kept their pride" ushers in the "Now" of the imminent "last riot" that introduces the last third of the poem's first section: "Now death shall sweep the countryside." However, a jarring temporal conflation is evident in the end of this section, since the riot that "shall" happen has already happened by the very next line ("All is gone . . .") and the speaker "look[s] upon the midst of ruins," which suggests that the ruins are still and inert.

The second section of "The Last Riot" then further destabilizes the reader's temporal expectations since, following the "ruins," the poem depicts a present-tense riot in medias res. In contrast to the first section's expository narrative form, the second section begins in the language of compact, percussive violence. The window onto these "ruins" is full of brutal action and motion in the form of multiple gerunds and participles, in strings of twos or threes without punctuation—"screaming crying," "fighting killing," "bleeding screaming fearing"—that sustain and suspend the activity of riot. This is a living museum of the destruction that hatred and injustice wreak. Halfway through this second section, the bombs drop—"And then the Bombs"—in a manner that, again, keeps them active rather than consigning them to the past. The bombs unleash a string of anaphoric "last" occurrences, in which only the central item on this list—"Last bleeding face"—continues the ongoing action from the stanza's opening, in an image that maintains and extends the violence of the moment and its impact on the human body, and can be seen as a metonymic figure for the dying human body writ large. In fact, the poem culminates by witnessing the final "Last of the human race."

In the second section's depiction of the "Last riot," the suffering of children is central, and noticeably absent are the end-rhymes of the first section, that had carried over even across the stanza breaks toward the successive "Now[s]" of the impending riot. Images of "Babies stomped" and "Children bleeding screaming fearing" are the poem's most vivid evocations of suffering, and indicate a culmination of the destructiveness of the riot. The final specific reference to human action or persons is the line "Last baby drops," a heartrendingly powerful convergence of birth and death: the phrase "baby drops" can be used to refer to infants in their process toward birth (i.e., settling into their mother's pelvis weeks prior to birth), yet in this case it appears to suggest either small tear-drops or drops of blood, or a baby being dropped from human care during the riot's upheaval. It is a devastating result of this study of youth agency that I argue for recognition of the artistry and temporal command in a young poet's damningly gorgeous representation of the killing of children as a result of racism. In this selection of her poems from *THE VOICE of the Children* anthology, Vanessa Howard's temporal fluency—her command over the use of multiple temporal strategies—is evident in testing the temporal limits of identity and agency ("The Question"), measuring almost-unmeasurable elemental timespans of ancestors' suffering due to racial oppression ("Monument in Black"), and manipulating temporal expectations in representing the anticipation, occurrence, and aftermath of a race riot ("The Last Riot")

Tragically, the final collaboration of The Voice of the Children workshop was a memorial booklet in 1973 for one of their young participants whose death was attributed to racism ("We Remember Michael"). Michael Angelo Thompson died at the age of thirteen, hit by a city bus and then denied care by a hospital in Bedford-Stuyvesant that "refused to treat him" due to institutional racism, as June Jordan describes in her account of this event ("The Voice of the Children" 30). Jordan's poem "For Michael Angelo Thompson" is included in the memorial booklet along with remembrances and poems by other participants, writings by Michael that had appeared in the weekly publication *The Voice of the Children*, and photographs by Anna Winand and Wayne Figueroa. The memorial booklet reflects the respectful inclusion of Michael's writing and art as its first section, the intense love and care of The Voice of the Children community of young people and adult mentors for this child who Jordan calls "One of the most beautiful children ever born into this world" ("The Voice of the Children" 30), and the heartbreaking honor his father and mother bestow by each writing memorials to Michael, in verse.

> "We called ourselves *The Voice of the Children,* for through
> writing we had a voice in a place where nothing was
> unimportant, and everyone was listening"

Of the young participants in The Voice of the Children workshop, Vanessa Howard was the most recognized and successful *as a young poet.* In addition to the publishing of her own poetry collection, she received public attention through articles in teen magazines that afforded her opportunities to articulate her ideas about young people and the purpose of writing.

Her consciousness of her role as a mentor to younger children is evident in an essay she wrote about The Voice of the Children workshop in which she quotes a poem in full written by a younger poet, Eric Smith. This chapter ends with a discussion of Smith's poem and Howard's essay, in which she articulates her sense of how writing conveys young people's perspectives and can counter adult domination.

In 1971, Howard was described in the teen magazine *Today's Girl* as "well on her way to becoming a major twentieth century poet" ("Vanessa Howard Speaks to Be Heard" 10), obviously a forward-looking statement. Howard's moving essay titled "We Speak to Be Heard" is preceded by a statement written by staff at *Today's Girl* explaining that when they asked her "whether we could tell her story here," Howard was "reluctant" to do so "until she herself thought up a way to have the readers of the magazine hearken to the voices of all her friends" (10). The unnamed author of the brief introduction to Howard's essay "We Speak to Be Heard" informs readers of *Today's Girl* that Howard's essay is "just as she wrote it. It is unedited. Read it and decide for yourself whether the predictions are true that she is to become a major writer" (10). The adult editor frames Howard's piece as a "prediction" of her future success rather than as a present achievement, and they attest to its *unadulterated* form ("unedited" by adults) as proof of its legitimacy and quality. This forward-looking view can potentially undercut the importance of Howard's writing given that she did not go on to publish further collections of poetry as an adult. Her achievement as a poet, though specific to that portion of her life that she spent as a young person, is nonetheless significant, as is her ability to articulate, as a young person, the value of poetry by and for young people.

In Howard's account of The Voice of the Children workshop published in *Today's Girl* magazine, she attests to the power of herself and her fellow participants to create poetry, despite their age and social role. When the workshop began, she and the other writers "were only twelve then, but just as real and alive as anyone twenty-five or a hundred. There our thoughts and ideas were not childhood fantasies shushed quiet by an alien adult world, but took shape, in the form of words and letters, creating poems" (Howard, "We Speak to Be Heard" 10). Howard claims for herself and her co-participants a status as "just as real and alive" as any adult, and she recognizes their poetry as a platform for shaping their "thoughts and ideas" beyond the typical discouragement and disparagement by adults. Howard goes on to articulate an original perspective on children's growth and change, one in which awareness is constant rather than incremental despite "emerging" differently over time: "In us, poetry was born while we were being born and born again, each time emerging as something different and new and constantly aware. And as all children do, we grew. But not just up. In so many different dimensions. We called ourselves *The Voice of the Children*, for through writing we had a voice in a place where nothing was unimportant, and everyone was listening" (10). Birth and rebirth recur ("we were being born and born again") and change is continual ("each time emerging as something different and new and constantly aware"). Anticipating alternatives to the standard developmental narrative of growing "up" such as Katherine Bond Stockton's notion of queer children "growing sideways," Howard holds that change is not unidimensional, and growth is "not just up" but involves growing "in so many different dimensions." Writing provides for Howard and her fellow young writers a location where their "voice" has significance and audience—"through writing we had a voice in a place where nothing was unimportant, and everyone was listening"—an audience occasioned in part by the "Hot Time" during which these young poets of color lived (to use Gwendolyn Brooks's phrase for racial unrest from her poem "Near-Johannesburg Boy" 4).

The purpose of The Voice of the Children workshop, according to Howard, is "for children to be heard" (12), yet she acknowledges that those who have turned sixteen are "no longer children" (11) and can no longer share in articulating children's voices, though they can play a mentoring and facilitative role in relation to present-day children. Howard states, "Being no longer children, we ceased to speak for them" (11), acknowledging the contingency of young people's agency as specific to the time of youth. Instead, Howard writes, "we began to help them to speak, developing in them voices that will bounce back against the mountains and echo in anger" (12). Here Howard depicts a landscape in which young people assist even younger people to claim agency and express their perspectives and ideas in ways that take advantage of the contours of that landscape, so their "voices . . . will bounce back against the mountains and echo in anger."

In concluding her essay, "We Speak to Be Heard," Howard chooses to include a poem by "Eric Smith (Age 12)," one of the younger participants in the later phase of The Voice of the Children workshop. In introducing Smith's poem, Howard refers to a "strengthening" ("We Speak to

Be Heard" 13) that children gained through The Voice of the Children workshop, by which "These children don't feel intimidated, or not as intimidated as they were, by the adult world anymore. They know that what they have to say is important, and they say it anyway it comes out" (13). Howard pays tribute to Smith's poem "I Am Clearly Real" by saying, "I can think of no way to say it better than the way Eric Smith said it in his poem" (12):

> I am not an imagination
> or an illusion of darkness.
> I am not an artificial person
> compared to anybody.
> I am not just a piece of art
> created to be laughed at as
> I walk in this world of chaos and confusion.
> I refuse to be an imagination,
> or an illusion,
> I refuse to be an artificial person,
> and I refuse to be a piece of art.
> I am clearly real.

Eric Smith's poem "I Am Clearly Real" is a clear-eyed song of praise to the present humanity of its speaker, established through powerful, explicit, and repeated rejection of perspectives or approaches that would diminish his status. Smith implicitly cautions adult readers—including myself and readers of this book—not to reduce the humanity and the reality of a young poet or a young speaker to "a piece of art." Smith uses great care in constructing his speaker's first-person claims of being—recall Bin Ramke's notion that poetry concerns "the dignity of being" (158)—through anaphoric negation. Smith balances three "I am not" phrases against three "I refuse to be" statements on either side of the poem's longest line in which the speaker moves steadily through an unsteady world ("I walk in this world of chaos and confusion"). The poem concludes with its only positive statement of being—"I am clearly real"—an emphatic claim of the speaker's irreducible personhood in the present that rings with bell-like clarity through assonance, alliteration, and the mirror-like reversal of "clearly" and "real."

"I Am Clearly Real" cleverly and self-consciously dismisses those who

CHAPTER 5

might dismiss or belittle the poem. Smith's speaker rejects reducing him to a "piece of art," a poem, that is "created to be laughed at." These lines equally critique disparaging assessments of artwork created by youth and also adult-created art that belittles youth in its representations. In addition, Smith takes issue with forces that would interrupt the continuity of his speaker's present-oriented action. The poem's sentences are all simple declarative ones until the sentence at the center of the poem, where the word "as" rebukes efforts to ridicule or unsettle the speaker's steady present action of moving forward "as / I walk in this world of chaos and confusion." Eric Smith claims for his speaker an unadulterated, uninterrupted present, one that is self-authored, purposeful, and "clearly real."

The purpose of considering questions of agency and temporality in relation to young poets is not only to appreciate otherwise undervalued examples of poetic craft or to offer original lyric times and perspectives but also to value the present voice and personhood of young writers. In his poem, Eric Smith contrasts "real" to "artificial," an adjective not often used to modify "person": "I am not an artificial person, / compared to anybody" across dimensions that could include age, race, class, gender, sexualities, generation, community, family, and individuality. How can we understand the claim that Eric Smith makes here? Smith's speaker is not a fantasy or "illusion" of others; he is not reducible through comparison to other persons; he is not the imaginative construction of adults; he is not fixed at the limits of a white gaze. Smith accomplishes this through hewing to the present tense, without reference to pasts or futures in which such fantasies and imaginative constructions—of young people, of youth of color—are often located. Yet "I Am Clearly Real" embodies a paradox, for while it is written by a young poet, Eric Smith does not identify the age or age-based identity of his first-person speaker. Of course, the speaker *is* an imaginative construction, an element of a work of art. The "illusion" here is youth-created, and the artifice accentuates Smith's critique.

"I Am Clearly Real" holds this paradoxical claim for the autonomy and dimensionality of youth-created art and the agency of an individual young poet, and Vanessa Howard herself was presumably influenced by Smith's poem in her own poem "For My Children" that appeared subsequently in her solo collection *A Screaming Whisper*. Howard's poem begins "My children are Unique / They are not animated ill-created / figments of someone else's imagination / in disguise" (20) and ends by referring to the children "ever growing in their blackness / ever striving to be real" (21). While Howard refers to the young participants in The Voice of the Children workshop as "these children" (13) in her essay "We Speak to Be Heard," in her six-stanza poem "For My Children," Howard trains her eyes directly on "my children" (20), alternating stanza openings with "My children are" and "They are not" (20) until the concluding statements of identification with them ("My children are me" 21) and valorization of their "blackness" and their "ever striving to be real" (21). Howard maintains the present tense in "For My Children," as does Smith in "I Am Clearly Real," and she repudiates a notion of children as harbingers of the future or as lingering traces of the past: "They are not images of tomorrow / or shadows of yesterday" (21). Howard also champions the individuality and dignity of children's identities that should not be reducible to adult fantasies, stock characters, or parental ownership: "They are not story book characters / from forgotten fairy tales / or Mrs. So and So's children / my children have names" (20). Reading Howard's poem "For My Children" alongside her essay "We Speak to Be Heard" suggests that as she grew older into her teen years, mentoring younger children was intertwined in a continuous way with her own poetics.

While Jordan and Bush chose Vanessa Howard's prose poem "Ghetto" with its indictment of anti-black racism as the foreword to *THE VOICE of the Children* anthology, Howard positions her own conception of poetry as the preface to her volume *A Screaming Whisper*. Howard's preface (here included in its entirety) opens by attending to the "eternal" and "everlasting" nature of words and poems, the notion that poetry, as "another way of life," is unending (ix):

> Poetry to me is another way of life, one that never ceases. A word is eternal even when forgotten and a poem is everlasting. Poems sometimes take the place of medicines, talks, hatred, violence, anger, pain, love or tears, preserving beautiful moments and easing bad ones. In writing my poetry, I have tried to capture all that fascinates me, contain all that's beautiful, restore all that's destroyed, and soothe all that's painful.

Striking here is the temporal expansiveness ("one that never ceases," "everlasting") and thematic capaciousness of Howard's poetic vision in incorporating "all that's beautiful" and "all that's destroyed," "all that fascinates me" and "all that's painful," and her evocation of the active work of the poet, which is "to capture," "contain," "restore," and "soothe."

Vanessa Howard's collection *A Screaming Whisper* includes an "About the Author" note at the end that positions Howard as an "Author" whose writing connects with her concerns while a younger child. Writing as an "Author" still in high school, she indicates that the poems convey ideas that are consistent with her earlier life: "Actually I have been writing and living them all my life, but just now they are being made known to the public" (58). It may seem an obvious point that a writer referring to "all my life" assumes a temporal ongoingness to her earlier existence, yet a teenaged writer doing so implicitly challenges adults' temporal assumptions about one's early years as only a prelude to the "all" of one's life. Here Howard's temporal canvas reflects respect for the span of her lived years during her childhood as continuous with her present, and as full of ideas about "all things that should be changed, all things that should be recognized, all things that should be done" (58)—in other words, her social and political critique, long in formation across her still-under-eighteen life.

Vanessa Howard articulates a radical critique of adult power over children's lives, and upholds the role of writing in counteracting that power. In her essay "We Speak to Be Heard," Howard indicates the role that writing can play for young people in relation to adult domination, and how older youth can help support younger children in this process. "Those of us who are sixteen and have successfully lived through being pushed aside, shushed quiet, intentionally confused, and other childhood diseases, are working with other, younger children to bring them through this chaos, using writing as a vaccination of immunity" (12). Howard explicitly and powerfully condemns the multiple and varied forms of adult domination and hegemony—the displacement of children's purposes, the silencing of children's voices, the deliberate obfuscations adults practice on children—as "childhood diseases" for which writing offers a potent "vaccination of immunity." Howard states, "It is easier for us who have survived these errors of adults—parents and teachers alike"—to help younger children "overcome and maybe change these errors, creating in our own way a small revolution" (12). Given the prevalence of adult power, for youth writing to produce "a small revolution" in adult-child relations and/or in young people's views of themselves and their capacities also involves its finding a serious audience and being "heard" (11). This "revolution" can help bring to the surface the value of young people's agency—their roles in their social worlds, their ideas, their cultural productions—so that it can be more readily recognized by youth and adults. Youth-written poetry is an expression of youth agency that can offer visions of "time for childhoods" that depict young people's imagined temporalities, their redrawn and remapped timescapes.

The Voice of the Children poets discussed here exercise temporal agency in remaking the present, sometimes in relation to pasts or futures. This involves lengthening or shortening the present, crafting an alternative present, shifting from an active to a passive present, speeding up the present or slowing it down, using the present to honor elemental timespans of ancestors' suffering, and/or suspending the present so it doesn't succumb to the past. Vanessa Howard practices a temporal fluency by speaking with and across multiple temporalities, such as testing the temporal limits of agency, memorializing the timescales of ancestors, and shifting the timeframes of racial violence. Howard shapes time strategically and artistically to figure histories of racial oppression, racial injustice, or racial violence, as do Michael Goode, Christopher Meyer, and Glen Thompson in poems I discussed earlier in this chapter. While not discounting present imperatives, Howard, Goode, Meyer, Thompson, and Smith go through and beyond them in representing a range of temporal positions that include standing in the present in relation to conditional futures, or remaking temporalities of agency against racial and age-based domination. The temporal agency of these young black poets is evident in the poetic control they exercise over pasts, presents, and futures.

In her essay "We Speak to Be Heard," Vanessa Howard highlights the importance of youth status in the name that she and the other young writers chose for their workshop and publication—"We called ourselves *The Voice of the Children*" (10)—and in her claim that they were "as real and alive" as anyone older. The name "The Voice" (capitalized in red typeface as "THE VOICE" on the cover of the anthology) "of the Children" has particular resonance for these children of color claiming not only the right to be recognized as children but also the right to be at the center of and guiding representations of children and childhood. The image on the cover of *THE VOICE of the Children* anthology—a somewhat grainy photomontage by Anna Winand—accentuates this claim to power, with the children in active poses, many with their fists raised in a gesture resonant of the Black Power movement, yet with variation in their bodily expression that conveys their youth and individuality. Representation of the children's individuality is enhanced by Anna Winant's individual photographs of each participant at the end of the volume, interspersed throughout June Jordan's afterword.

The participants in The Voice of the Children workshop wrote as young people whose lives encompassed their racial identities and experiences and observations of racial injustice, and this is reflected in the range of poems in *THE VOICE of the Children* anthology that take up themes of racial conflict or racial pride. As young writers of color writing in a racially tumultuous time, the participants in The Voice of the Children workshop located themselves at the center of the kind of "reorganized view of universality" (10) that Arnold Rampersad proposes in his discussion of African American poetry, a view that is "intellectually authentic in . . . rendition of both the particular and the universal" (13). In such a "reorganized" view of the universal, every child has particular lived experiences, possibly shared identities, and a stake in the struggles of local communities as well as potentially universal aspects of children and childhoods. This "reorganized view of universality" encompasses the shifting meanings, conceptions, and experiences that cohere around younger humans in their particular personal, cultural, political, and historical worlds. The Voice of the Children poets wrote at a charged political time when, for that moment, "everyone was listening" (Howard, "We Speak to Be Heard" 10) to these young writers of color in the United States. Their poetic voices continue to remind us that young people are "just as real and alive as anyone twenty-five or a hundred" (10) and unquestionably deserving of others' "listening," of being "heard" (10–11).

CONCLUSION

"Poems are voiceprints of language"

"Poems are voiceprints of language"
—June Jordan (*Soulscript*, xvi)

AT THE END of my interview with Terri Bush, she recited a short poem by June Jordan, "In the Times of My Heart," that she feels conveys the mission and tenor of The Voice of the Children workshop.

> In the times of my heart
> the children tell the clock
> a hallelujah
> > > listen people
> > > listen

Terri Bush remarked about Jordan's poem that "it's sort of the spirit of The Voice of the Children" (Bush, personal interview). In Jordan's poem, "the children" have voices with which they address "the clock" that governs "the times of my heart," and for which they deserve an audience. The adult speaker invites a respectful audience ("listen people / listen") for the children's voices, which provide depth and meaning ("a hallelujah") to the clock that directs the "heart" of the speaker. Young poets, through their agency, "tell the clock," or control and direct poetic representations of temporality. In youth-authored poems, representations of temporality bear the imprint of youth agency through the act of writing and the crafting of temporalities, and can help us envision and theorize the agency of young people.

It is, need I say, striking that two of the fiercest adult advocates for young poets in the twentieth-century United States—Gwendolyn Brooks and June Jordan—wrote poems in which the clock plays a central role in explicit or implicit connection to childhood. Recall from chapter 1 that Brooks's poem "The Busy Clock," written as a child and included in her autobiography *Report from Part One*, takes the perspective of a clock that, in a critique of adult-controlled time, is "never free" and has "no time to play" because it is at the bidding of "Bustling men and women." Given my focus on temporal representations in youth-written poetry preserved in the context of adult-facilitated projects, it has seemed apt to open my discussion of young poets writing lyric times with "The Busy Clock" by Brooks as a young poet and end with "In the Times of My Heart" by Jordan as an adult poet writing about how "the children tell the clock / a hallelujah." The argument of *Time for Childhoods* is that "tell[ing] the clock" is what happens when young poets take on a lyric voice, and that young poets' artistry is evident in *how* they "tell the clock" (or tell off the adult clock).

Gwendolyn Brooks and June Jordan both enjoined their audiences to "listen" to the voices of children. Brooks recited poems by young poets and directly invited her live and print audiences to "Listen to Moral Thirus" (*Report* 208), and Jordan writes in "In the Times of My Heart," "listen people / listen." In order for adults to take poetry written by young poets seriously, they must acknowledge young poets' claims of agency, loosen the reins of their own cultural power, and respect the integrity and complexity of poems written by young people. In June Jordan's essay "Old Stories: New Lives," delivered as the keynote address at a conference of the Child Welfare League of America in 1978—years after The Voice of the Children workshop ended—she writes, "I am convinced that our children pose the question whereby we must justify our power over their lives, or give it up. It seems tragically evident that we have to give it up: our power, our coercion of new life into old stories; we have to solicit and cultivate and respect major differences of behavior and habit and perspective as they emerge from our new life, our children" ("Old Stories: New Lives" 282). In order to avoid the "coercion of new life into old stories" and make space for the new stories that children invent, in order to "solicit and cultivate and respect" young people's perspectives as they craft their new stories into words, lines, and stanzas, it is necessary for adults to "give . . . up" the extent of their power over children's lives. Even the act of reading this book involves setting aside standard adult expectations and judgments about children and their artistic works, about which texts should qualify as literary and deserve study and critical attention.

Young poets are not just following or resisting adult clocks but constructing and articulating their own ways of time-making in their imaginative projects. A poem is a space to create one's temporal vision, and the young poets I discuss in *Time for Childhoods* figure time through their standpoints as children (at the time of writing the poems) in ways that further their artistry, enrich practices of lyric time, and demonstrate the importance of temporal agency. Whether or not they explicitly figure childhood itself or the standpoint of child speakers, young poets write in their present—as children—to figure new lyric times. In so doing, young poets reclaim both time and childhood from the limits of the pasts or futures of adulthood or the timelessness of ideologies of childhood.

Young poets bring a temporal fluency to lyric poetry in speaking with and across varied temporalities, and figuring temporality across multiple poetic purposes and contexts. While young people are confined to the temporal location of childhood with its social-political constraints, as poets they can remake their temporal limits by implicitly or explicitly questioning a temporal hierarchy in which children are considered to be not there *yet*. Through their *temporal standpoints* as youth, young poets can craft poetic worlds that reflect, subvert, or transform standard chronologies of daily time, age, and epoch. They can explode temporal possibilities in the lyric while maintaining varied rather than uniform valuations of age, action, and possibility.

Reading poetry written by poets under the age of eighteen thus expands our understanding of the lyric impulse, of what Reginald Shepherd has called "the traditional lyric's exploration of subjectivity and its discontents" (xi), to include and animate multiple temporal positions. Our prior understanding of lyric poetry has been limited by solely reading poetry written by adults. Adult writers typically imagine childhood positions retrospectively as a finished past, yet young poets write in the midst of time shifting across lived experience while they are still able to reflect back on "all my life" (Howard, *A Screaming Whisper* 58), envision a shimmering present-time, or collapse the distance to imagined futures. Daily temporal constraints may prime young poets to craft new stories about times that they realize they have the capacity to invent. Perhaps the many dimensions of change that young people experience contribute to young poets' ability to locate their poetic speakers at different and sometimes multiple points within a shifting temporal terrain. Physicist Carlo Rovelli has written that there are "a vast multitude" of times, "a different one for every point in space" (16), and that time is really just a way of talking about how things change in relation to one another: "Physics does not describe how things evolve 'in time' but how things evolve in their own times, and 'times' evolve relative to each other" (17). It is not the goal of this book to proclaim that the subjective experience of time may differ between children and adults, though that may be worth exploring. Instead, I have been concerned with young people's use and making of time in and through artistic projects in order to argue for the value of youth-written poetry and to theorize youth temporal agency.

Flexible temporal strategies—the creative remaking of time and temporal action that I term *dynamic temporality*—can have particular resonance in young poets' thematic engagements with injustice. As we have seen in the work of young black poets involved in contests and workshops sponsored by Gwendolyn Brooks and by June Jordan and Terri Bush, crafting lyric times can be an act of artistic intervention against persistent oppression. This is not simply a matter of calling out injustice but of asserting poetic control in inventing new temporal realities. Making and shaping time according to one's own priorities is a liberatory act. In *Freedom Dreams*, Robin D. G. Kelley introduces his study of the "black radical imagination" by discussing "poetic knowledge" (9)—drawing from Aimé Césaire's essay "Poetry and Knowledge"—as an imaginative re-envisioning of the world. Kelley writes, "the most radical art is not protest art but works that take us to another place, envision a different way of seeing, perhaps a different way of feeling" (11). Poetry can convey young people's indictment of adult power, of age-based injustice, of racial oppression and other social-political failures. Young poets' figuration of lyric time is thus a key dimension of re-envisioning artistic, social, and political possibilities.

While we all live and die in time, we can choose how we imagine and create in and with time. Young poets' uses and manipulations of time instantiate their agency as children. They can counter the temporally-derived limitations on their social and political power by imaginatively altering time itself. Young poets craft temporal landscapes—timescapes—that reveal their agency in constructing temporal realities that emerge from their own priorities and standpoints, while also constructing standpoints of poetic speakers. They marshal their poetic skills to make temporal worlds that might conform to standard clocks or manipulate temporality. Martin

Laureles "bring[s] back the Past" or invites "the Past" into the future ("I will order it at a restaurant"), Moral Thirus opens up the time of death as a moment of sensorial power ("And even when I die, I know I'd like to hear" in "Things"), and Theo Candlish imagines the deep future of Earth in relation to its past ("The Earth is going back to the way it was"). Young poets exercise temporal agency by reimagining temporality as a means to express their artistry, assert their ideas, counter injustice, and/or critique adult power. Janet Docka speaks against "the portals of time" involved in age-based oppression, Michael Goode stretches out the present of racial violence into the future ("I will long remember this dark day"), Vanessa Howard rewrites the timescales of racial suffering ("For he's suffered more than three light years" in "Monument in Black"), and Aurelia Davidson envisions emergence from past racial injustice ("OUT I COME—/ from the past").

Writing time results from, reveals, and represents the agency that young people practice in or out of the view of adults. Though adult poets often work with time as a literal "deadline,"[1] young poets confront the powerful constraints of social-political temporality with its age-based trajectory and adult-driven temporal priorities that structure social, cultural, and political institutions. While the daily lives of young people are defined and delimited by temporal restrictions and expectations, as writers they can destroy, reinvent, and transcend those times. As such, young poets invite and prompt audiences to step aside from—even decenter—standardized time, and open up temporal possibilities for poetic projects.

I argue that temporality is an important dimension or parameter of youth agency rather than a field in which youth agency is practiced. Time is fundamental to youth agency, given that youth agency is demarcated and constrained by the temporal aspects of youth as a social position and the ways in which young people's experiences of time are shaped by their status as young. It is not possible to fully theorize youth agency in the absence of young people's *temporal agency*, their agency in relation to time. Without recognizing the centrality of this temporal dimension, our conception of youth agency is incomplete. Akin to the interplay of space and time in the notion of space-time, there is no youth agency without *time for childhoods*.[2]

Remaking time for one's own purposes—even if "only" imaginatively—is a means of practicing agency that is available to all children. Adults bear responsibility for removing impediments to acknowledging all young people's temporal agency, not only those who pursue their artistry through poetic forms. Yet it is not surprising that youth-written poetry, particularly poetry that challenges conventional temporalities and ideologies, is not more visible. After all, adult-directed cultural, social, and political institutions have a vested interest in not recognizing children's agency, and perhaps especially children's temporal agency. For adults to recognize the temporal priorities of children requires that they decenter their own temporal desires and ideas—for instance, not to see children as figures from a fondly remembered or longed-for past or hoped-for future but to acknowledge them as full persons standing in the present of their own time, with their own desires and plans, and the ticking of their own clocks according to temporal permutations that they imagine.

Adults use time to be adults: to act according to a unidirectional temporal order proceeding from past to present to future with key age-based markers of increasing (and toward the end, likely decreasing) power.[3] In this standard model, children have value for adults as literal embodiments of the past, and as embodiments of movement toward the future (as they "develop") as figures of hope and potential. In the course of children's daily lives in time, their goals are sometimes served by adopting a unidirectional temporal narrative, such as emphasizing one's age as four and three-quarters instead of four as a means of claiming age status. Yet for children in adult-dominated societies, age is a limiting axis of power. Manipulating temporality itself can be a wider-ranging means to pursue one's goals, at least in mind, imaginatively, or on paper.

Young people's shaping of time in the poems they write expresses their artistry, ideas, and priorities. As adults, the only way to see these "time machines" (to alter William Carlos Williams's famous description of a poem as a "machine made of words," *Selected Essays* 256)—to save them, value them, learn from them, promote them—is to recognize poems written by young people as works of art that enrich our cultural lives and times. *Time for Childhoods: Young Poets and Questions of Agency* argues for literary criticism that engages seriously with poems written by young poets, for temporalities that encompass the range of times that young people experience and artistically construct, and for conceptions of youth agency that include time for childhoods. To admit poetry written by young poets into literary canons; to provide access for young poets to print, Internet, or performance audiences; and to focus critical attention on young people's poems requires that adults recognize and acknowledge this agency, and wake up to the value of time for childhoods for life and for literature. It is past time for us to do so.

Notes

Preface

1. Twenty-five years ago, Richard Flynn wrote an incisive essay titled "Can Children's Poetry Matter?" that is just as pertinent today.

2. I use the terms "children," "young people," and "youth" interchangeably to refer to people under the age of eighteen. The United Nations Convention on the Rights of the Child ("Convention") defines a child as "every human being below the age of eighteen years unless under the law applicable to the child, majority is attained earlier" (Article 1).

3. I acknowledge that *Time for Childhoods* is constrained by centering "Western" or "European American" practices and standards. Sarada Balagopalan compellingly argues that childhood studies scholarship needs to conceptualize children's lives inclusively across majority and minority worlds (using terms that reflect current global population numbers). Allison James and Alan Prout's essay "Re-presenting Childhood" remains an excellent consideration of time and childhood from a sociological perspective.

4. Indeed, Barbara Adam refers to children's education as "learning the habits of clock time" (59).

5. Homi Bhabha uses the phrase "The question of agency" (*Location of Culture* 171) in his discussion of postcolonial subjects of oppression. My use of this phrase is meant to signal a process of engagement with (and not conclusions about) theorizing youth agency, rather than direct reference to Bhabha's discussion, which I briefly take up in chapter 1.

6. I primarily explore June Jordan's co-sponsorship of The Voice of the Children workshop with educator Terri Bush, whose deep commitment to the young people in the workshop was evident throughout an interview I conducted with her in 2017.

7. "Who has the right to be an artist? How does one claim that right?" Helen Vendler (*The Ocean* 24) has raised these questions in arguing for the central place of the arts and artists in our societies, and they are also relevant to thinking about

children as members of their societies who can contribute to cultural and artistic life.

8. While the poems I discuss in *Time for Childhoods* were written when the poets were under the age of eighteen, the only poets who are still children as of this writing are those discussed in chapter 4. My broader argument is that youth-written poetry deserves to be read seriously *while* the writers are children.

Chapter 1: "The Busy Clock"

1. After the shooting, young survivors from Parkland led the way in staging school walkouts, lobbying state and federal legislators, and demanding gun control measures (Turkewitz and Yee). Bond et al. refer to crowd estimates at March for Our Lives events and note that young speakers at the Washington, D.C., event were drawn across contexts of interpersonal violence, community violence, and school shootings.

2. See also Eva Lewis, who has written about her experience co-organizing a Black Lives Matter protest against racism and gun violence (that incorporated youth spoken-word poetry performance) in Chicago. Lewis describes working with "three other incredible black teen girls to lead more than 1,000 people from Chicago's Millennium Park through Michigan Avenue, shutting down both directions of traffic" and writes that the power of their shared leadership should be recognized: "For being at the forefront of change, we deserve recognition that we as a community of black women don't often get."

3. The youth-led environmental organization Earth Guardians is an organizational plaintiff in the case.

4. Trial dates had been set for February 5, 2018, and then for October 29, 2018, yet both times attorneys for the U.S. government sought to prevent the suit from going to trial. A new trial date had not been set as of this writing (Our Children's Trust).

5. Throughout *Time for Childhoods*, my reference to "typical," "common," or "standard" ideologies of childhood rests on the continued dominance of developmental psychological frameworks for viewing children and childhood in the United States, as well as the continued power differential in U.S. society between adults and children. One could argue, as did an anonymous reviewer, that literary criticism offers other models that afford power to the young, such as Harold Bloom's metaphor of literary "influence" as poets' deliberate "misreading" (5) of earlier poets, but surely Bloom in his reference to the "young citizen of poetry" (10) did not have a child in mind. For discussion of cultural apprenticeship, see Barbara Rogoff. For critique of socialization models, see Myra Bluebond-Langner and Berry Mayall. Perry Nodelman and Mavis Reimer clearly outline common Western adult assumptions about children.

6. Michael Lewis offers a useful critique of progress in relation to child development.

7. See also Martin Woodhead.

8. See, for example, Spyros Spyrou.

9. Carolyn Steedman, Karen Sánchez-Eppler, and Robin Bernstein have each accomplished such integration in their scholarship.

10. Worth thinking about also is sociologist Allison James's injunction to consider the "dialectical interplay" among the terms "child," "children," and "childhood" in order to view children "as individuals who participate in the social world and as members of a social category defined by particular social, historical, and ideological processes" ("Understanding Childhood" 36).

11. See, for example, the work of Allison James, Chris Jenks, and Alan Prout; Mary Jo Maynes; and Steven Mintz.

12. In writing about the inclusion of "voices of children" in anthropological and sociological research, Allison James ("Giving Voice" 261) cautions us to attend to the role of adult mediation in selecting, editing, contextualizing, and interpreting children's words and statements, yet not to the point of compromising a notion of children's agency.

13. See Tatek Abebe; Karl Hanson and Olga Nieuwenhuys's edited collection *Reconceptualizing Children's Rights in International Development*; and Mehmoona Moosa-Mitha. See also Anne Wihstutz, who draws on feminist perspectives to pursue a relational idea of agency, which she re-envisions "as the expression of a specific relational interpretation of social conditions, in which children position themselves as belonging participants" (70).

14. See also Mark Rimmer's discussion of "musical agency" (563) from a relational perspective.

15. For nuanced contemporary discussions of youth agency, see Sarah White and Shyamol Choudhury on agency and children's participation in international development in Bangladesh, and Kelli Lyon Johnson on the complexities of youth agency and voice in studies of contemporary children who have escaped conditions of slavery. Florian Esser et al. ("Reconceptualising Agency and Childhood: An Introduction") review a range of current approaches to reconceptualizing agency, primarily from European sociological and education studies perspectives.

16. Cook-Gumperz uses "childness" to refer to "children's self-generated social categorization," an understanding that only children can have of "their own sense of what it means to be a child" (208); and in this way her use of the term differs dramatically from Peter Hollindale's use of "childness" in his discussion of children's literature's "Uniqueness" (7) to refer to "the quality of being a child—dynamic, imaginative, experimental, interactive and unstable" (46), which he considers to be a potential "shared ground, though differently experienced and understood, between child and adult" (47). Like Cook-Gumperz, I favor a notion of "childness" that refers to perspectives that only children can convey, of children's engagements with what it means and what it feels like to be a child.

17. James and Prout further write, "the 'time of childhood' both defines and is defined by 'time in childhood'" ("Re-presenting Childhood" 231).

18. Jean Piaget's work is the pre-eminent psychological approach to assessing children's

understanding of time against strict standards of the development of abstract thinking.

19. I recall as a young child confidently telling my mother, "When I grow up, you['ll] be the baby and I['ll] be the mommy," and being stunned when she told me in effect that our age roles vis-à-vis each other were fixed and permanent.

20. James and Prout articulate a notion of children's present-oriented "being" as an alternative to the developmental focus on children's future "becoming," in which the present-time of children's lives is always downplayed in adults' focus on the remembered pasts and hoped-for futures of childhood ("Re-presenting Childhood"). Emma Uprichard's model of children as "being and becoming" attempts to balance a present and future orientation yet is still determinative toward the direction of future adulthood. Alan Prout suggests that adults as well as children should be viewed through multiple and incomplete becomings. Lesley-Anne Gallacher and Michael Gallagher's proposal of a nondeterminative sense of becoming or "emergent subjectivity" focused on "process without predetermination" in the "present continuous tense" (510), and Hanne Warming's discussion of the "fluid and performative"—as opposed to "fixed and essential" (49)—nature of children's perspectives are potentially productive directions.

21. For example, Pia Christensen and Allison James used participatory methods and interviews to discern children's experiences of time in school settings in the United Kingdom; and Christensen in the United Kingdom and Gry Haugen in Norway explored children's perspectives on time with their families in post-divorce contexts. Sophie Sarre used semistructured and task-based interviews to consider temporalities of school work and family life among adolescents and their parents in the United Kingdom. Anne Solberg examined Norwegian children's and parents' negotiation over the use of time in relation to age; and Kathrine Vitus studied the temporal experiences of children living in asylum centers in Denmark while their family's cases were pending.

22. With gratitude to my daughter Emma for her careful transcription of Sammy's words as, so often during productive conversations in those years, I was driving.

23. Daisy Turner's archived oral account accords with the transcription in Bernstein (196) and Beck (21), while Beck (163) quotes a slightly different version.

24. Interestingly, Turner's poetic speaker joins her "dolly" in the present through her future action ("I'll stand right by your side"; Turner; Bernstein 195).

25. I discuss my use of "distinctive" later in this chapter in relation to Daylanne English's use of that term (in "Race, Writing, and Time") in discussing temporalities in African American literature.

26. Anthropologist Barbara Yngvesson applies my idea of dynamic temporality in learning from adult women speaking about their experiences being adopted transnationally as children and returning as adults "to the orphanages, hospitals, and families that were sites of their abandonment" (365); and in their verbal narratives accomplishing "transgressions of linear time and fixed spaces of belonging" that

enable "a more general rethinking of conventional narratives of development and the fixed categories that underpin them" (358).

27. One common method in developmental psychology and psychoanalysis is a retrospective approach in which children are known through adults' retrospective accounts comparing child-as-past with the adult present (see Virginia Blum). This "having been" child surfaces in contemporary social studies of childhood, in research that introduces adults' retrospective accounts of childhood while considering (e.g., Julia Brannen) or not considering (e.g., Dorothy Moss) methodological complications of these approaches. As with approaches that consider children's value for the future, backward-looking perspectives locate full subjectivity with adults: children's psychologies are considered preparatory and partial.

28. Additionally, Barrie Thorne has usefully articulated the need to theorize "different types of *temporality*—historical, generational, chronological, phenomenological, developmental, biological [that] should be central to the study of children and childhoods" (150).

29. As Bhabha explains, "*Time-lag keeps alive the making of the past*" (254): "The time-lag of postcolonial modernity moves *forward*, erasing that compliant past tethered to the myth of progress, ordered in the binarisms of its cultural logic: past/present, inside/outside" (253).

30. Mehmoona Moosa-Mitha proposes centering children's specific lived experiences, including their identity as children, as a means to theorize children's rights to citizenship, and "defining children's citizenship in ways that take their rights and status as citizens seriously on the basis, rather than to the exclusion, of their identity as children" (370).

31. See Alexander Siegel and Sheldon White for a thorough overview of the child study movement and its relation to developmental psychology in the United States. Elsewhere (Conrad "Baby's Darwin") I explore how Charles Darwin rewrote his original diary observations of his oldest child, which encompassed his own self-transformation as he responded to being recognized by his infant son, into a journal article that adhered to conventions of scientific objectivity including a disembodied observer.

32. See Kurt Danziger's discussion of the "triumph of the aggregate" (68) which involved "making psychological knowledge claims by attributing psychological characteristics to collective rather than individual subjects" (74); as well as the work of critical developmental psychologists including Erica Burman and John Morss.

33. See, for example, essays in *Childhoods: A Handbook*, edited by Gaile S. Cannella and Lourdes Diaz Soto; and Allison James and Adrian James. Sarada Balagopalan has recently argued persuasively for reconceptualizing the notion of "multiple childhoods" (37) in order to do justice to the lives of children in majority and minority worlds; see also Samantha Punch.

34. The term "children's literature" has been the subject of much scholarly discussion.

See, for example, Perry Nodelman's discussion of the "hidden adult" in children's literature, or Katharine Jones's proposal that "child literature" be used to refer to literature written by adults for young audiences in order to make clear that adult-authored literature for children "belongs to adults, with the child reader usually being the target of the book" (305–6), which "frees up space for a revised notion of something actually called children's literature—that is, a literature written by children" (306–7).

35. Phillis Wheatley's exact birthdate is unknown.

36. Elizabeth Goodenough et al. claim that works written by children "effectively have dual authors" (4) given that it is "the adult editor or publisher, using criteria of which the child is unaware, who determines the final content of work written by children" (4).

37. Hart adapted his "Ladder of Children's Participation" from Sherry Arnstein's "Ladder of Citizen Participation."

38. In other words, the initial mimeographed publication seems to reach the highest rung of Hart's ladder—level 8, "Child-initiated, shared decisions with adults" (Hart 41)—with the young writers launching the idea for the publication and sharing leadership with the adult co-facilitators, while the print anthology "collected by" June Jordan and Terri Bush (THE VOICE of the Children title page) could be seen as positioned between level 5, "Consulted and informed" (where children "understand the process, are consulted, and have their opinions treated seriously," Hart 43) and level 6, "Adult-initiated, shared decisions with children" (where adults launch a project and children are "involved in some degree in the entire process," Hart 41, 44), since the young people were aware of the goals of the project and involved in decision making around the weekly publication, yet the adults initiated, carried out, and made editorial decisions for the book project.

39. Relevant here is Sharon Olds's discussion of what she terms "apparently personal poetry" in a 1993 interview with Laurel Blossom: "I would use the phrase 'apparently personal poetry' for the kind of poetry that I think people are referring to as 'confessional.' Apparently personal because how do we really know? We don't" (30).

40. For current discussions of poetry writing in elementary classrooms see, for example, Certo; Flint and Laman. See Jonna Perrillo for a discussion of the continuities and discontinuities in trends in teaching poetry writing since the early twentieth century.

41. For instance, Margaret Anne Doody discusses the older Austen's efforts, in order to gain her novels' publication, to tone down her earlier "ruthless and exuberant style of comic vision" (119); and Juliet McMaster in her recent book *Jane Austen, Young Author* considers "the discontinuities and the continuities" (2) between Austen's juvenilia and adult novels and attends to the "vigorous imagination, delight in language and its possibilities, and the zest and energy" (15) that characterizes Austen's juvenilia.

42. In her review of *The Child Writer*, Mavis Reimer points out that references to the authenticity of children's perspectives or productions—as in Alexander and McMaster's claim that "The child's expression of his or her own subjectivity is there and available for us" ("Introduction" 1)—are problematic outside of "a systematic interrogation . . . [of] the category of 'the child' " (282).

43. In addition, Katharine Kittridge accounts for the dozens of books by young writers that appeared in the late eighteenth and early nineteenth century by identifying converging factors of "the role of composition in contemporary education, the increasing number of periodicals being published, and the expanding market for poetry by nontraditional writers" (unpaginated). David Sadler writes of the commodification of young writers in the United States and United Kingdom during the 1920s, when publishing works by children that conformed to a "childlike" (28) image became "almost a fad" (24) after the publication in 1919 of Daisy Ashford's popular novel *The Young Visiters*. Cathryn Halverson extends this analysis in writing that adult readers would gauge "authenticity" in terms of "how well a text corresponds to their already formed notion of 'the child' " (243), including such qualities as spontaneity, closeness to nature, and primacy of sensory perception, especially in texts by girls.

44. The Stephen family's *Hyde Park Gate News* is available in a facsimile edition (Woolf et al.).

45. Karen Sánchez-Eppler, concluding her discussion of the Hale libraries, sees "children as participants in cultural formation, creatively deploying flotsam salvaged from the adult world" (451).

46. See Christine Alexander ("Play and Apprenticeship"); Katherine Dalsimer; and Karen Sánchez-Eppler for discussion of family publications.

47. See David Sadler's discussion.

48. Adults are also present as competition judges or coaches of slam teams. For further discussion of youth spoken word and slam poetry, see Ibrahim; and Muhammad and Gonzalez. Morrell and Duncan-Andrade focus specifically on Hip-Hop as a mode of literacy.

49. See also Coval.

50. Other writers on the power of spoken word poetry in the lives of urban youth include Maisha Fisher and Susan Weinstein.

51. Anthologies produced by teachers of young poets include those compiled by Lyne and Nye. Anthologies produced by youth writing programs include Writers-Corps' *Tell the World*; Youth Speaks' *My Words Consume Me*; and Get Lit's *Get Lit Rising* (Diane Luby Lane and the Get Lit Players). Anthologies of young people's writing produced through contests include the series of Scholastic anthologies subtitled "the best young writers and artists in America" (e.g., Levithan, editor, *What We Remember, What We Forget*) and the River of Words anthologies (e.g., Michael, editor, *River of Words: Young Poets and Artists on the Nature of Things*). And anthologies produced by editors of literary magazines include *Leave This*

Song Behind from *Teen Ink* (Stephanie H. Meyer et al.); the annual *Rattle Young Poets Anthology* (Green), which is the subject of chapter 4; and those produced by *Hanging Loose*, which notes in its most recent anthology that "since our very first issue"—in 1968—"we have been publishing work by high school students along-side that of adult writers" (Pawlak 9).

52. In Ashford's manuscript, each chapter consisted of a single paragraph, yet J. M. Barrie describes in his introduction that these were "subdivided for the reader's comfort" (xix).

53. In fact, Daisy Ashford's *The Young Visiters* engendered disputes over its authorship: J. M. Barrie, who wrote the introduction praising it as "a remarkable work for a child" (xviii–xix), was believed by some to have authored it himself, as McMaster ("What Daisy Knew") discusses.

54. Elsewhere I explore this in Brooks's adult-written poetry for adults (Conrad, *Children Coming Home*) and for children (Conrad, "And stay, a minute more, alone").

55. Reprinted by consent of Brooks Permissions.

56. Another youth-written poem, "Clock" by Robert Kimmel, which appears in Nye's edited anthology *Salting the Ocean* (the subject of chapter 3), resonates with Brooks's poem in its concern with the clock's present well-being ("Clock, you must be tired, / after all, you stay up all night").

57. See Judith Plotz for further discussion of Romantic representations of childhood.

58. This accords with research by Pernille Hviid showing that children can have complex perceptions of themselves as "both big and small" (188) in relation to cultural expectations of children's change over time.

59. Irish poet Seamus Heaney famously invoked the pen as a shovel in his poem "Digging" (published in his twenties in his first collection, *Death of a Naturalist*) in which he contrasts the metaphorical shovel the son uses to write with the actual "spade" his father and grandfather used in the garden or for cutting turf.

60. I am less convinced by Bernstein's idea that performing childhood is necessarily backward-looking in "restoring the half-remembered, imagined original" of the "ideals of childhood" (24). Conceptualizing childhood in a manner that leaves room for young people's agency in relation to time requires broadening our temporal frameworks and expectations.

61. Virginia Jackson's historical discussion of lyric poetry begins as follows: "In Western poetics, almost all poetry is now characterized as lyric, but this has not always been the case" (826). Vendler has very simply referred to lyric poems as "smaller kinds of relatively short poetry" (*Poems, Poets, Poetry* 111) in contrast to longer narrative and epic poems.

62. Bonnie Costello writes about lyric time in the poetry of Wallace Stevens and Robert Frost in a manner that recalls Cameron's "lyric compression of temporality": for Costello, Stevens "expresses lyric's longing to evade time's force" (73), and Frost includes among his different "models of time" (39) a "lyric time" that involves "denying time and calling us back to beginnings" (40), a temporal "completeness" (42). Christopher R. Miller, in writing about "the poetry of evening"

(1), offers "a set of qualifications" to Cameron's claims about lyric timelessness in his exploration of "how evening poetry registers increments and lapses of time" (7).

63. Though Baker suggests that the centrality of time to the lyric poem is due to a human "wish . . . to prevent time" and mortality (236), which seems to overlap with Cameron's view, he concludes by offering an expansive view of lyric temporality that has more in common with Vendler's ideas: "A poem intends not so much to stop time as, instead, to formulate a parallel universe with its own temporality" (Baker 246).

64. See also Barbara Herrnstein Smith.

65. Alongside work by English; Thomas Allen; Michael O'Malley; and Lloyd Pratt, *Time for Childhoods* adds to our growing scholarly understanding of American time by considering how the artistic work of young people participates in temporal discourses.

66. For instance, in English's reading of slave narratives such as Harriet Jacobs's *Incidents in the Life of a Slave Girl*, she discerns a layering of temporality or "accretive time" ("Race, Writing, and Time" 234) wherein one is not locked into a uniform timeline but "one can always imagine and access other, and possibly better, times" (236) that might afford more opportunities for agency. Notably, English uses "accretive time" to "connote *layers* of time" (234), "an expansive process" of formation of "human identity and its layers" (239), in contrast to "intersectionality," which "implies a point" (239). English's use of "accretive time" is influenced by Michelle Wright's work on blackness and nonlinear time in *Physics of Blackness,* which is briefly discussed in chapter 2.

67. By William Carlos Williams, from *The Autobiography of William Carlos Williams*, copyright © 1951 by William Carlos Williams. Reprinted by permission of New Directions Publishing Corp.

68. My discussion of Jordan's advocacy also highlights the committed engagement of educator Terri Bush, who collaborated with Jordan in co-constructing and co-mentoring The Voice of the Children workshop that I discuss in chapter 5.

69. One interesting project is Red Beard Press, which describes itself as "the nation's first youth-driven press" that "provide[s] a unique platform for youth to curate and publish work by both peers and well known authors." Red Beard Press, http://www.redbeardpress.org (accessed 12 Oct. 2018).

Chapter 2: "to bloom in its own time"

1. Many of the transcripts of these readings are available at Dickinson Electronic Archives, www.emilydickinson.org/titanic-operas/folio-one (accessed 20 July 2016).

2. My transcription from the audio-recording is slightly different from the transcription on the website ("Emily & I Are Absolutely Different").

3. Aurelia Davidson ("Age 12, Grade 7") is listed in a press release of Chicago radio station WBEZ as one of the 1980 "Elementary School" prizewinners for her poem

"Trapped"; the awards are erroneously called the "Gwendolyn Brooks Awards" (WBEZ).

4. See Nodelman and Reimer for a useful delineation of such adult assumptions about children and children's literature. See also Jack Meacham for a discussion of adults' metaphors for children's actions.

5. As mentioned in chapter 1, Brooks's poems were first published in the newspaper *Hyde Parker* when she was eleven years old, an experience that she said "really set me up" (Presson 139); her poem "Eventide" was published in the magazine *American Childhood* in 1930, when she was thirteen; and beginning at the age of sixteen, Brooks published seventy-five poems (as she recounts in a 1967 interview with Roy Newquist 27) in the weekly "Lights and Shadows" column in the *Chicago Defender*, the influential newspaper that "played a powerful role in the Black Chicago Renaissance" (MacAustin 57).

6. The appearance on the notepaper's reverse side of a poem by another young poet, Ebony Tillman, a 1978 Illinois Poet Laureate prizewinner, suggests that Brooks may have been on her way to a reading other than the 1986 event at Seton Hall, where she read Davidson's poem but not Tillman's.

7. The spacing in Brooks's handwritten transcription of this seventeen-line poem could be read as indicating a stanzaic structure of couplets with a central single-line stanza. However, given that this stanzaic structure is not certain, and I did not locate an original typescript of Davidson's poem, I do not reprint such stanza breaks here. It is also not clear whether the full capitalizations in lines 4, 9, and 16 and underscoring in line 11 were present in Davidson's original poem or were added by Brooks as prompts for her public recitation of the poem.

8. There is interesting resonance here with James Weldon Johnson's "Lift Every Voice and Sing," which includes the lines "We have come . . . / Out from the gloomy past." Thanks to L. Brown Kennedy for this suggestion.

9. The website of the Illinois State Office discusses Brooks's use of poetry as both "social and aesthetic" in engaging with communities including "under-served areas of Chicago," and as "heartily encourag[ing] young writers to lend their voices to poetry communities" given that, for Brooks, poetry was "a personal way to make something beautiful that also possesses communal value" (Illinois State Office).

10. On the centenary of Gwendolyn Brooks's birth in 2017, Illinois Humanities in partnership with the Poetry Foundation "revitalize[d]" the prize, open to "young people" of elementary and high school age, and titled it the "Gwendolyn Brooks Youth Poetry Awards." Interestingly, Illinois Humanities does not acknowledge the original name of the award in recounting its history. Illinois Humanities, www .ilhumanities.org/program/gwendolyn-brooks-youth-poetry-awards/ (accessed 3 Sept. 2018).

11. For this inaugural contest, the rules stipulated that entrants could submit only a single poem of thirty lines or less, and the Illinois Arts Council facilitated collection of the entries ("About writers and writing").

12. In a 1984 self-interview in *TriQuarterly*, in which she formulated her own questions, Brooks asked herself "Talk about the Poet Laureate Awards" and responded that after being appointed poet laureate of Illinois, she launched the awards because "I wanted to substantiate the honor with assistance to the young" ("Interview" 408). In 1999 she was honored by Illinois' Cook County Juvenile Court for her work on behalf of Cook County's children (Krebs).

13. See Ann Barzel on behalf of the Illinois Arts Council.

14. Although Brooks initially received funding from the Illinois Arts Council to support this annual contest, she retained control over the process and outcomes of the contest, and it appears that she eventually had to absorb the cost of the awards themselves, though the award ceremony and luncheon continued to be hosted by the University of Chicago. D. J. R. Bruckner notes that Brooks did a great deal more than just sponsor this contest: "She solicits all the entries, judges them and pays a cash award to each winner out of her own pocket." Her daughter Nora Brooks Blakely recounts the outcome of Brooks's judging the contest: "She had three bags—one for yes, no and maybe" (Kantzavelos).

15. On July 7, 1980, Brooks received a letter from Charles W. Beirne, staff assistant at the Bureau of Telecommunications and Broadcasting, about a broadcast of the poetry award ceremony on WBEZ FM, and he asked, "Do you have any objection to my publishing the award winning entries in the all school creative writing anthology of the Chicago Public Schools?" Running down the right-hand margin of this letter in blue pen is Brooks's handwritten reply: "No, I won't allow any anthologizing until I have brought out 'Poet Laureate Awards—Illinois' (consisting of selections from my 11 years of awards)—G. Brooks" (note on letter from Charles W. Beirne).

16. In a letter dated September 16, 1980, to Robert Rosenthal, curator at the Joseph Regenstein Library at the University of Chicago, D. J. R. Bruckner, the university's Vice-President for Public Affairs, mentioned that the winning Illinois Poet Laureate Award poems were collected at the University of Chicago library and that he contemplated producing an anthology: "And each year I have sent the signed poems to the library, for our collections. Some day I hope we can make a book out of them."

17. In honor of Brooks's seventieth birthday, she also gave awards to adult poets, including Walter Bradford, Haki Madhubuti, Eugene Redmond, and Carolyn Rodgers (Melhem, "Afterword" 262). Her solicitation notice for the 1987 Poet Laureate Awards, the eighteenth awarded, make the parameters of the award clear. The contest was "open to all Illinois high school and elementary school students," and Brooks stipulated that entries must be short poems, "sixteen lines or less," and "Rhyme is permissible, but not required." Winners won a monetary award and were invited to read their poem and attend a celebratory luncheon with their parents at the University of Chicago: "Twenty $50.00 prizes will be awarded: ten prizes for elementary school students, and ten prizes for high school students.

Winners will read their work during a ceremony at the University of Chicago, June 7th, 1987. This is a special celebration honoring the student winners, major Illinois writers, and Ms. Brooks' 70th birthday!" (Brooks, solicitation notice).

18. All text in the original is capitalized (Brooks, "Mailgram").

19. These notes were written on the reverse side of an order form for David Company, Gwendolyn Brooks's own book imprint—named in honor of her father David Brooks (Melhem, "Afterword" 261)—and lists her collected poems BLACKS as "available February, 1987," which provides an approximate date for the notes.

20. Brooks might have had Davidson's and Tillman's poems in mind; these notes were archived in the same folder as their poems.

21. Brooks's lecture notes are handwritten on the reverse side of a typed reminder giving details about the event. The typed form lists the lecture title as "Poetry and the Education of Children: How to Use Poetry With Students."

22. The website of the Academy of American Poets has an extensive set of poems for children (in addition to lesson plans and resources for teachers), yet it focuses exclusively on poetry written by adults for children. Academy of American Poets, www.poets.org/poems-kids (accessed 26 May 2019).

23. The youth writing workshop The Voice of the Children co-facilitated by June Jordan and Terri Bush did produce such a regular publication with editorial and managerial positions, as I discuss in chapter 5.

24. Exceptions are "I Am in a Trap" by Janet Docka and the poems included in letters discussed at the end of the chapter.

25. Among the seven poems from the Brooks archives in the Bancroft Library discussed in this chapter, four appear at least twice: "Things" by Moral Thirus, "Baby Days" by Belinda, "When I Was Small" by Karen Cox, and "[My city]" by Ebony Tillman. These four plus "Trapped" by Aurelia Davidson passed through Brooks's hand either through her handwriting them or (ostensibly) typing them over. Brooks's handwriting is distinctive and easy to recognize, and the retyped poems I discuss often include notes in Brooks's hand (e.g., the retyped copy of "Things" has the author's name written beneath the poem in Brooks's hand; "When I Was Small" includes a note in a first-person voice.

26. Contests began at Burnside and Cornell Elementary Schools, and by 1967, Brooks had sponsored contests in two elementary and two high schools, as she indicated in an interview with Paul Angle, though she chose to have teachers judge these early contests rather than judge them herself.

27. For example, teachers are listed as the contest judges in the Burnside Poetry Contest program.

28. Burnside "Primary Winners"; Cornell Excerpts; Burnside Poems.

29. Ricardo Sims's footnote, which refers to the first line of his poem "The Day of Thanks"—"Many people think of it as food and fest,* / But you and I know the rest"—reads in its entirety: "*fest, n.- to feast (now obsolete)."

30. The interview begins as follows: "QUESTION: Why are you interviewing yourself? GB: Because I know the facts and the nuances" (Brooks, "Interview" 405).

31. Brooks initially wrote the parenthetical final sentence in the present tense—"I know a boy who feels that even <u>death</u> is a part of <u>distillable Life</u>! Says Moral Thirus:"—and subsequently changed it to past tense and added "13 year old," as her corrections in heavy pen markings indicate. This amendment correctly locates Moral Thirus as a thirteen-year-old person in the past, since that was his age in 1963–64, when he entered the contest. In the preceding list, another correction involved replacing "Stokely Carmichael" with "Malcolm X" (Brooks, "Carl Sandburg").

32. This coincides with the time period, discussed earlier in the chapter, that Brooks referred to as "the kindergarten of my new consciousness" (*Report* 86).

33. Moral Thirus's "Things" (author's name handwritten) is archived with other Cornell Elementary School poems from the 1963–64 contest. The other copy of "Things" (typescript) and "Death" are archived in a folder labeled "Gwendolyn Brooks Poetry Contest—High Schools 1965–1976; n.d." but are in similar typescript and format as other poems from the 1963–64 Cornell contest, and "Things" is dated 1964 by Brooks (*Report* 209).

34. The retyped version of "Things" (author's name handwritten) also adds a period at the end of the poem's opening line.

35. "Things" by Moral Thirus is reprinted in the excerpt from Brooks's "Report from Part One" in *Black World* (7–8) and in *Report from Part One* (208), without stanza breaks.

36. Lillian Myricks's poem "Freedom" also appears (twice) in the Gwendolyn Brooks Papers in The Bancroft Library at the University of California at Berkeley, along with other poems from Cornell Elementary School from 1963–64 (box 4, folder 2 and box 11, folder 31). In *Report*, Brooks prints her last name as "Myrick" (208).

37. Thus, the appearance of Moral Thirus's poem "Things" in Brooks's *Report from Part One* confirms my deduction that Brooks had read "Things" at the lecture whose notes are discussed at the outset of this section.

38. Belinda's last name is not recorded in Brooks's notes. See note below.

39. "When I Was Small" appears in a handwritten set of notes (not in Brooks's hand) with the poem bracketed in pen and "Quote entire" in Brooks's hand appearing outside the bracket. "Baby Days" also appears in that handwritten set of notes, with only the first four lines circled with "Quote" marked in the left margin in Brooks's hand. Both poems additionally appear in a typed set of notes—typed "(Burnside)" at the bottom of each page—most likely typed by Brooks herself and indicating her own selections. In the typed notes, Brooks includes the entire poem "Baby Days" (marked in the handwritten notes as one of the "Primary Winners") with a typed note underneath the poet's first name: "(I'll get her last name from the principal.)."

40. Karen Cox is listed as reciting her work at the poetry contest event at the Burnside School on May 28, 1964, whereas Belinda (the youngest participant) is not listed (Burnside Poetry Contest program).

41. In the Gwendolyn Brooks Papers in The Bancroft Library, "I Am in a Trap" appears on page 11 of a stapled booklet of prizewinning poems from the "Fourth

Annual Poet Laureate Awards 1973." Janet Docka was a sixteen-year-old high school student when she wrote the poem (e-mail message to the author).

42. Indeed, Brooks may have regularly given these booklets to young poets. A note on a poem sent to Brooks by Randy Wilkins indicates, in Brooks's hand, "Send 'Young Poets Primer, etc.'" (Gwendolyn Brooks Papers, BANC MSS 2001/83 z, The Bancroft Library, U of California Berkeley, box 11, folder 32).

43. While Sara Schwebel argues that children's letters to authors "do not reveal . . . children's agency" (282), I think even letters produced in classrooms or other organized contexts can indicate children's ideas and impressions of a text or author, as I demonstrate in this section.

44. While a common editorial practice would involve inserting [sic] following words that do not conform to standard spelling, as a practice of respect for the artistry of the young poets that I discuss, I do not "correct" their spelling. As I mention in chapter 1, spelling is a contentious issue in young people's writing and publication.

45. See previous note.

Chapter 3: "My future doesn't know / ME"

1. Unfortunately the anthology is out of print.

2. The book's copyright page indicates, "The individual poets represented in this volume hold the copyrights to their poems."

3. An argument in favor of including ages is that it makes it easier for young readers to identify with the poets. For instance, in a workshop that students in my college class conducted with elementary school–aged people, after the college students announced that the poem they recited was written by a person who was eight years old, one participant announced "I'm eight years old!"

4. I refer to all adults who select or gather young people's poems as editors for ease of reference.

5. Such an attempt to indicate the geographic and demographic location and reach of an anthology helps readers judge how inclusive an anthology is likely to be across dimensions such as race and class. When an anthology provides no such indication of its scope or practices in soliciting participation (e.g., Meyer et al., *Leave This Song Behind*), it is difficult to gauge its inclusiveness.

6. Even without thematic sections, though, editors are of course deciding how to position poems in relation to one another across a volume.

7. Occasionally a "formerly young" poet will provide an essay that frames an anthology, e.g., Fuhrman's "Still at It: Notes from a Former Teen Poet," which appears as an afterword to Pawlak et al., *When We Were Countries*.

8. Another exception is the decision by June Jordan and Terri Bush to position young poet Vanessa Howard's prose poem "Ghetto" as the foreword to the anthology *THE VOICE of the Children*, and Vanessa Howard's own preface to her solo volume *A Screaming Whisper*, both discussed in chapter 5.

9. See Mayall for a relevant discussion of children and "free time."

10. I do not take up questions of poets' "reputation" or judgments of "quality" that some readers might bring to these poems. Instead, I point out the irony and injustice of the attention to Nye's poem given that it was inspired by the poem by Afshar, Jr.

11. Reviewed by Sabrina, Module 6 Poetry by Kids, 6 May 2013, reviewedbysabrina .blogspot.com/2013/05/poetry-ls5663-module-6-poetry-by-kids.html (accessed 15 February 2018).

Chapter 4: "My sole desire is to move someone through poetry, and allow for my voice to be heard"

1. Quotations from contributors' notes and poems from the *Rattle Young Poets Anthology* are included by permission of the poets and their parents, with the exception of Christell Victoria Roach, the author of the note used in the title of this essay, whose family could not be reached.

2. See also Erica Burman ("Local, Global or Globalized?") and Jo Boyden. Sarada Balagopalan provides a valuable perspective on current predicaments concerning critical conceptualization and mobilization on the rights of children in majority and minority worlds.

3. See Gerison Lansdown; and Didier Reynaert et al.

4. Again, by "children," I mean people under the age of eighteen, as defined in the United Nations CRC ("Convention").

5. As mentioned in chapter 1, Victoria Ford Smith offers compelling consideration of this issue in her work on artistic collaborations between children and adults in the United Kingdom during the nineteenth and early twentieth century.

6. While guidelines for the 2014 *Rattle Young Poets Anthology* stipulated, "Poems must be submitted by a parent or legal guardian. We would be happy to have teachers encourage their students to submit work, but the submission itself must come from a parent" (Green 88), guidelines for subsequent volumes (Rattle Foundation, www.rattle.com/children/guidelines/, accessed 28 Apr. 2015) permit teachers to submit their students' work as long as they can guarantee parental permission for publication.

7. For instance, Article 12 of the CRC indicates that "the views of the child [will be] given due weight in accordance with the age and maturity of the child" ("Convention").

8. Developmental psychologist Deanna Kuhn discusses children's "metacognition," their knowing about knowing, and how this awareness "comes to operate increasingly under the individual's conscious control" (178).

9. E-mail correspondence, 29 Sept. 2015. Katie Bickell later reflected on her own choices in transcription: "Perhaps I should have written the poem just as it was spoken: running on, perhaps no breaks or punctuation whatsoever except where obvious in the full stops of her speech. That may have been more honest, in a way. There is so much to consider about transcribing and publishing children's work that I hadn't considered until now" (e-mail correspondence, 2 Oct. 2015).

10. E-mail correspondence, 29 Sept. 2015; 2 Oct. 2015.

11. Years ago, while attending a poetry event at my children's elementary school in which the young people had been invited to recite a poem they had either read in a book or written themselves, I was struck by the word another child used in asking my son whether he was going to read a poem he had "made," which carries resonance of craft and shaping by hand.

12. All quotations from Shawna Foster are from e-mail correspondence, 30 Sept. 2017.

Chapter 5: "We Speak to Be Heard"

1. Terri Bush, interview with the author, 6 June, 2017, New York, NY.

2. The poem was later reprinted in the 1969 collection *Here I Am!* edited by Virginia Olsen Baron. Copyright for all poems in *THE VOICE of the Children* anthology was registered by The Voice of the Children, Inc.

3. Reprinted by permission of Christopher Meyer. The lineation is slightly different in the version of the poem in the Teachers College *Record*, January 1969, vol. 70, no. 4, 359.

4. Capitalization and punctuation are slightly different in the version of this poem published in *Soulscript*. Glen Thompson is identified as "Age 13" in *THE VOICE of the Children*.

5. Vanessa Howard's poem "Truly My Own," which I also discuss later in this chapter, appears in the anthology's final section titled "Very Personal."

6. See the discussion of Kali Grosvenor in chapter 1; also see Christine Alexander, "Defining and Representing Literary Juvenilia."

7. Roger Hart's "Ladder of Children's Participation," discussed in chapter 1, provides a useful way of characterizing youth leadership and youth-adult collaboration, including planning and decision making, in projects involving adults and young people.

8. A couple of years following the publication of *THE VOICE of the Children*, the notion of "afterword" takes on additional resonance for Jordan with *Dry Victories*—her 1972 book for a young audience that she wrote in Black English, including the prefatory "Note to the Readers" (viii)—after the publisher requested that she include "An Afterword" in Standard English: "This whole book," she writes, "is an 'afterword.' It is written *after* the Civil War, *after* the Reconstruction Era, *after* the Civil Rights' Era, *after* the assassination of Malcolm X, the Kennedys, Dr. King, little girls in a Birmingham Sunday School, and *after* the assassination of countless hopes and acts of faith" (75).

9. In essays Jordan wrote in the early 1970s (such as those combined in "White English/Black English: The Politics of Translation"), she writes about the politics of language and race that black children must negotiate, particularly in schools: "*White power uses white English as a calculated, political display of power to control and eliminate the powerless.* . . . School, compulsory public school education, is the process whereby Black children first encounter the punishing force of this white

power" (65, emphasis in original). She argues for the value of Black English and literature alongside "standard" English and literature, in order to preserve "this carrier of Black-survivor consciousness" (69) with its qualities of emotion, identity, shared history, and collective memory.

10. The workshop received enough attention that June Jordan wrote a letter to "Visitors and Adult Friends of the Children" dated "1969–70" in which she requested that adult visitors to the workshop limit their conversation, not discuss the children in their presence, respect the privacy of the children by "not attempt[ing] to 'look over the shoulder' of children while they are writing," and avoid "Criticism of the children's writings" since "It is the workshop policy that children's writings are not subject to adult 'correction'" while "on the other hand, excessive praise can discomfort children and impeded their willing exploration of potentiality" (Jordan, "Visitors and Adult Friends of the Children").

11. A number of other anthologies of young people's writing appeared in the early 1970s, often in association with community-engaged projects, such as Herbert Kohl and Victor Hernández Cruz, editors, *Stuff: A Collection of Poems, Visions, & Imaginative Happenings from Young Writers in Schools*; and Irving Benig, editor, *The Children: Poems and Prose from Bedford-Stuyvesant*.

12. Richard Flynn has noted the cross-purposes in Koch's project between his goals of supporting children's writing and his prioritizing of his own actions and emotions. Flynn finds in Koch's words an "unspoken conflict between competing aims—the stated goals of empowering children as writers go hand-in-hand with nostalgic, adult impulses to romanticize childhood" ("Can Children's Poetry Matter?" 38).

13. Mark Nowak and Timothy Gray each refer to the attention Koch received for his approach at that time compared to other poets teaching in schools.

14. *THE VOICE of the Children* also received positive reviews at the time, including Eve Merriam's review in the *New York Times* and "Voice of the Children Is Poignant Cry for Love and Understanding," though most reviews, including Merriam's, consist mainly of quoting from the young contributors' work, and others characterize the young writers using terms such as "ghetto kids" (Hulett) that the young writers themselves explicitly critique or reject (see the discussion of Vanessa Howard's "Ghetto" later in the chapter).

15. This is evident, for example, in Valerie Kinloch's account of June Jordan's lifelong advocacy for children.

16. See Muller et al. for accounts of the history and goals of Poetry for the People, and Jocson for its continuing resonance.

17. Correspondence between June Jordan and editor Milton Meltzer, a prolific white writer of nonfiction books for young audiences with whom Jordan had worked on *Who Look At Me*, her first book for a young audience, makes clear that *Soulscript* was aimed at school-aged children (e.g., letter dated 22 Jan. 1969, from Meltzer to June Meyer [Jordan]).

18. Meltzer, who along with Loretta Barrett at Doubleday served as co-editor for *Soulscript*, had asked Jordan to reduce the number of poems by young people:

"Breaking it down by section, you have 19 poems in Part I, where the kids speak. It's more than in any other section. We like very much your way of opening the book with this. But isn't 19 out of balance? . . . Could you cut the total to about 10 poems? Perhaps by letting no one have more than one poem, or dropping the poorer?" Letter dated 22 Jan. 1969, from Milton Meltzer to June Meyer [Jordan].

19. Letter dated 28 Jan. 1969, from June Meyer [Jordan] to Milton Meltzer.

20. In the published version of *Soulscript*, there are fifteen poems by nine young poets (compared with the draft version's nineteen poems by eleven young poets), clearly the result of Jordan's tenacity in attempting to "hold for all the poems of the children." In the 2004 reprint of *Soulscript*, one poem is omitted.

21. Page numbers refer to the original 1970 edition of *Soulscript*.

22. "Monument in Black" is the only poem from The Voice of the Children workshop that appears in *My Black Me*; the only other young poet featured in that anthology is Kali Grosvenor, whose work is briefly discussed in chapter 1.

Conclusion: "Poems are voiceprints of language"

1. See discussion of the work of Cameron in chapter 1.

2. In Einstein's (1905) theory of special relativity, time intersects dynamically with spatial dimensions. See Galison for a clear discussion of the development of Einstein's views on relativity. See also Gravity Probe B.

3. See Emmanuelle Tulle.

Works Cited

Abdullah, Thandiwe. "What This Black Lives Matter Teen Activist Thinks Never Again MSD Misses about the Gun Debate." *Bustle*, 24 Mar. 2018, www.bustle.com/p/what-this-black-lives-matter-teen-activist-thinks-never -again-msd-misses-about-the-gun-debate-8587893. Accessed 30 Oct. 2018.

Abebe, Tatek. "Interdependent Rights and Agency: The Role of Children in Collective Livelihood Strategies in Rural Ethiopia." Hanson and Nieuwenhuys, *Reconceptualising Children's Rights in International Development*, 71–92.

"About writers and writing." *Negro Digest*, vol. 19, no. 1, Nov. 1969, 97.

Adam, Barbara. *Timewatch: The Social Analysis of Time*. Polity, 1995.

Adoff, Arnold. *My Black Me: A Beginning Book of Black Poetry*. Dutton, 1974.

Afshar, Jamshid, Jr. "Roller-Skate!" Nye, *Salting the Ocean*, 97.

Alexander, Christine. "Defining and Representing Literary Juvenilia." Alexander and McMaster, *Child Writer*, 70–97.

———. "In Search of Juvenilia: A Survey of the Birth, Childhood and Growth of a New Genre." Owen and Peterson, *Home and Away*, 2–25.

———. "Play and Apprenticeship: The Culture of Family Magazines." Alexander and McMaster, *Child Writer*, 31–50.

Alexander, Christine, and Juliet McMaster, editors. *The Child Writer from Austen to Woolf*. Cambridge UP, 2005.

———. "Introduction." Alexander and McMaster, *Child Writer*, 1–7.

Allen, Thomas M. *A Republic in Time: Temporality and Social Imagination in Nineteenth-Century America*. U of North Carolina P, 2008.

American Library Association. Coretta Scott King Book Awards. www.ala.org /emiert/coretta-scott-king-book-awards-all-recipients-1970-present. Accessed 16 June 2017.

Angle, Paul. "An Interview with Gwendolyn Brooks." 1967. Gayles, *Conversations with Gwendolyn Brooks*, 13–25.

Arnstein, Sherry R. "A Ladder of Citizen Participation." *Journal of the American Planning Association*, vol. 35, no. 4, 1969, 216–24.

Ashford, Daisy. *The Young Visiters or, Mr. Salteena's Plan*. George H. Doran Company, 1919.

Austen, Jane. *Love and Freindship: and Other Youthful Writings*. Penguin, 2016.

Baker, David. "To Think of Time." *Radiant Lyre: Essays on Lyric Poetry*, edited by David Baker and Ann Townsend, Graywolf Press, 2007, 235–46.

Balagopalan, Sarada. "Childhood, Culture, History: Redeploying 'Multiple Childhoods.'" *Reimagining Childhood Studies*, edited by Spyros Spyrou et al., Bloomsbury, 2019, 23–39.

Baron, Virginia Olsen, editor. *Here I Am!* Dutton, 1969.

Barrie, J. M. Preface. Ashford, *Young Visiters*, vii–xix.

Barth, Kelly. "Poetry *Is* the Life of Gwendolyn Brooks." *Bluefield (WV) Daily Telegraph*, vol. 90, no. 67, 8 Mar. 1985, A1–A2.

Barzel, Ann. Letter to Gwendolyn Brooks. 12 Apr. 1971. Gwendolyn Brooks Papers, BANC MSS 2001/83 z, The Bancroft Library, U of California, Berkeley, box 4, folder 17.

Beck, Jane C. *Daisy Turner's Kin: An African American Family Saga*. U of Illinois P, 2015.

Beirne, Charles W. Letter to Gwendolyn Brooks. 7 July 1980. Gwendolyn Brooks Papers, BANC MSS 2001/83 z, The Bancroft Library, U of California, Berkeley, box 4, folder 17.

Belinda [last name unknown]. "Baby Days." Gwendolyn Brooks Papers, BANC MSS 2001/83 z, The Bancroft Library, U of California, Berkeley, box 11, folder 31.

Belinda [last name unknown]. "Baby Days." Gwendolyn Brooks Papers, BANC MSS 2001/83 z, The Bancroft Library, U of California, Berkeley, box 11, folder 31. Manuscript.

Benig, Irving, editor. *The Children: Poems and Prose from Bedford-Stuyvesant*. Grove Press, 1971.

Bernstein, Robin. *Racial Innocence: Performing American Childhood from Slavery to Civil Rights*. New York UP, 2011.

Berry, Deborah. "Gwendolyn Brooks." Apr. 1973. Gwendolyn Brooks Papers, BANC MSS 2001/83 z, The Bancroft Library, U of California, Berkeley, box 11, folder 23.

Bezner, Kevin. "A Life Distilled: An Interview with Gwendolyn Brooks." 1986. Gayles, *Conversations with Gwendolyn Brooks*, 117–24.

Bhabha, Homi K. *The Location of Culture*. Routledge, 1994.

Bickell, Cailena. "Contributor Note." Green, *Rattle Young Poets Anthology*, 81.

———. "Don't Worry, Mom, Don't Panic." Green, *Rattle Young Poets Anthology*, 10–12.

Bickell, Katie. "Cailena Bickell's Rattle Poem." Received by Rachel Conrad, 29 Sept. 2015.

———."Cailena's mother's super long response." Received by Rachel Conrad, 30 Sept. 2015.

———. "Re: Cailena's mother's super long response." Received by Rachel Conrad, 2 Oct. 2015.

Blake, Jamilia J., et al.. "The Role of Colorism in Explaining African American Females' Suspension Risk." *School Psychology Quarterly*, vol. 32, no. 1, 2017, 118–30.

Bloom, Harold. *The Anxiety of Influence: A Theory of Poetry*. 1973. 2nd ed., Oxford UP, 1997.

Blossom, Laurel. "Sharon Olds: An Interview." *Poets and Writers*, Sept./Oct. 1993, 30–32.

Bluebond-Langner, Myra. *The Private Worlds of Dying Children*. Princeton UP, 1978.

Blum, Virginia. *Hide and Seek: The Child between Psychoanalysis and Fiction*. U of Illinois P, 1995.

Bond, Kanisha, et al. "Did You Attend the March for Our Lives? Here's What It Looked Like Nationwide." *Washington Post*, 13 Apr. 2018.

Bourdieu, Pierre. *The Logic of Practice*. 1980. Translated by Richard Nice, Stanford UP, 1990.

Boyden, Jo. "Childhood and the Policy Makers: A Comparative Perspective on the Globalization of Childhood." James and Prout, *Constructing and Reconstructing Childhood*, 2nd ed., 190–229.

Brannen, Julia. "Childhoods across the Generations: Stories from Women in Four-Generation English Families." *Childhood*, vol. 11, no. 4, 2004, 409–28.

Brewbaker, James, and Dawnelle J. Hyland, editors. *Poems by Adolescents and Adults: A Thematic Collection for Middle School and High School*. Urbana: National Council of Teachers of English, 2002.

Brooks, Gwendolyn. *Annie Allen*. Harper, 1949.

———. "The Busy Clock." Brooks, *Report from Part One*, 56.

———. "Carl Sandburg, my predecessor as Poet Laureate of Illinois." Lecture notes, n.d. Gwendolyn Brooks Papers, BANC MSS 2001/83 z, The Bancroft Library, U of California, Berkeley, box 3, folder 48. Manuscript.

———. Congratulatory note. n.d. Gwendolyn Brooks Papers, BANC MSS 2001/83 z, The Bancroft Library, U of California, Berkeley, box 3, folder 56.

———. "Emily & I Are Absolutely Different In The Details Of Our Lives." Dickinson Electronic Archives, www.emilydickinson.org/titanic-operas/folio-one/gwendolyn-brooks. Accessed 20 July 2016.

———. "Fourth Annual Poet Laureate Awards, 1973." Prefatory note. Gwendolyn Brooks Papers, BANC MSS 2001/83 z, The Bancroft Library, U of California, Berkeley, box 4, folder 18.

———. "Interview." *TriQuarterly* 60, 1984, 405–10.

———. Mailgram. 30 May 1983. Gwendolyn Brooks Papers, BANC MSS 2001/83 z, The Bancroft Library, U of California, Berkeley, box 4, folder 17.

———. *The Near-Johannesburg Boy and Other Poems*. Third World Press, 1986.

———. Note on letter from Charles W. Beirne. 7 July 1980. Gwendolyn Brooks

Papers, BANC MSS 2001/83 z, The Bancroft Library, U of California, Berkeley, box 4, folder 17. Manuscript.

———. "Poetry And The Educating of Children. How To Use Poetry With Students." Lecture at the Independent School Association of Central States, Nov. 1987. Gwendolyn Brooks Papers, BANC MSS 2001/83 z, The Bancroft Library, U of California, Berkeley, box 3, folder 45. Manuscript.

———. *Report from Part One.* Broadside, 1972.

———. "Report from Part One: An Excerpt from the Autobiography of Gwendolyn Brooks." *Black World,* vol. 21, no. 11, Sept. 1972, 4–13.

———. Solicitation notice for 18th Annual Poet Laureate Awards, 1987. Gwendolyn Brooks Papers, BANC MSS 2001/83 z, The Bancroft Library, U of California, Berkeley, box 4, folder 17.

———. *Very Young Poets.* Third World Press, 1983.

———. "Young people across the country are writing poetry." Lecture notes, n.d. Gwendolyn Brooks Papers, BANC MSS 2001/83 z, The Bancroft Library, U of California, Berkeley, box 11, folder 32. Manuscript.

———. *Young Poet's Primer.* Brooks Press, 1980.

Bruckner, D. J. R. Letter to Robert Rosenthal. 16 Sept. 1980. Gwendolyn Brooks Papers, BANC MSS 2001/83 z, The Bancroft Library, U of California, Berkeley, box 4, folder 17.

Bryan, Ashley, illustrator. *Ashley Bryan's ABC of African American Poetry.* Atheneum, 1997.

———, illustrator. *Sail Away: Poems by Langston Hughes.* Atheneum, 2015.

Burman, Erica. *Deconstructing Developmental Psychology.* Routledge, 1994.

———. "Local, Global or Globalized? Child Development and International Child Rights Legislation." *Childhood,* vol. 3, no. 1, 1996, 45–66.

Burnside Elementary School. "Primary Winners." 1964. Gwendolyn Brooks Papers, BANC MSS 2001/83 z, The Bancroft Library, U of California, Berkeley, box 11, folder 31.

Burnside Poems. Burnside Elementary School, 1964. Gwendolyn Brooks Papers, BANC MSS 2001/83 z, The Bancroft Library, U of California, Berkeley, box 11, folder 31.

Burnside Poetry Contest program. 28 May 1964. Gwendolyn Brooks Papers, BANC MSS 2001/83 z, The Bancroft Library, U of California, Berkeley, box 4, folder 25.

Bush, Terri. Personal interview. 6 June 2017. New York, NY.

———. "Introduction." "Selections from *The Voice of the Children.*" *Record,* Teachers College, Columbia U, vol. 70, no. 4, 1969, 353–59.

Cameron, Sharon. *Lyric Time: Dickinson and the Limits of Genre.* Johns Hopkins UP, 1979.

Candlish, Theo. "When People Leave This Earth." Green, *Rattle Young Poets Anthology,* 16.

Cannella, Gaile S., and Lourdes Diaz Soto, editors. *Childhoods: A Handbook.* Peter Lang, 2010.

Capshaw, Katharine. *Civil Rights Childhood: Picturing Liberation in African American Photobooks*. U of Minneapolis P, 2014.

Certo, Janine. "Poetic Language, Interdiscursivity and Intertextuality in Fifth Graders' Poetry: An Interpretive Study." *Journal of Literacy Research*, vol. 47, no. 1, 2015, 49–82.

Césaire, Aimé. "Poetry and Knowledge." *Lyric and Dramatic Poetry, 1946–1982.* Translated by A. James Arnold, UP of Virginia, 1990, xlii–lvi.

Christensen, Pia. "Why More 'Quality Time' Is Not on the Top of Children's Lists: The 'Qualities of Time' for Children." *Children and Society*, vol. 16, 2002, 77–88.

Christensen, Pia, and Allison James. "What Are Schools For: The Temporal Experience of Learning." *Conceptualising Child-Adult Relations*, edited by Leena Alanen and Berry Mayall, Routledge, 2001, 70–85.

Clarke, Cheryl. *"After Mecca': Women Poets and the Black Arts Movement*. Rutgers UP, 2005.

Collins, Bill. "[When I used to go to the beach]." Nye, *Salting the Ocean*, 66.

Committee on the Rights of the Child. "General Comment No. 12: The Right of the Child to Be Heard." *Office of the High Commissioner for Human Rights*, United Nations Human Rights, 20 July 2009, www2.ohchr.org/english/bo dies/crc/docs/AdvanceVersions/CRC-C-GC-12.pdf. Accessed 13 Apr. 2015.

———. "General Comment No. 17: On the Right of the Child to Rest, Leisure, Play, Recreational Activities, Cultural Life and the Arts (Art. 31)." *Office of the High Commissioner for Human Rights*, United Nations Human Rights, 17 Apr. 2013, tbinternet.ohchr.org/_layouts/15/treatybodyexternal/Download. aspx?symbolno=CRC%2fC%2fGC%2f17&Lang=en. Accessed 23 May 2019.

Conkling, Hilda. *Poems by a Little Girl*. Frederick A. Stokes, 1920.

Conrad, Rachel. "'And stay, a minute more, alone': Time and Subjectivities in Gwendolyn Brooks's *Bronzeville Boys and Girls*." *Children's Literature Association Quarterly*, vol. 38, no. 4, 2013, 379–98.

———. "Baby's Darwin and Darwin's Baby: Mutual Recognition in Observational Research." *Human Development*, vol. 41, 1998, 47–64.

———. *Children Coming Home*: The Anticipatory Present in Gwendolyn Brooks's Poems of Childhood. *Callaloo: Journal of African Diaspora Arts and Letters*, vol. 37, no. 2, 2014, 369–88.

———. "Children's Right to Write: Young People's Participation as Producers of Children's Literature." *Handbook of Children's Rights: Global and Multidisciplinary Perspectives*, edited by Martin D. Ruck et al., Taylor and Francis, 2017, 481–97.

"Convention on the Rights of the Child." United Nations Human Rights, Office of the High Commissioner for Human Rights, 20 Nov. 1989, www.ohchr .org/en/professionalinterest/pages/crc.aspx. Accessed 13 Apr. 2015.

Cook-Gumperz, Jenny. "Children's Construction of Childness." *Play and the Social Context of Development in Early Care and Education*, edited by Barbara Scales et al., Teachers College Press, 1991, 207–18.

Cornell Excerpts. Cornell Elementary School. Gwendolyn Brooks Papers, BANC MSS 2001/83 z, The Bancroft Library, U of California, Berkeley, box 11, folder 31.

Corsaro, William. *We're Friends, Right? Inside Kids' Culture.* Joseph Henry Press, 2003.

Costello, Bonnie. *Shifting Ground: Reinventing Landscape in Modern American Poetry.* Harvard UP, 2003.

Coval, Kevin. "Louder Than a Bomb: The Chicago Teen Poetry Festival and the Voices That Challenge and Change the Pedagogy of Class(room), Poetics, Place, and Space." *Handbook of Public Pedagogy: Education and Learning Beyond Schooling*, edited by Jennifer A. Sandlin et al., Routledge, 2010, 395–408.

Cox, Karen. "When I Was Small." Gwendolyn Brooks Papers, BANC MSS 2001 /83 z, The Bancroft Library, U of California, Berkeley, box 11, folder 31.

———. "When I Was Small." Gwendolyn Brooks Papers, BANC MSS 2001 /83 z, The Bancroft Library, U of California, Berkeley, box 11, folder 31. Manuscript.

Crenshaw, Kimberlé. "Mapping the Margins: Intersectionality, Identity Politics, and Violence against Women of Color." *Stanford Law Review*, vol. 43, no. 6, 1991, 1241–99.

Culler, Jonathan. *Theory of the Lyric.* Harvard UP, 2015.

Dalsimer, Katherine. *Virginia Woolf: Becoming a Writer.* Yale UP, 2002.

Danziger, Kurt. *Constructing the Subject: Historical Origins of Psychological Research.* Cambridge UP, 1994.

Darian-Smith, Eve, and Philip C. McCarty. "Beyond Interdisciplinarity: Developing a Global Transdisciplinary Framework." *Transcience,* vol. 7, no. 2, 2016, www.researchgate.net/publication/311486261_Beyond_Interdisciplinarity_Developing_a_Global_Transdisciplinary_Framework. Accessed 8 Oct. 2019.

Davidson, Aurelia. "Trapped." Gwendolyn Brooks Papers, BANC MSS 2001/83 z, The Bancroft Library, U of California, Berkeley, box 11, folder 32.

Davis, Kenneth. Illustrated thank-you card to Gwendolyn Brooks. Gwendolyn Brooks Papers, BANC MSS 2001/83 z, The Bancroft Library, U of California, Berkeley, box 2, folder 36.

Docka, Janet A. "I Am in a Trap." Gwendolyn Brooks Papers, BANC MSS 2001/83 z, The Bancroft Library, U of California, Berkeley, box 4, folder 18.

Doody, Margaret Anne. "Jane Austen, That Disconcerting 'Child.'" Alexander and McMaster, *Child Writer*, 101–21.

Dove, Rita, and Marilyn Waniek (Nelson). "A Black Rainbow: Modern Afro-American Poetry." *Poetry after Modernism*, edited by Robert McDowell, Story Line Press, 1991, 217–75.

Earth Guardians. www.earthguardians.org. Accessed 20 Aug. 2017.

Edelman, Lee. *No Future: Queer Theory and the Death Drive.* Duke UP, 2004.

Edwards, Jennifer. "Masters." *Ten-Second Rainshowers: Poems by Young People*, compiled by Sandford Lyne, Simon and Schuster Books for Young Readers, 1996, 19.

Einstein, Albert. "On the Electrodynamics of Moving Bodies." June 30, 1905. *The Principle of Relativity*. Methuen, 1923, 1–24.

Emirbayer, Mustafa, and Ann Mische. "What Is Agency?" *American Journal of Sociology*, vol. 103, no. 4, 1998, 962–1023.

English, Daylanne K. *Each Hour Redeem: Time and Justice in African American Literature*. U of Minneapolis P, 2013.

———. "Race, Writing, and Time." *Time and Literature*, edited by Thomas M. Allen, Cambridge UP, 225–41.

Epstein, Rebecca, et al. "Girlhood Interrupted: The Erasure of Black Girls' Childhood." Georgetown Law, Center on Poverty and Inequality, 2017, SSRN, papers.ssrn.com/sol3/papers.cfm?abstract_id=3000695. Accessed 4 Dec. 2018.

Esser, Florian, et al. "Reconceptualising Agency and Childhood: An Introduction." Esser et al., *Reconceptualising Agency and Childhood*, 1–16.

———, editors. *Reconceptualising Agency and Childhood: New Perspectives in Childhood Studies*. Routledge, 2016.

Finch, Annie. *The Body of Poetry: Essays on Women, Form, and the Poetic Self*. U of Michigan P, 2010.

Fisher, Maisha T. *Writing in Rhythm: Spoken Word Poetry in Urban Classrooms*. Teachers College P, 2007.

Fitzgerald, Robyn, et al. "Children's Participation as a Struggle over Recognition: Exploring the Promise of Dialogue." *A Handbook of Children and Young People's Participation*, edited by Barry Percy-Smith and Nigel Thomas, Routledge, 2010, 293–305.

Fitzhugh, Louise. *Harriet the Spy*. 1964. Random House, 2001.

Flint, Amy Seely, and Tasha Tropp Laman. "Where Poems Hide: Finding Reflective, Critical Spaces Inside Writing Workshop." *Theory into Practice*, vol. 51, 2012, 12–19.

Flynn, Richard. "'Affirmative Acts': Language, Childhood, and Power in June Jordan's Cross-writing." *Still Seeking an Attitude: Critical Reflections on the Work of June Jordan*, edited by Valerie Kinloch and Margret Grebowicz, Lexington Books, 2004, 119–43.

———. "Can Children's Poetry Matter?" *The Lion and the Unicorn*, vol. 17, no. 1, 1993, 37–44.

"For the Children." Brochure. The Voice of the Children, Inc. Collection of Terri Bush.

Foster, Rose. "Eulogy for a Balloon." Green, *Rattle Young Poets Anthology*, 31.

Foster, Shawna. "Re: Follow up to scholarly article on Rattle Young Poets Anthology." Received by Rachel Conrad, 30 Sept. 2017.

Fox, Aaron. "Contributor Note." Green, *Rattle Young Poets Anthology*, 83.

———. "It's Raining." Green, *Rattle Young Poets Anthology*, 32.

Freire, Paulo. *Teachers as Cultural Workers*. Westview Press, 2005.

Fuhrman, Joanna. "Still at It: Notes from a Former Teen Poet." Pawlak et al., *When We Were Countries*, 264–65.

Fuller, Hoyt, et al. "Interview with Gwendolyn Brooks." 1973. Gayles, *Conversations with Gwendolyn Brooks*, 67–73.

Galison, Peter. *Einstein's Clocks, Poincaré's Maps*. Norton, 2003.

Gallacher, Lesley-Anne, and Michael Gallagher. "Methodological Immaturity in Childhood Research? Thinking through 'Participatory Methods.'" *Childhood*, vol. 15, no 4, 2008, 499–516.

Gayles, Gloria Wade, editor. *Conversations with Gwendolyn Brooks*. UP of Mississippi, 2003.

Gershowitz, Elissa. "Writing for Themselves and Each Other." *Children's Literature Association Quarterly*, vol. 27, no. 1, 2002, 40–45.

Goff, Phillip Atiba, et al.. "The Essence of Innocence: Consequences of Dehumanizing Black Children." *Journal of Personality and Social Psychology*, vol. 106, no. 4, 2014, 526–45.

González, Emma. Speech at March for Our Lives, Washington, D.C., 24 Mar. 2018, YouTube, www.youtube.com/watch?v=u46HzTGVQhg. Accessed 30 Oct. 2018.

Goode, Michael. "April 4, 1968." Jordan and Bush, *THE VOICE of the Children*, 56–57.

Goodenough, Elizabeth, et al. "Introduction." *Infant Tongues: The Voice of the Child in Literature*, edited by Elizabeth Goodenough et al., Wayne State UP, 1994, 1–15.

Gravity Probe B: Testing Einstein's Universe. einstein.stanford.edu/. Accessed 27 Dec. 2016.

Gray, Leticia. "Patterns." Nye, *Salting the Ocean*, 28.

Gray, Timothy. *Urban Pastoral: Natural Currents in the New York School*. U of Iowa P, 2010.

Green, Timothy, editor. *Rattle Young Poets Anthology*. Rattle Foundation, 2014.

Grosvenor, Kali. *Poems by Kali*. Doubleday, 1970.

Grube, Vicky. "Admitting Their Worlds: Reflections of a Teacher/Researcher on the Self-Initiated Art Making of Children." *International Journal of Education and the Arts*, vol. 10, no. 7, 2009.

Hackney, Sheldon. "A Conversation with Gwendolyn Brooks." 1994. Gayles, *Conversations with Gwendolyn Brooks*, 155–64.

Halberstam, J. Jack. *In a Queer Time and Place: Transgender Bodies, Subcultural Lives*. New York UP, 2005.

Hall, Stuart. "Cultural Identity and Diaspora." *Colonial Discourse and Post-Colonial Theory: A Reader*, edited by Patrick Williams and Laura Chrisman, Harvester Wheatsheaf, 1993, 392–401.

Halverson, Cathryn. "Reading Little Girls' Texts in the 1920s: Searching for the 'Spirit of Childhood.'" *Children's Literature in Education*, vol. 30, no. 4, 1999, 235–48.

Hanson, Karl, and Olga Nieuwenhuys. "Living Rights, Social Justice, Translations." Hanson and Nieuwenhuys, *Reconceptualizing Children's Rights*, 3–25.

————, editors. *Reconceptualizing Children's Rights in International Development: Living Rights, Social Justice, Translations.* Cambridge UP, 2013.

Harding, Sandra. *Whose Science? Whose Knowledge? Thinking from Women's Lives.* Cornell UP, 1991.

Hardman, Christel. "The Beautiful Words." Apr. 1973. Gwendolyn Brooks Papers, BANC MSS 2001/83 z, The Bancroft Library, U of California, Berkeley, box 11, folder 23.

Hart, Roger. *Children's Participation: The Theory and Practice of Involving Young Citizens in Community Development and Environmental Care.* London, Earthscan Publications, 1997.

Haugen, Gry Mette D. "Children's Perspectives on Everyday Experiences of Shared Residence: Time, Emotions and Agency Dilemmas." *Children and Society*, vol. 24, 2010, 112–22.

Heaney, Seamus. *Poems, 1965–1975.* Farrar, Straus and Giroux, 1980.

Heming, Anna B. Letter to Gwendolyn Brooks. 12 Apr. 1973. Gwendolyn Brooks Papers, BANC MSS 2001/83 z, The Bancroft Library, U of California, Berkeley, box 11, folder 23.

Hitlin, Steven, and Glen H. Elder, Jr. "Time, Self, and the Curiously Abstract Concept of Agency." *Sociological Theory*, vol. 25, no. 2, 2007, 170–91.

Hodge, Chinaka. Foreword. Youth Speaks, *My Words Consume Me*, ix.

Hodgson, Lucia. "Infant Muse: Phillis Wheatley and the Revolutionary Rhetoric of Childhood." *Early American Literature*, vol. 49, no. 3, 2014, 663–82.

Hollindale, Peter. *Signs of Childness in Children's Books.* Thimble, 1997.

hooks, bell. *Teaching Community.* Routledge, 2003.

Horner, Shirley. "Emily Dickinson Tribute." *New York Times*, 6 Apr. 1986.

Howard, Vanessa. "For My Children." Howard, *Screaming Whisper*, 20–21.

————. "Ghetto." Jordan and Bush, *THE VOICE of the Children*, ix.

————. "The Last Riot." Jordan and Bush, *THE VOICE of the Children*, 8–9.

————. "Monument in Black." Jordan and Bush, *THE VOICE of the Children*, 43.

————. Preface. Howard, *Screaming Whisper*, ix.

————. "The Question." Jordan and Bush, *THE VOICE of the Children*, 45.

————. *A Screaming Whisper.* Holt, Rinehart, 1972.

————. "Truly My Own." Jordan and Bush, *THE VOICE of the Children*, 83.

————. "We Speak to Be Heard." *Today's Girl*, vol. 1, no. 3, Nov. 1971, 10–13.

Hulett, Fred. "The Voices." *Courier-Post*, Camden, NJ, 31 Dec. 1970.

Hullert, Ricki. "Mrs. Brooks." Apr. 1973. Gwendolyn Brooks Papers, BANC MSS 2001/83 z, The Bancroft Library, U of California, Berkeley, box 11, folder 23.

Hviid, Pernille. "'Next year we are small, right?': Different Times in Children's Development." *European Journal of Psychology of Education*, vol. 23, no. 2, 2008, 183–98.

Ibrahim, Awad. "Youth: Our New Cultural Theorists." *Jeunesse: Young People, Texts, Cultures*, vol. 7, no. 2, 2015, 129–33.

Illinois State Office. Illinois Poet Laureate, Former Laureates, Gwendolyn Brooks.

Illinois.gov, www2.illinois.gov/sites/poetlaureate/pages/brooks.aspx. Accessed 23 May 2019.

Jabbour, Alan, and Ethelbert Miller. "A Conversation with Gwendolyn Brooks." 1986. Gayles, *Conversations with Gwendolyn Brooks*, 125–32.

Jackson, Virginia. "Lyric." *The Princeton Encyclopedia of Poetry and Poetics*, edited by Roland Greene et al., 4th ed., Princeton UP, 2012, 826–34.

James, Allison. "Giving Voice to Children's Voices: Practices and Problems, Pitfalls and Potentials." *American Anthropologist*, vol. 109, no. 2, 2007, 261–72.

———. "Life Times: Children's Perspectives on Age, Agency, and Memory across the Life Course." *Studies in Modern Childhood: Society, Agency, Culture*, edited by Jens Qvortrup, Palgrave Macmillan, 2005, 248–66.

———. "Understanding Childhood from an Interdisciplinary Perspective." Pufall and Unsworth, *Rethinking Childhood*, 25–37.

James, Allison, and Adrian L. James. "Childhood: Toward a Theory of Continuity and Change." *Annals of the American Academy of Political and Social Science*, vol. 575, 2001, 25–37.

James, Allison, and Alan Prout, editors. *Constructing and Reconstructing Childhood: Contemporary Issues in the Sociological Study of Childhood*. 1997. 2nd ed., RoutledgeFalmer, 2002.

———. "Re-presenting Childhood: Time and Transition in the Study of Childhood." James and Prout, *Constructing and Reconstructing Childhood*, 230–50.

James, Allison, Chris Jenks, and Alan Prout. *Theorizing Childhood*. Polity Press, 1998.

Jocson, Korina M. *Youth Poets: Empowering Literacies in and out of Schools*. Peter Lang, 2008.

Johnson, James Weldon. "Lift Every Voice and Sing," *Complete Poems*, edited by Sondra Kathryn Wilson, 1927/1935, Penguin, 2000, 109–10.

Johnson, Kelli Lyon. "'If I got a chance to talk to the world . . .': Voice, Agency, and Claiming Rights in Narratives of Contemporary Child Slavery." *Child Slavery before and after Emancipation: An Argument for Child-Centered Slavery Studies*, edited by Anna Mae Duane, Cambridge UP, 2017, 234–50.

Jones, Katharine. "Getting Rid of Children's Literature." *Lion and the Unicorn*, vol. 30, no. 3, 2006, 287–315.

Jordan, June. "Afterword." Jordan and Bush, *THE VOICE of the Children*, 93–99.

———. *Directed by Desire: The Collected Poems of June Jordan*, edited by Jan Heller Levi and Sara Miles, Copper Canyon P, 2005.

———. *Dry Victories*. Holt, Rinehart and Winston, 1972.

———. "For Michael Angelo Thompson." Jordan, *Directed by Desire*, 170–72.

———. Interview. *I Know What the Red Clay Looks Like: The Voice and Vision of Black Women Writers*, edited by Rebecca Carroll, Crown, 1994, 141–51.

———. "Introduction." Jordan, *Soulscript*, 1970, xvi–xix.

———. Letter to Milton Meltzer. 28 Jan. 1969. June Jordan Papers, 1936–2002, MC 513. Schlesinger Library, Radcliffe Institute for Advanced Study, box 53, folder 10.

————. "Old Stories: New Lives." *Some of Us Did NOT Die.* Basic/Civitas Books, 2002, 275–83.

————. *Soldier: A Poet's Childhood.* Basic Books, 2000.

————, editor. *Soulscript: Afro-American Poetry.* Doubleday, 1970.

————, editor. *Soulscript: A Collection of Classic African American Poetry.* 1970. Harlem Moon / Broadway Books, 2004.

————. "Visitors and Adult Friends of the Children." 1969–1970. June Jordan Papers, 1936–2002, MC 513. Schlesinger Library, Radcliffe Institute for Advanced Study, box 54, folder 10.

————. "The Voice of the Children." 1967. *Civil Wars.* Beacon Press, 1981, 29–38.

————. "'The Voice of the Children' Saturday Workshop Diaries." *Journal of a Living Experiment*, edited by Phillip Lopate, Teachers and Writers Press, 1979, 134–57.

————. "White English/Black English: The Politics of Translation." 1972. *Civil Wars.* Beacon Press, 1981, 59–73.

Jordan, June, and Terri Bush. Acknowledgment. Jordan and Bush, *THE VOICE of the Children*, v.

————, collectors. *THE VOICE of the Children.* Holt, Rinehart and Winston, 1970.

Juliana v. U.S. "First Amended Complaint for Declaratory and Injunctive Relief," U.S. District Court, District of Oregon-Eugene Division, Case 6:15-cv-01517-TC, document 7, filed 10 Sept. 2015. Our Children's Trust, www.ourchildrens trust.org/court-orders-and-pleadings. Accessed 2 Mar. 2018.

Juvenilia Press. UNSW Sydney, School of the Arts and Media, www.arts.unsw .edu.au/juvenilia/. Accessed 10 Mar. 2016.

Kantzavelos, Maria. "Writing with Rhyme and Reason." *Chicago Tribune*, 8 June, 2001.

Kass, James. "Introduction." Youth Speaks, *My Words Consume Me*, xi–xv.

Kelley, Robin D. G. *Freedom Dreams: The Black Radical Imagination.* Beacon, 2003.

Kent, George E. *A Life of Gwendolyn Brooks.* UP of Kentucky, 1990.

Kim, Ruth H. "'Never Knew Literacy Could Get at My Soul': On How Words Matter for Youth, or Notes toward Decolonizing Literacy." *Review of Education, Pedagogy, and Cultural Studies*, vol. 35, 2013, 392–407.

Kimmel, Robert. "Clock." Nye, *Salting the Ocean*, 83.

King, Willie Marvel. Letter to Gwendolyn Brooks. 16 Dec. 1969. Gwendolyn Brooks Papers, BANC MSS 2001/83 z, The Bancroft Library, U of California, Berkeley, box 2, folder 35.

Kinloch, Valerie. *June Jordan: Her Life and Letters.* Women Writers of Color series. Praeger, 2006.

Kittridge, Katharine. "Early Blossoms of Genius: Child Poets at the End of the Long Eighteenth Century." *Looking Glass: New Perspectives on Children's Literature*, vol. 15, no. 2, 2011. www.lib.latrobe.edu.au/ojs/index.php/tlg/article /view/274/271. Accessed 20 July 2017.

Kivlehan, Sophie. "Why I Sued the Federal Government over Harmful Air

Pollution." *Morning Call (Pennsylvania)*, 22 June 2017, www.mcall.com /opinion /mc-climate-change-lawsuit-paris-accord-kivlehan-ithink-0623–20 170622-story.html. Accessed 27 May 2019.

Koch, Kenneth. "Teaching Children to Write Poetry." 1970. *Wishes, Lies, and Dreams: Teaching Children to Write Poetry*, edited by Kenneth Koch, Harper and Row, 1980, 7–55.

Kohl, Herbert, and Victor Hernández Cruz, editors. *Stuff: A Collection of Poems, Visions, & Imaginative Happenings from Young Writers in Schools*. World Publishing, 1970.

Krebs, Elisabeth. "Tickets Still Available for Court Gala." *NWITimes.com*, 16 Apr. 1999.

Kuhn, Deanna. "Metacognitive Development." *Current Directions in Psychological Science*, vol. 9, no. 5, 2000, 178–81.

Lane, Diane Luby, and the Get Lit Players. *Get Lit Rising: Words Ignite. Claim Your Poem. Claim Your Life*. Simon and Schuster, 2016.

Langbauer, Laurie. *The Juvenile Tradition: Young Writers and Prolepsis, 1750–1835*. Oxford UP, 2016.

Lansdown, Gerison. "The Realisation of Children's Participation Rights: Critical Reflections." *A Handbook of Children and Young People's Participation: Perspectives from Theory and Practice*, edited by Barry Percy-Smith and Nigel Thomas, Routledge, 2010, 11–23.

Laureles, Martin. "Charm to Bring Back the Past." Nye, *Salting the Ocean*, 88.

Leader, Anna. Prefatory comment. Meyer et al., *Leave This Song Behind*, 2016.

Lee, Felicia R. "A Feminist Survivor with the Eyes of a Child." *New York Times*, 4 July 2000, E1.

Leonard, Madeleine. *The Sociology of Children, Childhood, and Generation*. Sage, 2016.

Levithan, David, editor. *What We Remember, What We Forget: The Best Young Writers and Artists in America*. A PUSH Anthology. Scholastic, 2012.

Lewis, Eva. "Teen Activists Shut Down Chicago Streets with Peaceful Black Lives Matter Protest." *Teen Vogue*, 15 July 2016.

Lewis, Ida. "'My People Are Black People.'" 1971. Gayles, *Conversations with Gwendolyn Brooks*, 54–66.

Lewis, Michael. *Altering Fate: Why the Past Does Not Predict the Future*. Guilford, 1997.

Livingston, Myra Cohn. *The Child as Poet: Myth or Reality?* The Horn Book, 1984.

Luk, Karen A. "[Where does my free time go?]." Nye, *Salting the Ocean*, 100.

Lyne, Sandford, compiler. *Ten-Second Rainshowers: Poems by Young People*. Simon and Schuster Books for Young Readers, 1996.

———, compiler. *Soft Hay Will Catch You: Poems by Young People*. Simon and Schuster Books for Young Readers, 2004.

MacAustin, Hilary. "The *Defender* Brings You the World: The Grand European

Tour of Patrick B. Prescott Jr." *The Black Chicago Renaissance*, edited by Darlene Clark Hine and John McCluskey, Jr., U of Illinois P, 2012, 57–75.

Mandell, Nancy. "The Least-Adult Role in Studying Children." *Journal of Contemporary Ethnography*, vol. 16, no. 4, 1988, 433–67.

Matejka, Adrian. "Remembrance." *Revise the Psalm: Work Celebrating the Writing of Gwendolyn Brooks*, edited by Quraysh Ali Lansana and Sandra Jackson-Opoku, Curbside Splendor, 2017, 319.

Matthews, Gareth B. *Dialogues with Children*. Harvard UP, 1984.

———. *The Philosophy of Childhood*. Harvard UP, 1994.

Mayall, Berry. *Towards a Sociology for Childhood: Thinking from Children's Lives*. Open UP, 2002.

Maynes, Mary Jo. "Age as a Category of Historical Analysis: History, Agency, and Narratives of Childhood." *Journal of the History of Childhood and Youth*, vol. 1, no. 1, 2008, 114–24.

McMaster, Juliet. "'Adults' Literature,' by Children." *Lion and the Unicorn*, vol. 25, no. 2, 2001, 277–99.

———. *Jane Austen, Young Author*. Ashgate, 2016.

———. "What Daisy Knew: The Epistemology of the Child Writer." Alexander and McMaster, *Child Writer*, 51–69.

Meacham, Jack. "Action, Voice, and Identity in Children's Lives." Pufall and Unsworth, *Rethinking Childhood*, 69–84.

Melhem, D. H. "Afterword." Kent, *Life of Gwendolyn Brooks*, 259–64.

———. *Gwendolyn Brooks: Poetry and the Heroic Voice*. UP of Kentucky, 1987.

Meltzer, Milton. Letter to June Meyer [Jordan]. 22 Jan. 1969. June Jordan Papers, 1936–2002, MC 513. Schlesinger Library, Radcliffe Institute for Advanced Study, box 53, folder 10.

Merleau-Ponty, Maurice. *Phenomenology of Perception*. 1962. Routledge. 1995.

Merriam, Eve. "For Young Readers." *New York Times*, 24 Jan. 1971.

Meyer, Christopher. "[sitting on the dock]." Jordan and Bush, *THE VOICE of the Children*, 52.

Meyer, Stephanie H., et al., editors. *Leave This Song Behind: Teen Poetry at Its Best*. Health Communications. 2016.

Michael, Pamela, editor. *River of Words: Young Poets and Artists on the Nature of Things*. Milkweed Editions, 2008.

Miller, Christopher R. *The Invention of Evening: Perception and Time in Romantic Poetry*. Cambridge UP, 2006.

Mintz, Steven. "Reflections on Age as a Category of Historical Analysis." *Journal of the History of Childhood and Youth*, vol. 1, no. 1, 2008, 91–94.

Moosa-Mitha, Mehmoona. "A Difference-Centred Alternative to Theorization of Children's Citizenship Rights." *Citizenship Studies*, vol. 9, no. 4, 2005, 369–88.

Morrell, Ernest, and Jeffrey M. R. Duncan-Andrade. "Promoting Academic Literacy with Urban Youth through Engaging Hip-Hop Culture." *English Journal*, vol. 91, no. 6, 2002, 88–92.

Morrison, Toni. "The Future of Time: Literature and Diminished Expectations." *What Moves at the Margin: Selected Nonfiction*, edited by Carolyn C. Denard, UP of Mississippi, 2008, 170–86.

Morrison, Toni, with Slade Morrison. *The Big Box*. Hyperion, 1999.

Morrison, Toni, and Slade Morrison. *The Book of Mean People*. Hyperion, 2002.

Morss, John R. *Growing Critical: Alternatives to Developmental Psychology*. Routledge, 1996.

Moss, Dorothy. "Memory, Space and Time: Researching Children's Lives. *Childhood*, vol. 17, no. 4, 2010, 530–44.

Muhammad, Gholnescar "Gholdy," and Lee Gonzalez. "Slam Poetry: An Artistic Resistance toward Identity, Agency, and Activism." *Equity and Excellence in Education*, vol. 49, no. 4, 2016, 440–53.

Muller, Lauren, and the Poetry for the People Collective, editors. *June Jordan's Poetry for the People: A Revolutionary Blueprint*. Routledge, 1995.

Myricks, Lillian. "Freedom." Brooks, *Report*, 208–9.

Nadler, Janna. "The Unauthorized Child Author." *Image of the Twentieth Century in Literature, Media, and Society*. Society for the Interdisciplinary Study of Social Imagery Conference Proceedings. Colorado State University–Pueblo, 2000, 413–18.

National Council of Teachers of English. "NCTE Beliefs about the Students' Right to Write." National Council of Teachers of English, www2.ncte.org/statement/students-right-to-write/. Accessed 16 Mar. 2018.

Neufeldt, Victor A. "The Child Is Parent to the Author: Branwell Bronte." Alexander and McMaster, *Child Writer*, 173–87.

Newquist, Roy. "Gwendolyn Brooks." 1967. Gayles, *Conversations with Gwendolyn Brooks*, 26–36.

Nodelman, Perry. *The Hidden Adult: Defining Children's Literature*. Johns Hopkins UP, 2008.

Nodelman, Perry, and Mavis Reimer. "Common Assumptions about Childhood." *The Pleasures of Children's Literature*, edited by Nodelman and Reimer, 3rd ed., Allyn and Bacon, 2003, 79–107.

Nowak, Mark. "Panthers, Patriots, and Poetries in Revolution." Organize Your Own, 12 Dec. 2016, organizeyourown.wordpress.com/16/12/12/panthers-patriots-and-poetries-in-revolution-by-mark-nowak/. Accessed 20 July 2017.

Nye, Naomi Shihab. *A Maze Me: Poems for Girls*. Greenwillow Books, 2014.

———, selector. *The Flag of Childhood: Poems from the Middle East*. Simon and Schuster, 1998/2002.

———. *19 Varieties of Gazelle: Poems of the Middle East*. Greenwillow, 2002.

———. "The Rider." *The Place My Words Are Looking For*, edited by Paul B. Janeczko, Simon and Schuster, 1990, 6.

———, selector. *Salting the Ocean: 100 Poems by Young Poets*. Illustrated by Ashley Bryan. HarperCollins, 2000.

―――, selector. *This Same Sky: A Collection of Poems from Around the World*. 1992. Simon and Schuster, 1996.

Ocen, Priscilla A. "(E)racing Childhood: Examining the Racialized Construction of Childhood and Innocence in the Treatment of Sexually Exploited Minors." *UCLA Law Review*, vol. 62, 2015, 1586–640.

O'Malley, Michael. *Keeping Watch: A History of American Time*. Smithsonian, 1996.

Osborn, Ian Jasper. "Contributor Note." Green, *Rattle Young Poets Anthology*, 85.

Oswell, David. *The Agency of Children: From Family to Global Human Rights*. Cambridge UP, 2013.

Our Children's Trust. "Juliana v. United States: Youth Climate Lawsuit." www.our childrenstrust.org/juliana-v-us. Accessed 20 Aug. 2019.

Owen, David, and Lesley Peterson, editors. "Introduction." *Home and Away: The Place of Child Writers*. Cambridge, 2016.

Parke, Ross D., et al. "The Past as Prologue: An Overview of a Century of Developmental Psychology." *A Century of Developmental Psychology*, edited by Parke et al., American Psychological Association, 1994, 1–70.

Pawlak, Mark. Preface. Pawlak et al., *When We Were Countries*, 9–11.

Pawlak, Mark, et al., editors. *When We Were Countries: The Hanging Loose Press High School Writing Collection*. Brooklyn: Hanging Loose Press, 2010.

Peacock, Cyndea. "[I touched]." Nye, *Salting the Ocean*, 84.

Perrillo, Jonna. "The Popularization of High School Poetry Instruction, 1920–1940." *Research in the Teaching of English*, vol. 50, no. 1, 2015, 111–18.

Piaget, Jean. *The Child's Conception of Time*. 1927. Translated by A. J. Pomerans, Basic Books, 1969.

Plotz, Judith. *Romanticism and the Vocation of Childhood*. Palgrave, 2001.

"Poetry 180 / A Poem a Day for American High Schools." Hosted by Billy Collins. Library of Congress, www.loc.gov/poetry/180/p180-more.html. Accessed 15 Feb. 2018.

Pratt, Lloyd. *Archives of American Time: Literature and Modernity in the Nineteenth Century*. U of Pennsylvania P, 2009.

Presson, Rebekah. "Interviews with Gwendolyn Brooks." 1988. Gayles, *Conversations with Gwendolyn Brooks*, 133–39.

Prout, Alan. *The Future of Childhood*. RoutledgeFalmer, 2005.

Pufall, Peter B. and Unsworth, Richard P., editors. *Rethinking Childhood*, Rutgers UP, 2004.

Punch, Samantha. "Exploring Children's Agency across Majority and Minority World Contexts." Esser et al., *Reconceptualising Agency and Childhood*, 183–96.

Ramke, Bin. "A Poetics, of Sorts." Shepherd, *Lyric Postmodernisms*, 157–59.

Rampersad, Arnold. "The Universal and the Particular in Afro-American Poetry." *College Language Association (CLA) Journal*, vol. 25, no. 1, 1981, 1–17.

Redcay, Anna. *"The Long-Defended Gate": Juvenilia, the Real Child, and the Aesthetics of Innocence, 1858–1939*. Unpublished dissertation, U of Pittsburgh.

Reimer, Mavis. Review of *The Child Writer from Austen to Woolf*, edited by Christine

Alexander and Juliet McMaster. *English Studies in Canada*, vol. 33, no. 1–2, 2007, 279–83.

Reynaert, Didier, et al. "A Review of Children's Rights Literature since the Adoption of the United Nations Convention on the Rights of the Child." *Childhood*, vol. 16, no. 4, 2009, 518–34.

Rimmer, Mark. "Music, Middle Childhood and Agency: The Value of an Interactional-Relational Approach." *Childhood*, vol. 24, no. 4, 2017, 559–73.

Roach, Christell Victoria. "Contributor Note." Green, *Rattle Young Poets Anthology*, 86.

Rogoff, Barbara. *The Cultural Nature of Human Development*. Oxford UP, 2003.

Roiphe, Katie. "A Lovely Way to Burn." *New York Times Book Review*, 12 Apr. 2009, 14.

Rovelli, Carlo. *The Order of Time*. Riverhead Books, 2018.

Rufo, David. "Artistic Agency in the Elementary Classroom." *Art Education*, vol. 64, no. 3, 2011, 18–23.

Sadler, David. "Innocent Hearts: The Child Authors of the 1920s." *Children's Literature Association Quarterly*, vol. 17, no. 4, 1992, 24–30.

Sánchez-Eppler, Karen. "Castaways: *The Swiss Family Robinson*, Child Bookmakers, and the Possibilities of Literary Flotsam." *The Oxford Handbook of Children's Literature*, edited by Julia L. Mickenberg and Lynne Vallone, Oxford UP, 2011, 433–54.

Sandburg, Carl. *The Complete Poems of Carl Sandburg*. Harcourt, 2003.

Santillana, Alberto. "[I feel like a puppy that]." Nye, *Salting the Ocean*, 13.

Sarre, Sophie. "Parental Regulation of Teenagers' Time: Processes and Meanings." *Childhood*, vol. 17, no. 1, 2010, 61–75.

Schwebel, Sara L. "The Limits of Agency for Children's Literature Scholars." *Jeunesse: Young People, Texts, Contexts*, vol. 8, no. 1, 2016, 278–90.

Shepherd, Reginald. "Introduction." Shepherd, *Lyric Postmodernisms*, xi–xvii.

———, editor. *Lyric Postmodernisms*. Counterpath Press, 2008.

Siegel, Alexander W., and Sheldon H. White. "The Child Study Movement: Early Growth and Development of the Symbolized Child." *Advances in Child Development and Behavior*, vol. 17, 1982, 233–85.

Sims, Ricardo. "The Day of Thanks." Gwendolyn Brooks Papers, BANC MSS 2001/83 z, The Bancroft Library, U of California, Berkeley, box 11, folder 31.

Smith, Barbara Herrnstein. *On the Margins of Discourse: The Relation of Literature to Language*. U of Chicago P, 1978.

Smith, Eric. "I Am Clearly Real." *Today's Girl*, vol. 1, no. 3, Nov. 1971, 13.

Smith, Victoria Ford. *Between Generations: Collaborative Authorship in the Golden Age of Children's Literature*. UP of Mississippi, 2017.

Solberg, Anne. "Negotiating Childhood: Changing Constructions of Age for Norwegian Children." James and Prout, *Constructing and Reconstructing Childhood*, 126–44.

Sorby, Angela. *Schoolroom Poets: Childhood, Performance, and the Place of American Poetry, 1865–1917*. U of New Hampshire P, 2005.

Spyrou, Spyros. "Time to Decenter Childhood?" *Childhood*, vol. 24, no. 4, 2017, 433–37.

Stalling, Jonathan. "Finding a Democratic Speech: The Intercultural Poetics and Pedagogy of June Jordan's Poetry for the People." *Still Seeking an Attitude: Critical Reflections on the Work of June Jordan*, edited by Valerie Kinloch and Margret Grebowicz, Lexington Books, 2004, 209–32.

Steedman, Carolyn. *The Tidy House: Little Girls Writing*. Virago, 1982.

Stevenson, Robert Louis. *A Child's Garden of Verses*. 1885. Chronicle Books, 1989.

Stockton, Kathryn Bond. *The Queer Child, or Growing Sideways in the Twentieth Century*. Duke UP, 2009.

Svitak, Adora. "What Adults Can Learn from Kids." Feb. 2010, TED2010, www .ted.com/talks/adora_svitak?language=en. Accessed 1 Nov. 2018.

Teachers and Writers Collaborative. "About Us: History." www.twc.org/about-us/. Accessed 24 July 2017.

Thirus, Moral. "Death." Gwendolyn Brooks Papers, BANC MSS 2001/83 z, The Bancroft Library, U of California, Berkeley, box 4, folder 26.

———. "Things." Gwendolyn Brooks Papers, BANC MSS 2001/83 z, The Bancroft Library, U of California, Berkeley, box 4, folder 26.

———. "Things." [Author's name handwritten.] Gwendolyn Brooks Papers, BANC MSS 2001/83 z, The Bancroft Library, U of California, Berkeley, box 11, folder 31.

———. "Things." Brooks, *Report*, 208.

———. "Things." Brooks, "Report from Part One: An Excerpt from the Autobiography of Gwendolyn Brooks," 7–8.

Thomas, Joseph T., Jr. *Poetry's Playground: The Culture of Contemporary American Children's Poetry*. Wayne State UP, 2007.

Thompson, Elizabeth. "Different Worlds." Lyne, *Soft Hay Will Catch You*, 13.

Thompson, Glen. "Hands." Jordan and Bush, *THE VOICE of the Children*, 15.

Thorne, Barrie. "Crafting the Interdisciplinary Field of Childhood Studies." *Childhood*, vol. 14, no. 2, 2007, 147–52.

Tillman, Ebony. "[My city]." Untitled poem on plain white paper. Gwendolyn Brooks Papers, BANC MSS 2001/83 z, The Bancroft Library, U of California, Berkeley, box 11, folder 32.

———. "[My city]." Untitled poem on Amtrak notepaper. Gwendolyn Brooks Papers, BANC MSS 2001/83 z, The Bancroft Library, U of California, Berkeley, box 11, folder 32.

Tulle, Emmanuelle, editor. *Old Age and Agency*. Nova Science Publishers, 2004.

Turkewitz, Julie, and Vivian Yee. "With Grief and Hope, Florida Students Take Gun Control Fight on the Road." *New York Times*, 20 Feb. 2018.

Turner, Daisy. Interview with Jane C. Beck. *Journey's End: The Memories and Traditions of Daisy Turner and Her Family*, Program 14: Daisy's Black Doll, Vermont Folklife Center, beta.prx.org/stories/16120. Accessed 1 May 2018.

Uprichard, Emma. "Children as 'Beings and Becomings': Children, Childhood and Temporality." *Children and Society*, vol. 22, 2008, 303–13.

"Vanessa Howard: Young Author of 'A Screaming Whisper.' " *Scholastic Scope*, 29 Jan. 1973, 4–7.

"Vanessa Howard Speaks to Be Heard." *Today's Girl*, vol. 1, no. 3, Nov. 1971, 10.

Vendler, Helen. "The Art of Criticism, No. 3." Interview by Henri Cole. *Paris Review*, vol. 141, 1996, 166–212.

———. *The Ocean, the Bird, and the Scholar*. Harvard UP. 2015.

———. *Poems, Poets, Poetry*. 3rd ed., Bedford / St. Martin's, 2009.

———. *Poets Thinking: Pope, Whitman, Dickinson, Yeats*. Harvard UP, 2004.

Viner, Christopher. "Anonymous." Nye, *Salting the Ocean*, 25.

Vitus, Kathrine. "Waiting Time: The De-subjectification of Children in Danish Asylum Centres." *Childhood*, vol. 17, no. 1, 2010, 26–42.

Vodicka, Christine. Illustrated thank-you card to Gwendolyn Brooks. Gwendolyn Brooks Papers, BANC MSS 2001/83 z, The Bancroft Library, U of California, Berkeley, box 2, folder 36.

Voice of the Children, Inc. Dedication. Jordan and Bush, *THE VOICE of the Children*, iv.

"Voice of the Children Is Poignant Cry for Love and Understanding." *Olympian*, Olympia, WA, 27 Dec. 1990.

Warming, Hanne. "Getting Under Their Skins? Accessing Young Children's Perspectives through Ethnographic Fieldwork." *Childhood*, vol. 18, no. 1, 2011, 39–53.

Watkins, Mel. "Gwendolyn Brooks, 83, Passionate Poet, Dies." *New York Times*, 5 Dec. 2000.

WBEZ. "WBEZ Presents Award-Winning Poetry." Press release. 30 June 1980. Gwendolyn Brooks Papers, BANC MSS 2001/83 z, The Bancroft Library, U of California, Berkeley, box 4, folder 17.

Weinstein, Susan. *Feel These Words: Writing in the Lives of Urban Youth*. State University of New York P, 2009.

Weiss, Jen, and Scott Herndon. *Brave New Voices: The Youth Speaks Guide to Teaching Spoken-Word Poetry*. Heinemann, 2001.

"We Remember Michael." Memorial booklet. The Voice of the Children, Inc. 1973. Collection of Terri Bush, New York.

Wheatley, Phillis. *Poems on Various Subjects, Religious and Moral*. London, 1773.

White, Sarah C., and Shyamol A. Choudhury. "The Politics of Child Participation in International Development: The Dilemma of Agency." *European Journal of Development Research*, vol. 19, no. 4, 2007, 529–50.

Wihstutz, Anne. "Children's Agency: Contributions from Feminist and Ethic of Care Theories." Esser et al., *Reconceptualising Agency and Childhood*, 61–74.

Williams, William Carlos. *The Autobiography of William Carlos Williams*. New Directions, 1967.

———. *Selected Essays*. New Directions, 1954.

———. "This Is Just to Say." *Selected Poems*. New Directions, 1969, 55.

Woodhead, Martin. "Childhood Studies: Past, Present, and Future." *Introduction to Childhood Studies*, edited by Mary Jane Kehily, 2nd ed., Open UP, 2008, 17–31.

Woolf, Virginia, et al. *Hyde Park Gate News: The Stephen Family Newspaper*, edited by Gill Lowe, Hesperus Press, 2006.

Wordsworth, William. "Ode: Intimations of Immortality from Recollections of Early Childhood." *The Prelude: Selected Poems and Sonnets*, edited by Carlos Baker, Holt, Rinehart and Winston, 1964, 152–58.

Wright, Michelle M. *Physics of Blackness: Beyond the Middle Passage Epistemology*. U of Minnesota P. 2015.

———. "Queer Temporalities: Space-ing Time and the Subject." *Time and Literature*, edited by Thomas M. Allen, Cambridge UP, 288–304.

WritersCorps. *Tell the World: Teen Poems from WritersCorps*. HarperCollins, 2008.

"Writers of High School Age." Hanging Loose Press, hangingloosepress.com /high_school.html. Accessed 28 Apr. 2015.

Yngvesson, Barbara. "The Child Who Was Left Behind: 'Dynamic Temporality' and Interpretations of History in Transnational Adoption." *Childhood*, vol. 20, no. 3, 2013, 354–67.

Youth Speaks. *My Words Consume Me: An Anthology of Youth Speaks Poets*. Youth Speaks / 826 Valencia, 2003.

———. "Pedagogy." *Youth Speaks*, youthspeaks.org/pedagogy-2/. Accessed 20 Oct. 2016.

Youth v. Gov. www.youthvgov.org/. Accessed 27 May 2019.

Index

Abdullah, Thandiwe, 2, 15
Abebe, Tatek, 167n13
Adam, Barbara, 165n4
Adoff, Arnold, 131
adoption, transnational, 168–69n26
adult assumptions about children, x, 6, 12, 22, 49, 58, 111–12, 166n5, 174n4
"adultification" (Blake), 20
adult mediation, xii, 7–10, 21, 42, 107, 110, 112, 117–18, 137–38, 167n12, 179n9; "unadulterated" correction, 151. *See also* young writers/youth writing: spelling and
adult status, 49, 75, 164; temporal goals or timelines and, 13, 104–5, 163–64
African American literature, and temporality, 40–41, 168n25
African American poetry, and universality, 158
Afshar, Jamshid, Jr., 93, 100–104, 179n10
age: as category of analysis, 6; genre and, 25, 37; in identifying writers, 87–88, 112; as metric of maturity, 39, 107, 112, 179n7 (*see also* development: developmental ideas and narratives); poetic speakers as unmarked and, 39–40

agency of young poets, 45–47; artistic agency, 7–8, 10, 110; practices that preserve, 87–91. *See also* collaboration, between children and adults; dynamic temporality; temporal agency; youth leadership
agency of youth, conceptions of: xi, 7–15, 163–64; as an active practice, 9; autonomy vs. interdependence, 8–9, 110. *See also* temporal agency
age status: poetic representations of, 32–34, 71–77; of writers, 23, 39–40, 48–49, 112, 135–36, 140, 161, 163–64
Alexander, Christine, 24–25, 29, 171n42, 171n46, 180n6
Allen, Thomas M., 173n65
American Library Association, 141
Angle, Paul, 176n26
Arnstein, Sherry R., 170n37
Ashford, Daisy, 28, 171, 172nn52–53
audience, for youth-written poetry, 3, 26–28, 46, 60, 64, 70–71, 76, 83, 89, 106, 111, 126, 137, 152, 156, 159, 181n17
Austen, Jane, 25, 29, 170n41
authority and authorship. *See* young writers/youth writing

www.ingramcontent.com/pod-product-compliance
Lightning Source LLC
Chambersburg PA
CBHW030325270326
41926CB00010B/1506